60 years of France and Europe

2017 marked the 60th anniversary of the signing of the Treaty of Rome and the starting point for today's European Union (EU). Since then, the project has indisputably come a very long way and has undergone major changes in direction. However, one constant has been the central role played by France.

This important milestone is used to take stock of the relationship between France and Europe. The enclosed chapters cover a broad range of issues relating to the past, present and future, investigating Franco-European relations via the optic of a wide range of debates. These include

- the issue of Europe in French presidential elections;
- the impact of the European question on the development of the two major political forces (of left and right) in France, and its role in their internal tensions;
- Europe as a key consideration in French macroeconomic policy;
- France's Algerian question and missed opportunities to extend 'Europe' to its North African neighbour; and
- Charles de Gaulle's role in defining the EU's structures for transnational democratic politics.

60 years of France and Europe assesses how and why Europe matters in our understanding of contemporary France and contributes to the important and ongoing research agendas for the study of France and the EU.

The chapters were originally published in a special issue of *Modern & Contemporary France.*

Helen Drake is Professor of French and European Studies, Loughborough University, UK and Director of the Institute for Diplomacy and International Governance, Loughborough University London, UK.

Chris Reynolds is Associate Professor of Contemporary French and European Studies, Nottingham Trent University, UK.

60 years of France and Europe

Edited by
Helen Drake and Chris Reynolds

LONDON AND NEW YORK

First published 2019
by Routledge
2 Park Square, Milton Park, Abingdon, Oxon, OX14 4RN, UK

and by Routledge
711 Third Avenue, New York, NY 10017, USA

Routledge is an imprint of the Taylor & Francis Group, an informa business

© 2019 Association for the Study of Modern & Contemporary France.

All rights reserved. No part of this book may be reprinted or reproduced or utilised in any form or by any electronic, mechanical, or other means, now known or hereafter invented, including photocopying and recording, or in any information storage or retrieval system, without permission in writing from the publishers.

Trademark notice: Product or corporate names may be trademarks or registered trademarks, and are used only for identification and explanation without intent to infringe.

British Library Cataloguing-in-Publication Data
A catalogue record for this book is available from the British Library

ISBN13: 978-1-138-49445-9

Typeset in Myriad Pro
by codeMantra

Publisher's Note
The publisher accepts responsibility for any inconsistencies that may have arisen during the conversion of this book from journal articles to book chapters, namely the possible inclusion of journal terminology.

Disclaimer
Every effort has been made to contact copyright holders for their permission to reprint material in this book. The publishers would be grateful to hear from any copyright holder who is not here acknowledged and will undertake to rectify any errors or omissions in future editions of this book.

Contents

Citation Information		vi
Notes on Contributors		viii
	Introduction: Sixty years on: France and Europe from the Treaty of Rome to the 2017 elections *Helen Drake and Chris Reynolds*	1
1	Presidential elections and Europe: the 2012 game-changer *Chris Reynolds*	7
2	From 'la petite Europe vaticane' to the Club Med: the French Socialist Party and the challenges of European integration *David Hanley*	25
3	Between Euro-Federalism, Euro-Pragmatism and Euro-Populism: the Gaullist movement divided over Europe *Benjamin Leruth and Nicholas Startin*	43
4	France and European macroeconomic policy coordination: from the Treaty of Rome to the euro area sovereign debt crisis *David Howarth and Joachim Schild*	61
5	Drawing Algeria into Europe: shifting French policy and the Treaty of Rome (1951–1964) *Megan Brown*	81
6	European democracy deferred: de Gaulle and the Dehousse Plan, 1960 *Eric O'Connor*	99
	Conclusion *Helen Drake and Chris Reynolds*	115
	Index	121

Citation Information

The following chapters were originally published in the journal *Modern & Contemporary France,* volume 25, issue 2 (May 2017). When citing this material, please use the original page numbering for each article, as follows:

Introduction

Sixty years on: France and Europe from the Treaty of Rome to the 2017 elections
Helen Drake and Chris Reynolds
Modern & Contemporary France, volume 25, issue 2 (May 2017). pp. 111–116

Chapter 1

Presidential elections and Europe: the 2012 game-changer
Chris Reynolds
Modern & Contemporary France, volume 25, issue 2 (May 2017). pp. 117–134

Chapter 2

From 'la petite Europe vaticane' to the Club Med: the French Socialist Party and the challenges of European integration
David Hanley
Modern & Contemporary France, volume 25, issue 2 (May 2017). pp. 135–151

Chapter 3

Between Euro-Federalism, Euro-Pragmatism and Euro-Populism: the Gaullist movement divided over Europe
Benjamin Leruth and Nicholas Startin
Modern & Contemporary France, volume 25, issue 2 (May 2017). pp. 153–169

Chapter 4

France and European macroeconomic policy coordination: from the Treaty of Rome to the euro area sovereign debt crisis
David Howarth and Joachim Schild
Modern & Contemporary France, volume 25, issue 2 (May 2017). pp. 171–190

Chapter 5

Drawing Algeria into Europe: shifting French policy and the Treaty of Rome (1951–1964)
Megan Brown
Modern & Contemporary France, volume 25, issue 2 (May 2017). pp. 191–208

CITATION INFORMATION

Chapter 6

European democracy deferred: de Gaulle and the Dehousse Plan, 1960
Eric O'Connor
Modern & Contemporary France, volume 25, issue 2 (May 2017). pp. 209–224

For any permission-related enquiries please visit:
http://www.tandfonline.com/page/help/permissions

Notes on Contributors

Megan Brown is Assistant Professor in History at Swarthmore College, Pennsylvania, USA.

David Hanley is Visiting Professor of European Studies at the Centre for European and International Studies Research, University of Portsmouth, UK.

David Howarth is Professor of Political Economy at the University of Luxembourg.

Benjamin Leruth is Assistant Professor in Public Administration at the University of Canberra, Australia.

Eric O'Connor is History and Economics Teacher at The Seven Hills School, Cincinnati, USA.

Chris Reynolds is Associate Professor of Contemporary French and European Studies at Nottingham Trent University, UK.

Joachim Schild is Professor of Comparative Government at the University of Trier, Germany.

Nicholas Startin is Head of Department of Politics, Languages & International Studies at the University of Bath, UK.

INTRODUCTION

Sixty years on: France and Europe from the Treaty of Rome to the 2017 elections

Helen Drake and Chris Reynolds

Introduction

The publication of this special issue is timed to coincide with the 60th anniversary of the signing of the Treaty of Rome in March 1957 by France and its five fellow founder members of the European Economic Community (EEC).[1] The Treaty of Rome committed France to integrate its economy ever more comprehensively with those of its fellow member states. If Parsons (2017) is to be believed, by far the majority of French organised interests at the time (political, economic, industrial, administrative, diplomatic) were just as resistant to this development as they had been to the 1951 Treaty of Paris establishing the European Coal and Steel Community, and the European Defence and Political Communities in 1954.

In this interpretation of history, a minority of French politicians carried the day in 1957 by virtue of luck and a constellation of circumstances, just as they had done in 1951 (and would do in later years at similar critical moments), whereas in 1954 these factors did not line up: former prime minister Georges Bidault had argued in the parliamentary debates on the European Defence Community in 1953 that building Europe could not come at the price of unmaking France or its empire (then, the Union française); 'il faut faire l'Europe,' Bidault argued, 'sans défaire l'Union française' (see Bossuat 2006, 52).

In contrast, the Treaty of Rome set up terms of engagement over which France had driven a hard bargain, which appeared unthreatening to national autonomy, and which survived the transition from the Fourth to the Fifth Republics in 1958. On the eve of the 2017 French presidential elections, our empirically rich collection of articles returns to those early years and to the 60 years since to inform our reflection on the state of France's EU membership today. Collectively, we assess how and why Europe matters in our understanding of contemporary France, and we seek to situate our findings in the ongoing research agendas for the study of France and the European Union.

Specifically, it would appear that studies of Europeanisation as an independent variable of change have in the case of France reached something of a dead end; or rather, from one reading of Parson's (2017) meta-review of recent literatures, reflect a 'distressing' stalemate in the reality of French politics, a 'national inertia' characterised by the 'resilience of the French party system and institutions' (599) and where 'French people have difficulty connecting their views on Europe to choices of representatives, and the only clear party positions on Europe come from extremists' (598).

Presidents and parties

Our contributors bring nuance to this picture. With regards to the presidency, and specifically the presidential elections of 2012, Reynolds's reading of the campaigns leads him to conclude that the question of Europe was clear and present, despite appearances to the contrary; it was, he argues, the elephant in the room finally revealed in all its bulk and immutability. President Sarkozy's response to the world financial and economic crisis of 2008 onwards and his enactment of the 2008 French presidency of the EU's Council of Ministers were the primary sources of this salience. In matter of fact, French presidential candidates throughout the Fifth Republic have all used presidential elections as occasions to solemnly and emphatically reaffirm their commitment to Europe, and the 2012 elections were no exception to the rule, certainly on the part of the mainstream candidates of right (Nicolas Sarkozy) and left (François Hollande). Moreover, French presidents routinely claim that they make no distinction between the national and European levels of governance, supporting Robert Ladrech's depiction of Europeanisation, coined as far back as 1994, as 'an incremental process reorientating the direction and shape of politics to the degree that EC [European Community] political and economic dynamics become part of the *organizational logic* of national politics and policy-making' (Ladrech 1994, 69, our emphasis).

So perhaps 'salient' is the wrong term to depict an issue that at presidential election time is both everywhere—as an 'organizational logic'; and nowhere—as a distinct political cleavage (Drake 2013). Behind this picture are France's parties of government which have been disturbed but not transformed by the addition of a European layer of governance in the Fifth Republic. Specifically, they have by and large eschewed any extensive revision of their ideological and ideational foundations. Parsons (2017) draws a direct line from the early days of the European Community to the present time in this regard, noting that '[t]he fragmentation that so confused French debates over the early communities, with parties struggling to digest or stifle European dilemmas, still troubles the relationship' (597).

In this collection, David Hanley for the French Socialist Party (Parti socialiste, PS) and Ben Leruth and Nick Startin for the 'Gaullist movement'—the mainstream right—arrive at broadly similar conclusions. Hanley returns to three key historical moments in the life of the intra-party management of the PS: the late 1950s ('joining the EEC and its immediate aftermath'); the 1983 policy U-turn of President François Mitterrand; and the presidency of François Hollande with specific reference to the Eurozone crisis. Taken together, Hanley finds strong evidence of continuity in the party's behaviour over the European issue; namely, that Europe was an 'active resource' for party management to impose unity, even at the cost of shedding 'disgruntled activists', but that over time this—holding a pro-EU line in the face of internal opposition—has come at serious cost to the party's inner strength (and electoral popularity). Unity was relatively easy to achieve in the case of the EEC: in comparison with the fissiparous impact on the party of the European Defence Community in 1954 and, above all, of the Algerian war, there was much to agree over in the Treaty of Rome. In 1983, Mitterrand's choices to forge ahead with European integration in the face of opposition within the party cost him some dissidents, entrenched fault lines within the party and also distinguished it from the French Communist Party, but simultaneously bolstered his power as President of the Republic. François Hollande, faced with the aftermath of the Eurozone crisis on coming to power in 2012, was similarly able to exert presidential power to marginalise dissenting voices in the PS on the question of macro-economic policy manoeuvre vis-à-vis the EU. However, the party entered the 2017 presidential elections seriously weakened: President Hollande declined to run for a second term in an unprecedented admission of weakness; incumbent prime minister Manuel Valls fell casualty to the party primaries which saw Benoît Hamon emerge from the left of the party as official presidential candidate; and former government minister Emmanuel Macron established his own movement and presidential platform, 'En Marche!'

On the right, Leruth and Startin show how the Gaullist legacy in European matters is also far from settled, and how it fragments support for the mainstream right. De Gaulle when president pursued a complex strategy towards *la construction européenne,* and so it is not surprising that his legacy is contested, meaning different things at different times to different people. Leruth and Startin do classify the legacy into three strands of Gaullist thought on Europe—federal, pragmatic and populist—and conclude that the Gaullist movement returns to the populist, *souverainiste* version like a moth to a flame, with the 2017 presidential elections so far conforming to type, confirming that at this time, 'the movement has failed to forge a coherent, common stance on Europe'. Here too we can ask whether this fragmentation is functional, in so far as this conservatism preserves differentials between individuals and their careers, and holds out the permanent hope of triumph over one's rivals. If so, and as with the PS, such a strategy comes at a cost, namely the opening of space for rival parties and movements with clearer messages on Europe in the case of 2017, by way of example, we can point to the National Front and its presidential election programme proposal for systematically reclaiming French legal, monetary, economic and political sovereignty from the EU.[2]

Policies and ideas

Howarth and Schild provide a complementary perspective on how the obduracy of French ideas on Europe has come at a high price, in this case, the loss of power relative to Germany, and an effective loss of economic autonomy in macro-economic policymaking to the point where the Economist Intelligence Unit in December 2011 branded French democracy 'flawed', specifically for the 'erosion of sovereignty and democratic accountability associated with the effects of and responses to the eurozone crisis' (Economist Intelligence Unit 2011). In their article for this collection, the authors trace the stability of French preferences in monetary policy since the late 1940s (with the exception of the 1958–1969 de Gaulle decade). This stability takes the form of consistent support for 'European-level mechanisms for balance of payments support'. In the current day, this amounts to a Keynesian belief that both debtor and creditor countries in the Eurozone should share responsibility for adjustments in order to reduce macro-economic imbalances between participating countries, as predicated in the post-war Bretton Woods system of 'embedded liberalism'. This is a policy line that runs counter to German ordo-liberalism thinking (a preference for macro-economic convergence [to the creditor country norm] and supranational governance of macro-economic fiscal policy), which has, time and time again, won out in the battle of ideas with France, despite the contributions of several significant and influential French figures (Robert Marjolin, Georges Pompidou, Jean-Pierre Fourcade, Valery Giscard d'Estaing, Raymond Barre, Pierre Bérégovoy) to the debate over the decades. Howarth and Schild argue that the Eurozone crisis did provide French leaders with a 'window of opportunity' to further their preferences, and that they had some limited success, but overall were capped by 'German hostility' to proposals such as Hollande's call for 'the mutualisation of public debt through the introduction of Eurobonds'. Howarth and Schild's carefully traced account 'from the Treaty of Rome to the euro area sovereign debt crisis' reveals very clearly how the Franco-German relationship functions as a self-regulating system of push and pull, give and take, where the interplay is determined as much by ideational difference as by diverging material interests. They conclude that the red line that France will not cross—to relinquish further autonomy in fiscal matters—has 'left the euro area in a dangerous in-between-territory'; and it has also left the French mainstream vulnerable to political attacks on the price it has paid over the years with regards to the battle of macro-economic ideas with its partner Germany.

Megan Brown and Eric O'Connor, finally for this collection, look back to the negotiations of the Treaty of Rome and the early years of its implementation to provide further examples of how domestic French preferences effectively limited alternative futures for the European Community (and by extension, today's European Union). Brown's study, 'Drawing Algeria into Europe', tells the fascinating story of 'Eurafrique' which never was: how the founding members of the EEC, at France's request, were ready to draw the boundaries of Europe beyond the Mediterranean to incorporate French Algeria. The account, drawing substantially on primary archival material, demonstrates how France's domestic turmoil—the loss of Algeria and the fall of the Fourth Republic—brought about an early contraction of the territorial reach of European integration, and set a course for how the EU would henceforth define its friends and neighbours: the momentum for EU–North African relations was never really regained, despite efforts along the way. The Eurafrique that never was, seen from today's perspective, was perhaps a lost opportunity to prevent the problems and human tragedies posed by today's ongoing flight of refugees from North Africa to the EU, and to which the EU still has little coherent answer.

Brown's article unpicks how France went about integrating l'Union française into the EEC as a key plank in its own 'Françafrique' strategy. Times had already moved on since the European Coal and Steel Community negotiations which did not include discussions of French empire. As that empire crumbled further during the 1950s, so did France look to the European level for support in maintaining (for example, via aid) what was left. France's sense of global mission at this time trumped concerns over national sovereignty: better Eurafrique than no Françafrique. French demands were met, market access would over time be accorded to French overseas possessions, and Algeria was set to become the 'most underdeveloped region of the European community'. Free movement of labour was a sticking point, for example for Italians fearing North African cheap labour; but, nevertheless, the Treaty of Rome lay 'the groundwork for an extension of Europe beyond the continent' and Brown talks of the 'long reach of the Treaty of Rome', geographically speaking.

As Algeria started to escape from the French grip, the EC6 struggled to picture Algeria as a third-party state: 'how would an independent state located on the continent of Africa be connected to the European Economic Community, and what legal and economic rights might this entail?' We note in passing that such questions are not irrelevant, in 2017, to the situation of the EU27 faced with Brexit. Ultimately, domestic French politics and the loss of Algeria meant that the Treaty plans for Algeria (Article 227) became redundant, but the influence of the negotiations over Eurafrique nevertheless skewed the EU's development policies from the start: 'In economic, political and geographical terms, Europe was never only on the continent. Indeed, its greatest advocates could not even agree where Europe ended and an African, Muslim or Arab world began' (Brown). As such, the case of Algeria and Europe informs our understanding of 'contemporary interrogations of Europe's borders and citizenship regimes' (Brown).

Eric O'Connor, in his article entitled 'European Democracy Deferred: de Gaulle and the Dehousse Plan, 1960', focuses on the period shortly after de Gaulle returned to power as President of the Fifth Republic. The matter in question is the debate that emerged in 1960 over the activation of the Treaty of Rome's Article 138 provisions for direct elections to the Assembly (the European Parliament [EP] as it subsequently became known). In this account of the debate, two unequal protagonists—Renaud Dehousse for the Assembly, and Charles de Gaulle (by proxy) for the Council of Ministers—clashed over their competing visions of democracy. Dehousse had given his name to the Assembly's report recommending the federalist-inspired move to transnational, direct elections to the Assembly; de Gaulle by 1960 had made clear his preference for plebiscitary democracy grounded in nations and their states. De Gaulle instructed his ministers to block the Assembly's 'Dehousse Plan' and in doing so drained support within the Community of Six from the already minority idea of a federal European future. In this regard, the Treaty of Rome was a casualty of having been 'created in one era, and implemented in another' and it is hard to disagree with O'Connor's conclusion that here too, we see the original Six store up ambiguity for future generations: this 'stalemate' over direct elections to the EP, argues O'Connor, 'perpetuated the original democratic design of European integration, in which democracy existed in shape and spirit, exemplified by a transnational parliament and its federalist representatives, but not in practice'. Despite direct elections to the EP finally coming on stream in 1979 and despite subsequent transfers of power to the EP in the EU's political system, this tension between the spirit and the practice of democracy at the level of the EU continues to be not only prominently writ large in EU-level discussion, but writ nationally at the level of French politics, as shown by our collection of articles discussed above.

In conclusion

The Fourth Republic that signed the Treaty of Rome 60 years ago did become undone but not over Europe. The Union française also became undone, again not because of Europe, and *despite* the EU5's willingness in the Treaty negotiations to extend 'Europe' to North Africa to accommodate French demands. The Fifth Republic inherited the 1957 settlement of the EU6 and implemented it *à sa guise*: we saw above the blocking moves of General de Gaulle with relation to direct elections to the EP, by way of example. But in the case of the Fifth Republic and 60 years on from the signing of the Treaty of Rome, it seems reasonable to ask the following question: by seeking not to become undone by the growing tensions of EU membership, perhaps contemporary France has fallen into the sort of transactionalist, cost–benefit relationship with the EU that we more readily associate with the United Kingdom's 'conditional and differential engagement' with the EU, and which made the UK vulnerable to its 2016 vote by referendum to withdraw from its 43-year membership (Geddes 2013). Seen from this perspective, the significance of 'Europe' to the 2017 French presidential elections becomes more obvious, and gives us a more realistic sense of the possible and probable outcomes from French policy towards Europe in the aftermath of those elections. Sixty years on from the signing of the Treaty of Rome, notions of 'Frexit' are both as far-fetched and as envisageable as was 'Brexit' in 2013, on the 40th anniversary of the UK's accession to the EEC.

Notes

1. Belgium, Luxembourg, the Netherlands, Italy and West Germany.
2. For detail, see https://www.marine2017.fr/wp-content/uploads/2017/02/projet-presidentiel marine-le-pen.pdf (accessed February 10, 2017).

Disclosure statement

No potential conflict of interest was reported by the authors.

References

Bossuat, G. 2006. *Faire l'Europe sans défaire la France. 60 ans de politique d'unité européenne des gouvernements et des présidents de la République française (1943–2003)*. Brussels: Peter Lang.

Drake, H. 2013. "Everywhere and Nowhere: Europe and the World in the French 2012 Elections." *Parliamentary Affairs* 66 (1): 124–141. doi:10.1093/pa/gss068.

Economist Intelligence Unit. 2011. "Democracy Index 2011: Democracy Under Stress." Accessed February 10, 2017. https://www.eiu.com/public/topical_report.aspx?campaignid=DemocracyIndex2011

Geddes, A. 2013. *Britain and the European Union*. Basingstoke: Palgrave, 11.

Ladrech, R. 1994. "Europeanization of Domestic Politics and Institutions: The Case of France." *Journal of Common Market Studies* 32 (1): 69–88.

Parsons, C. 2017. "France and the Evolution of European Integration." In *The Oxford Handbook of French Politics*, edited by R. Elgie, E. Grossman and A. Mazur, 585–605. Oxford: Oxford University Press.

Presidential elections and Europe: the 2012 game-changer

Chris Reynolds

ABSTRACT

As well as marking 60 years since the signature of the Treaty of Rome, 2017 will see the 10th presidential election of France's Fifth Republic. The overlap between the question of Europe and the election to France's highest office provides the framework for this article to explore the development of the European debate in France. Prior to 2012, and despite the increasing and undeniable salience of it for French domestic concerns, the question of Europe is widely considered to have been a secondary issue in presidential elections. Focusing in particular on the period since the pivotal debate and referendum on the Maastricht Treaty and the intervening transition from 'permissive consensus' to 'constraining dissensus', this article will explain how and why Europe has seemingly defied logic to remain on the margins of successive election campaigns, before presenting the 2012 presidential elections as a game-changer on how the question of Europe featured. The conclusion offers a discussion on the ramifications for future presidential elections, starting with that of 2017.

RÉSUMÉ

L'année 2017 marquera le soixantième anniversaire de la signature du Traité du Rome et verra la dixième élection présidentielle de la Ve République française. Une telle convergence fournit l'occasion idéale d'examiner le développement du débat européen en France. Avant 2012, et malgré son importance indéniable et croissante dans la politique domestique française, la question de l'Europe était largement perçue comme un enjeu d'importance secondaire dans les élections présidentielles. Se focalisant en particulier sur la période du tournant du référendum et débat sur Maastricht à la période suivante qui a vu s'opérer la transition du « permissive consensus » au « constraining dissensus », cet article expliquera comment et pourquoi l'Europe est restée, contre toute logique, en marge des campagnes électorales avant de démontrer comment les élections de 2012 ont changé la donne concernant la place de l'Europe dans le débat électoral. La conclusion s'interrogera sur les conséquences de ce changement pour les futures élections présidentielles, à commencer par celles de 2017.

Introduction

In the 60 years since the signing of the Treaty of Rome, the European project has become a central influence on French politics and society. Despite evidence of consistent general support, there has been increasing scepticism as sacrifices and negative consequences have become inevitable (Milner 2000). One would therefore be forgiven for assuming that the intervening period would have witnessed an elevation of the question of Europe to a crucial election issue. However, and as will be discussed in greater detail below, 'Europe has long been absent from French national electoral contests' (Dehousse and Tacea 2015, 152). Whilst opposition to Europe has been mounting, the political translation of it has been reserved to marginal and extreme elements. The dominant centre-right/centre-left forces have shared a consensus on the fundamental advancement of the EU project (Drake 2013, 127–128). As a result, Europe dominated by a 'rhetoric of unanimity' (Rozenberg 2011b) has never really been an issue with enough leverage to see it brought in from the margins of successive presidential campaigns. The strange set of circumstances that has seen the increasingly important issue of Europe astutely avoided has enabled analysts of its presence in election campaigns to describe it as 'invisible mais omniprésente' (Belot and Cautrès 2004).

This article begins by shedding some light on how this paradoxical set of circumstances has emerged, with the 1995 presidential elections as the logical starting point. Up until then, there had been little or no consultation between the political elite and the general population on this question. The belief, commonly described as the 'permissive consensus' (Lindberg and Scheingold 1970), was that widespread acceptance of the European project characterised the general view of the French (and general EU) population with much support for the French lead on its development and progression (Schmidt 2007, 999–1001). However, François Mitterrand's decision to ratify the Maastricht Treaty via a referendum in 1992 cast doubt on this assumption and revealed how the European question was far from consensual (Drake 2008, 197–198; Flood 2005, 43; Hurrelmann 2007, 352). The post-Maastricht era would see the 'permissive consensus' replaced by what has been described as a 'constraining dissensus' (Hooghe and Marks 2008). Europe, it is argued, has since then featured much more prominently on national political agendas as it has moved away from its status as the preserve of the mainstream elite. Despite this shift, the European question appears to have remained no more than an issue of secondary concern in successive election campaigns to France's highest office. The three presidential elections of 1995, 2002 and 2007 will be briefly analysed to demonstrate and explain how this period saw the European issue become an increasingly important, difficult, yet hidden, campaign theme. 2012 is then presented as a game-changing election signalling an important shift in how Europe featured. It will be concluded that Europe is now here to stay as a prominent issue in presidential election campaigns, reflecting its position as an unavoidable area of importance. The article will draw on material from speeches, manifestos, media appearances and polling data.

1995–2007: the European elephant

The 1995 elections were not only significant because they would turn the page on the Mitterrand era. They were equally the first post-Maastricht presidential elections. This was significant for two reasons. Firstly, the successful ratification of the Maastricht Treaty and its overwhelming backing by the bulk of France's mainstream politicians marked a significant step forward for the European project. As a result, the presence of Europe was set to weigh more heavily in the lives of the entire French population for years to come (Johnson 1997, 260–261). Secondly, despite the OUI victory, the referendum sparked considerable debate in France and exposed clear divisions over the issue amongst the electorate as well as within and between political parties (Milner 2000, 35–36; Rozenberg 2011a, 4–6). One would therefore have been forgiven for assuming that Europe's prominence as an election theme would increase accordingly. However, an examination of the 1995 campaign reveals that this did not materialise, with a 'conspicuous absence of a serious discussion on Europe' (Mazey 1995, 146; see also Flood 2005, 58; Ross 2000, 96–97) amongst candidates and only secondary importance afforded to the issue in opinion polls.[1] This paradoxical set of circumstances can be explained by the fact that the growing doubts and fears, as exposed by the Maastricht referendum debate, coupled with the continued consensus amongst the mainstream political elite over the advancement of the European project (Tiersky 1995, 116–119), meant that the interests of the main candidates were best served by avoiding this difficult issue.

By the time of the 2002 presidential elections, the progress of the European project had continued unabated, perhaps most symbolically represented with the introduction of the euro in January of the election year. With such developments came increasing doubts, fears and mounting Euroscepticism (Flood 2005, 42–63). Whilst President Chirac undoubtedly picked up the pro-European baton from his predecessor, there was an evident dampening in enthusiasm emanating from the Élysée, perhaps reflective of the doubts amongst the electorate. This was no more evident than in the changing nature of the Franco-German axis. The *moteur de l'Europe*, as previously represented by the Mitterrand–Kohl partnership, fell on difficult times as Chirac and German Chancellor Gerard Schroeder appeared to have very different priorities (Boussat 2006, 187–212). In such circumstances, once again, one would have assumed that Europe would have an increased bearing in the 2002 presidential election campaign. However, as had been the case in 1995, both in terms of the attention afforded by the candidates and polling data on important themes, the expected increase in prominence was not forthcoming. The increasing scepticism surrounding the question of Europe was a key factor in explaining why 'avoiding the issue of "Europe" unsurprisingly emerged in the 2002 elections and [was] an implicit campaign objective of the front-runners' (Drake 2003, 6). Despite Chirac's failings over Europe, his overall commitment to the project, juxtaposed with increasing doubts, rendered it an obsolete area for gaining political capital for all main candidates, thus explaining why it 'assez peu nourri les débats entre candidats tout au long de ce printemps electoral' (Belot and Cautrès 2004, 119). Such scant coverage unsurprisingly impacted on the importance afforded to the European question by the electorate, as evidenced in polling data where it continued to languish as a question of secondary importance or even as an issue of 'no significance' to voters (Lewis-Beck, Nadeau, and Bélanger 2012, 108–109).[2]

When the 2007 election came around, there was good reason to assume that Europe would feature as a salient campaign theme. Chirac's second term in office would be dominated by international affairs. Initially, his brave stance on the 2003 Iraq conflict earned him plenty of plaudits. However, before too long, he ran into serious difficulties and the issue of Europe was significant (Cole, Le Galès, and Levy 2008, 1–16). In particular, his 2005 decision to ratify the new European constitutional treaty via a referendum sparked an intense debate on the question of Europe on a scale not experienced since Maastricht. However, this time the result was inverted and any hope he had harboured of consolidating his popularity through a OUI victory evaporated when the French sensationally voted NON (Dulphy and Manigand 2006). This result (compounded by subsequent domestic difficulties) served to accentuate the significance of the 2007 elections as an opportunity to wipe the slate clean and start afresh. Given that Europe had so clearly defined the preceding period combined with the sheer intensity of debate, doubt and division as exposed by the referendum campaign, it is once again with a certain degree of puzzlement that the theme of Europe seemingly figured so little during the 2007 presidential campaign. The major candidates persisted with the approach of the two previous elections whereby the negativity (as exposed by the growing Euroscepticism brought so evidently to light during the referendum debate) saw them divert attention away from the problematic European question, instead choosing to focus heavily on domestic affairs (Cautrès 2007, 3). Once again, such minimal coverage cannot have been without significance on the persistence of Europe as a theme of only secondary importance in polling data.[3]

In summary, the discrepancy between the importance of Europe and its marginalisation in presidential election campaigns must be understood through the optic of widespread growing disenchantment that had seen the emergence of a growing gulf between political elites and their general populations (Bickerton, Hodson, and Puetter 2015, 710–711). Such a phenomenon is not exclusive to France, or indeed Europe, and is one that shows no sign of abating. However, this alone is insufficient. Explaining why the anticipated post-92 promotion of Europe as a central election issue did not materialise necessitates a consideration of the impact of the transition from 'permissive consensus' to 'constraining dissensus'. As Hooghe and Marks (2008) argue, with increasing public scepticism and deepening divisions within mainstream political parties, the elites were forced to look nervously over their shoulders when dealing with the European question (5). The upshot in presidential election campaigns was a tendency to avoid any overt discussion of Europe, with the obvious impact on how this was translated in the opinion polls (see Table 1).

Let us now turn our attention to the 2012 election as a game-changer in terms of how the European question featured.

Presidentials 2012—game changer

Nicolas Sarkozy was elected in 2007 on a *rupture* ticket, vowing to tackle the difficult reforms he deemed necessary to help France adapt to the demands of the twenty-first century global economy (Hewlett 2007, 407–410). His *hyperprésident* approach to reforms such as the pension regime combined with his inimitable presidential style soon led to a crisis in terms of his popularity (Cole 2012, 312–314; Gaffney 2012). It was however another crisis that would bring the question of Europe into stark focus. Despite declaring that 'la France est de retour en Europe' in his election victory speech, and his leading role in overcoming the 2005 setback with the renegotiated Lisbon Treaty, it was not until the onset of the global financial

Table 1. Salience of campaign themes, 1995–2007.

	Rank in importance		
	1995	2002	2007
Unemployment	1	1	1
Education	2	7	4
Personal security	8	2	7
Environment	9	6	6
Immigration	11	4	10
Europe	**13**	**11**	**12**

Note: Table adapted from CEVIPOF data ranking the importance of issues in presidential election campaigns (Lewis-Beck, Nadeau, and Bélanger 2012, 92).

crisis of 2008 that Europe became the central focus of Sarkozy's presidency. As the crisis gathered momentum and threatened the single currency via the Greece debacle, Sarkozy discovered the merits of the Franco-German axis and led France to centre stage in helping protect Europe's economy from a complete meltdown (Dimitrakopoulos, Menon, and Passas 2009, 451–465). By the beginning of 2012, the extent of the financial crisis had become clear and it inevitably dominated political debates and media coverage up and down the country. Such focalisation on the crisis was accentuated further by the President's calculation that his best chance of re-election lay by diverting attention away from his desperately unpopular domestic performance and instead focusing on presenting himself as the man that saved the euro from collapse. On the one hand, he was able to claim that the unprecedented financial meltdown prevented him from achieving all of his goals domestically. On the other, he could portray himself as a responsible leader who had been at the forefront of helping France and Europe face up to the crisis and prepare for the worst consequences it had to offer. His strategy was clearly to present himself as the candidate who needed to remain in post in order to see through the long-term plan he was responsible for putting in place.

The campaign—first round

The campaign for the first round of the 2012 election campaign involved 10 candidates (a drop in comparison to 2002 and 2007), five of whom inflected the campaign significantly. Outgoing President Sarkozy's official programme *Mes Propositions pour une France Forte et Juste* was a late arrival and was criticised for being light on detail but it certainly afforded considerable prominence to the question of Europe.[4] His campaign tour and public appearances saw him consolidate the main points of his policy on Europe—i.e. that Europe was of considerable importance for France, that the crisis had exposed the need for change and that he, having played such a central role in rescuing the project, was the best placed candidate to continue the job.[5] A typical example of Sarkozy's discourse on Europe came in his Récy speech of 15 March when he declared:

> Voilà à quoi nous avons consacré les quatre dernières années ! Maintenant que la crise financière est derrière nous, maintenant que nous avons résolu le problème grec – et ce n'est pas si simple – je veux vous le dire ici, en nous battant pour les autres nous nous sommes battus pour la France, en sauvant les autres nous nous sommes sauvés nous-mêmes, et où sont-ils tous ceux qui n'ont cessé de me critiquer lorsqu'avec Madame MERKEL nous nous battions pour sauver l'Euro, pour sauver l'Europe, pour sauver la Grèce ? Aujourd'hui que la crise financière est derrière nous…[6]

> François Hollande launched his campaign much earlier and, in his *60 Engagements pour la France*, outlined the importance of the European question.[7] His campaign speeches and appearances saw the Parti Socialiste (PS) candidate present himself as the alternative to Sarkozy's austerity-driven response to the crisis. He accepted the need for change but refused to accept the inevitability of the German-led line, insisting instead on the need for growth as the central focus.[8] For example, in his Paris speech of 17 March, Hollande declared:

> Nous sommes à un moment crucial, car l'élection présidentielle en France se tient au moment même où un nouveau traité est signé. Face à un pacte qui porte le nom de stabilité mais qui peut devenir un pacte d'austérité, j'oppose un pacte de responsabilité, de gouvernance et de croissance.[9]

The Sarkozy/Hollande duel was of course dominant. However, the unlikely clash between Jean-Luc Melenchon and Marine Le Pen provided an interesting battle that was not without significance and the question of Europe figured heavily.

The Front National candidate set out her programme in the manifesto entitled *Mon Projet* including the familiar anti-EU rhetoric of her party based around the demand for greater sovereignty via a withdrawal from the Eurozone and a renegotiation of all existing treaties.[10] Such themes punctuated her campaign tour as she insisted on the need to bring Europe into the debate more so as to avoid the usual cosy consensus of the mainstream elite.[11]Vous l'avez remarqué en effet, aucun des deux candidats siamois de l'UMP [Union pour un Mouvement Populaire] et du PS ne traite la question européenne, alors qu'elle engage très largement la France, les Français et leur avenir. Non, conscients de leur parfaite ressemblance sur le sujet de l'Europe, les siamois de l'UMP et du PS, qui souvenons-nous posaient fièrement ensemble en 2005 pour *Paris Match* afin d'appeler les Français à dire OUI à la Constitution de Monsieur Giscard, choisissent délibérément pendant cette campagne d'esquiver la question de l'Europe, au profit des coups de communication et des annonces sans lendemain, quand ce ne sont pas les noms d'oiseau ou les insultes![12]

Melenchon was equally critical of the European project but for very different reasons. In his *L'Humain d'abord* manifesto, the Front de Gauche candidate set out the need for a new direction.[13] Interpreting the post-Lisbon Europe as one firmly set on a neoliberal trajectory, he called for France to lead a new, post-crisis era for Europe based on social justice, ecology and the need to overcome the existing democratic crisis.[14]

> Il faut avoir la volonté et ne pas se coucher chaque fois que quelqu'un parle un peu fort, ne pas vouloir jouer le bon élève de la classe capitaliste, ne pas céder toutes les cinq minutes à Mme Merkel ou à je-ne-sais-qui quand ils font les gros yeux pour protéger la rente en Europe. […] Mais en plus nous aurons ouvert la brèche pour toute l'Europe car ce sera la première faille dans le dispositif des libéraux, que nous aurons réussie. Et après nous votent les Grecs. Après nous votent les Allemands. Et cette brèche s'élargira quand on verra que les Français ont commencé à abattre le mur, le mur de l'argent![15]

The final candidate of the five front-runners was the centrist François Bayrou. This stalwart of recent presidential elections reiterated his well-trodden, pro-European stance and sought to present himself as the consensual candidate in his *La France Solidaire* programme.[16] The manifesto and his campaign outlined his acceptance of how the crisis had exposed the frailties of the European project but that the response lay not in scapegoating Europe but instead in France leading a strengthening of the project, something it had always done and benefitted greatly from.[17]

> Je veux le dire face à tous les Français qui nous regardent et face au monde qui nous regarde, dans cette salle, dans ce grand courant d'opinion, dans ce peuple français qui est en train de se former pour son redressement : nous, l'Europe, nous l'aimons !Nous aimons l'Europe parce que nous aimons la France et nous aimons l'Europe du même amour que nous aimons la France, parce que c'est la même chose et le même destin. L'Europe est la clef du destin de la France comme la France est la clef du destin de l'Europe. Si l'Europe est faible, si l'Europe est vide, alors l'avenir de la France sera affaibli.[18]

Overall, the first-round campaign demonstrated just how significant the European question had become for the main candidates. Its prominence in manifestos, campaign literature and candidate speeches revealed, both directly and indirectly, how Europe had become an unavoidable issue for any serious contenders (Drake 2013, 124–141). It is interesting to consider, via a range of opinion polls, just what impact this had on the electorate (see Table 2 for overview of poll results).

An early Opinionway poll on 14–15 March 2012 asked respondents to outline the themes that would have the greatest influence on their choices in the first round.[19] Only 8% picked out *la construction européenne* with issues such as *le pouvoir d'achat* (43%), *l'emploi* (42%)

Table 2. Salience of 1st round campaign themes.

Opinionway		Ipsos		CSA		TNS Sofres		Harris Interactive	
Le pouvoir d'achat	46	Le pouvoir d'achat	43	Le pouvoir d'achat	45	La lutte contre le chômage	50	L'emploi	44
L'emploi	44	La crise économique et financière	42	L'emploi	38	La réduction de la dette et des déficits	31	La lutte contre les déficits, la dette	38
La protection sociale	30	Le chômage	38	La dette de l'État	30	L'amélioration de l'école et l'enseignement	29	Le pouvoir d'achat	36
La dette et les déficits	25	Les inégalités sociales	30	Les inégalités sociales	29	L'amélioration du pouvoir d'achat	26	L'éducation et la formation	32
Les inégalités sociales	24	L'immigration	25	L'immigration	20	Le financement du système de protection sociale	24	La lutte contre les inégalités	30
L'éducation et la formation	20	Les déficits publics	21	Les retraites	19	La lutte contre les inégalités et les injustices	23	Les impôts, la fiscalité	26
L'immigration	19	L'insécurité	21	La sécurité des biens et des personnes	17	La lutte contre la pauvreté	18	La moralisation de la vie politique	25
La sécurité	19	Les retraites	17	L'éducation et la recherche	13	La lutte contre l'insécurité	16	L'immigration	24
La fiscalité	17	Les impôts et les taxes	16	**L'avenir de l'euro**	**12**	La politique fiscale, les impôts et les taxes	15	Les retraites	21
L'environnement	17	Le fonctionnement du système de santé	9	L'accès aux soins	10	La lutte contre l'immigration clandestine	15	La santé	21
La construction européenne	**15**	**La construction européenne**	**8**	La protection de l'environnement	5	La protection de l'environnement	9	**L'Europe**	**20**
La France dans le monde	6	L'environnement	7	L'accès au logement	5	**La situation internationale**	**9**	La compétitivité des entreprises françaises	19
La corruption, les affaires	6	Le fonctionnement de la justice	6	Le nucléaire	2	L'intégration des minorités dans la société française	3	La sécurité des personnes et des biens	18
La mondialisation	4	L'accès au logement	3	Rien de tout cela	7			La lutte contre les délocalisations	16
NSP/NR	3	Les inégalités entre femmes et hommes	3					La réforme des institutions	14
		L'avenir de l'énergie nucléaire	0					La politique étrangère de la France	13

Note: Table 2 brings together the results of the five opinion polls referred to above and draws on the questions asking respondents to highlight the themes most important in determining their choices.

or *l'immigration* (21%) ranking higher. A similar question could be found in an Ipsos poll of 19–21 April, on the eve of the vote, where respondents were asked to identify the three dominant themes that would influence their decision.[20] Europe did not even figure, with similar domestic concerns taking priority. A CSA study conducted on polling day 22 April included a similar question with results showing how 12% chose the future of the euro to be a significant concern; again, hardly a top priority.[21] A TNS Sofres poll on the same day revealed no specific place for the question of Europe with 9% highlighting the international situation as important.[22] One poll that bucked the evident trend was a Harris Interactive study of 22 April where Europe figured much more prominently, drawing 20%, but still lagging behind the usual domestic concerns such as *la dette, l'éducation* or *les impôts*.[23]

Despite a certain degree of variation between the poll outcomes, there is a clear trend suggesting that, whilst Europe was certainly something that had some bearing on voter choices, the prominence afforded to this question by candidates was not replicated amongst the electorate. The first-round result contained no real surprises with Sarkozy (27.8%) and Hollande (28.63%) progressing to the second-round head-to-head (Kuhn 2013).

The campaign—second round

Neither candidate wasted any time getting back on the campaign trail following the first-round result. On 23 April Hollande was in Brittany and Sarkozy in Saint-Cyr-sur-Loire. Early evidence of the continued prominence of Europe was delivered by the PS candidate in his Quimper speech when he declared that he wanted to make 'l'élection présidentielle du 6 mai non pas une élection nationale mais une élection européenne'[24] He argued that this election provided the opportunity for France to set an example for other EU nations where there was an equal thirst for a new direction. Sarkozy countered with his insistence on the continuation of his successful approach. The impact of the strong first-round FN vote was clear to see in the outgoing President's tough rhetoric recognising that Europe was increasingly perceived as connected to difficulties over the economy and immigration. For example:

> Je veux m'adresser à ceux dont on méprise la douleur, à tous ceux auxquels on ne donne jamais la parole, parce que, au fond, on ne veut pas entendre leurs plaintes. À tous ceux qui ne supportent plus le déni de souffrance dont ils se sentent victimes, à tous ceux qui en ont assez d'entendre que l'insécurité n'est pas une réalité, que l'immigration, ce n'est pas un sujet. Le nombre d'insultes, d'injures que j'ai dû supporter parce que j'ai osé poser la question de l'immigration, c'est un scandale ![25]

Despite calls for more than the one televised debate scheduled for 2 May, the only other time the two candidates would share a television platform was for a special edition of *Des paroles et des actes* on 26 April.[26] However, instead of a conventional head-to-head debate, both appeared separately for a strictly regulated 35 minutes each. A wide range of issues were covered, including Europe. Hollande called into question the liberal, deregulationist approach of the EU and was highly critical of the 'Merkozy'-led austerity response to the crisis. Sarkozy also focused heavily on Europe and countered Hollande's negative assessment of his European policy, claiming that his record and approach was and would continue to be successful. Only through a continuation of his line, he argued, would France truly experience the growth his competitor was so keen on.

Beyond the polemical debate around the ownership of 1 May, *la fête du travail* provided a high-profile opportunity for both candidates (and Marine Le Pen) to address the nation (Leveque 2012). Hollande attended a meeting in Nevers to mark this important date and commemorate the passing of Pierre Bérégovoy. He made much of the past, including that of the former Prime Minister and François Mitterrand, and in particular the long-held pro-Europeanism of his party:

> Je suis européen. François Mitterrand nous a montré la voie. Pierre Bérégovoy a éclairé le passage. Je suis européen parce que je pense que dans un contexte comme nous le connaissons, la crise qui frappe, notre Europe peut être le levier, la solution – sauf si elle se condamne à l'austérité, ce que le candidat sortant a choisi comme orientation avec la chancelière d'Allemagne.[27]

He hammered home the point that his victory would provide a much-sought example for other EU nations seeking an alternative to austerity. Sarkozy held a huge rally at the Trocadero in Paris where, whilst re-affirming his pro-European credentials, he highlighted the increasing fears attached to the project and in particular the perceived detrimental impact on French workers. The solution he argued lay with the borders—Europe's external borders as well as those within:

> Il faut des frontières à l'Europe. Il faut des frontières à la France. Non pour s'enfermer, mais pour s'affirmer dans le monde. Pour clarifier les rapports avec les autres. La frontière, c'est le droit opposé à la force. C'est la règle opposée au désordre. C'est la régulation au lieu du laisser-faire. Les frontières, cela peut paraître loin des préoccupations quotidiennes de ceux qui se lèvent tôt et qui travaillent dur.[28]

The now traditional, and arguably pivotal, TV debate between the candidates took place on 2 May and, unsurprisingly, the marathon three-hour session saw a broad range of issues discussed.[29] There was no direct discussion of the European question. However, its importance in transcending a number of issues was evident throughout. Whilst the pro-European stance of both candidates may help explain why it did not feature more specifically, that is not say there were no differences on the subject. Inevitably, the crisis brought the discussion on Europe to the table. The now-familiar pattern of Sarkozy defending his approach thus far and the need for it to continue, countered by Hollande arguing that the time had come for a new European direction, was in evidence.

Both candidates brought their campaigns to a close on 3 May with speeches in Toulon (Sarkozy) and Toulouse (Hollande). Unsurprisingly, the familiar lines on Europe were maintained and remained prominent in both camps. The outgoing president sought to remind the electorate of his central role in steering France and Europe through the crisis.

> La France n'a pas été emportée comme tant d'autres pays comme un fétu de paille par la crise. Nous avons tenu. Nous avons pris les mesures, les mesures qui s'imposaient face à l'urgence [...] les réformes qui nous ont évité de connaître l'humiliation que connaît aujourd'hui la Grèce, les souffrances que connaissent l'Italie et le Portugal et aujourd'hui les affres que connaît l'Espagne.[30]

He argued that changing the president would lead to an absurd, new direction and inevitable disaster: 'Deux jours de mensonges, et des années pour régler la facture, voilà le projet socialiste'. The PS candidate consolidated his discourse on how he had given some credibility to the idea of an alternative approach for Europe. He argued that something considered impossible was now perfectly possible and even desirable. His victory, he argued, would be a victory not just for France but also for Europe.

> Le devoir qui est le nôtre, la responsabilité qui est la mienne, c'est que la victoire du 6 mai soit ressentie partout en Europe comme un moment d'espoir, comme un moment de confiance, de redressement possible. Je reçois des messages de la Grèce, du Portugal, de l'Espagne, de l'Italie, partout où ils nous disent : « Surtout ne laissez pas passer votre chance, vous, peuple français, permettez l'alternance pas simplement en France mais dans toute l'Europe ! ». Nous avons un devoir de victoire.[31]

The first-round trend that saw candidates afford significant importance to the European question clearly continued into round two. To establish whether or not this was replicated amongst the electorate, one can turn to a range of opinion poll results (see Table 3 for overview of poll results). Figures 1 and 2 below show two word clouds produced on the results of the following question posed in a 6 May Harris Interactive Poll: 'Quelles sont toutes les raisons pour lesquelles vous avez voté pour Nicolas Sarkozy/François Hollande?'[32]

On first view, it would appear that Europe remained very much a secondary concern for both Sarkozy and Hollande supporters. Nevertheless, that it featured at all could lend weight to the assessment that Europe was beginning to emerge as a more significant area of concern, interestingly more so for those having voted for Sarkozy. Another voting day poll by Opinionway asked respondents to identify the questions that counted most in their second-round choices.[33] *La construction européenne* garnered a significant 21% but still lagged behind the same domestic issues given priority in round one. A TNS Sofres poll on the same day presented results to a very similar question where Europe was not even mentioned and *la situation internationale* received 10%.[34] Such an absence for Europe was identifiable in an Ipsos rolling poll in the period leading up to the second-round vote.[35] Respondents were asked to identify three areas that concerned them most from a personal

Figure 1. Reasons for voting Hollande.

Figure 2. Reasons for voting Sarkozy.

Table 3. Salience of 2nd round campaign themes.

Opinionway		TNS Sofres		Ipsos (pour la France)		Ipsos (personnellement)	
L'emploi	50	La lutte contre le chômage	49	La crise économique financière	56	Le pouvoir d'achat	61
Le pouvoir d'achat	48	La réduction de la dette et des déficits	36	Le chômage	47	Les retraites	35
La dette et les déficits	47	L'amélioration de l'école et l'enseignement	32	Les déficits publics	36	Les impôts et les taxes	31
La protection sociale	46	L'amélioration du pouvoir d'achat	29	Le pouvoir d'achat	29	Le fonctionnement du système de santé	23
Les inégalités sociales	35	Le financement du système de protection sociale (retraites, santé…)	28	L'immigration	24	La crise économique financière	23
L'éducation et la formation	34	La lutte contre les inégalités et les injustices	23	Les inégalités sociales	17	Le chômage	21
L'immigration	34	La lutte contre la pauvreté	18	Le système éducatif	15	Le système éducatif	16
Le rôle de la France dans le monde	27	La lutte contre l'immigration clandestine	17	L'insécurité	15	L'insécurité	16
La sécurité	25	La lutte contre l'insécurité	15	Le fonctionnement du système de santé	13	Les inégalités sociales	14
La fiscalité	24	La politique fiscale, les impôts et les taxes	15	Les impôts et les taxes	12	L'immigration	13
La construction européenne	**21**	**La situation internationale**	**10**	Les retraites	10	Les déficits publics	9
La corruption, les affaires	20	La protection de l'environnement	7	Le fonctionnement de la justice	6	L'environnement	8
L'environnement	13	L'intégration des minorités dans la société française	6	L'accès au logement	5	L'accès au logement	7
La mondialisation	9	Sans réponse	1	L'environnement	4	Le fonctionnement de la justice	5
Aucun de ceux-là	5			L'avenir de l'énergie nucléaire	3	Les inégalités entre femmes et hommes	3

Note: Table 3 brings together the results of the three opinion polls referred to above and draws on the questions asking respondents to highlight the themes most important in determining their choices.

perspective and also for France more generally. Neither set of results received any explicit reference to Europe.

On the surface, it would appear that Europe was not of any serious concern to the French electorate in 2012. There certainly appears to have been a significant gap between the electorate and the main candidates in relation to the question of Europe and its importance. This ambiguity helps explain Drake's analysis of the European issue being 'everywhere and nowhere' during the campaign (Drake 2013). The following section provides an explanation for this paradoxical set of circumstances and explains why 2012 should nevertheless be considered a game-changer in relation to this question.

Making sense

The first point to make relates to the fact that in all presidential elections prior to, and including, 2012, polling data has revealed Europe to be little more than a secondary consideration for the electorate. It is undeniable that Europe has consistently featured well down the list of declared priorities. However, one must be careful not to draw over-simplistic conclusions. Whilst it may well be the case that Europe has not featured in explicit terms, it is impossible to dissociate those themes that have been most prominent from the question of Europe. As the years have passed and the European project has progressed, it has become an undeniably prominent feature in the way in which France functions (Schmidt 2007, 995–998). However, Europe is not something that exists outside France, it is stitched into the very fabric of how it works and importantly how France views itself. This relationship with Europe as somewhat of a fait accompli has been reinforced by the dominant political discourse which can be traced back as far as François Mitterrand's 1983 volte-face. When he then declared in 1987 that 'la France est notre patrie et l'Europe notre avenir', France signalled its choice to henceforth follow a very strong pro-European trajectory and from that point on everyone seemingly bought into the project (Boussat 2006, 182). So central has Europe become since then that it could argued as more of a domestic than a foreign policy issue (Rowdybush and Chamorel 2011, 170). The fact that it is viewed in this manner goes some way towards explaining how and why it has never really featured explicitly as a separate issue of importance for the electorate, as borne out by the polling data. The counter-intuitive consequence that has seen the increased salience of Europe find no replication in its perceived prominence as a principle concern for the electorate (Dehousse and Tacea 2015, 152) can in part be explained by the fact that its significance has been hidden by the conflation between Europe and key domestic issues such as unemployment, economy, immigration etc. As demonstrated above, 2012 did not reveal any significant shift in polling data, with Europe continuing in its position of secondary importance. Nothing then, it could be argued, sets 2012 apart. For the voting public, Europe remained 'the elephant in the room'. The real and significant change concerns the manner with which this issue was handled by the presidential candidates.

Prior to 2012, the question of Europe was not one that featured prominently in the campaigns of major candidates. Recognising the mounting scepticism towards Europe alongside the seemingly immovable French commitment to the project, no presidential candidates saw any real value in prioritising it in their campaigns. Instead, and central to maintaining the 'elephant in the room' status, the 'constraining dissensus' era saw mainstream parties continue to 'resist politicising the issue' (Hooghe and Marks 2008, 21). This is where 2012 becomes the game-changer. If the previous three elections saw Europe dodged or avoided, it is impossible to draw the same conclusion in 2012. In fact, as argued by Dehousse and Tacea (2015), it would be reasonable to discuss the 2012 presidential campaign as having been 'Europeanised', with this issue a consistently important theme right across the political spectrum (155).

Central to understanding the reasons behind this shift is the impact of the global financial crisis of 2008. However, it is first of all important to map out the context within which this crisis struck as it is one where Europe had already started to emerge as a prominent concern. Upon his election in 2007, Sarkozy was unambiguous in outlining his determination to make Europe a priority. In a bid to overcome what he perceived as the setbacks of the Chirac era, he set out to re-establish France's place as a leader of the European project. This Europeanisation of the French presidency was in full evidence in Sarkozy's central role in the process leading to the Lisbon Treaty which essentially sought to make up for the damage cause by the French 2005 NON vote (Dehousse and Menon 2009, 100–101). Sarkozy's prioritisation of Europe therefore pre-dated the onset of the financial crisis but it was unquestionably accentuated as a result. When the subprime crisis hit the world economy in 2007–2008, the impact on France was, to a certain extent, underestimated. In the early stages, there was even some suggestion that the structure of the French economy (previously lamented by Sarkozy) could somehow shelter France from the worst of what was to come (de la Brosse 2009). However, as the full impact unfolded, it became clear that France would not be spared and the 2008–2012 period was one that saw the crisis inevitably dominate public and political debates (Hewlett 2012). The multiple and interconnected consequences of the exceptional context lie at the heart of explaining why the 2012 presidential elections can be described as a game-changer for the European question.

Firstly, it would be no longer possible for Europe to be the 'elephant in the room' issue. How could a presidential campaign in 2012 hope to relegate Europe to a secondary issue when the economic crisis had effectively monopolised political and media debates and thus brought the question of Europe to everyone's attention? (Dehousse and Tacea 2012, 6; Lequesne 2012). Secondly, Sarkozy's response to focus all of his attentions on helping save the euro alongside Angela Merkel in the latter stages of his mandate meant that one of the principal candidates had effectively put all his eggs in the European basket and was intent on making as much political capital from the issue as possible. Thirdly, the long-held, mainstream discourse that Europe was a positive for France—under pressure for some time (Kramer 2006; Rozenberg 2011a, 2015)—became an extremely difficult line to toe in the wake of the financial crisis. As the euro emerged as the greatest victim of the depression, the feeling spread that France was being further dragged into the mire as a result. This was pounced upon by Eurosceptics and in particular the FN, who sought to exploit the crisis and place it front and centre in their own campaign.[36] The central argument that Europe could be a shield to protect France from the vicissitudes of globalisation became a very difficult one to support when this US-born crisis stood to cripple the French economy (for some) because of French membership of the EU.[37] The context of the crisis therefore forced the 'constraining dissensus' onto the presidential election agenda. As a result, the debate over Europe was no longer the preserve of extreme, populist parties on the left and right, and mainstream candidates were left with little choice but to engage with Europe as a central issue. The fourth and final point relates to the subsequent breakdown in the 'rhetoric of unanimity'. The hitherto dominant consensus between the mainstream candidates over the advancement and direction of the European project that had been so central during the eras of the 'permissive consensus' and 'constraining dissensus' also broke down as a result of the crisis. The two main candidates, whilst both adamant pro-Europeans, argued for two very different responses to the crisis. On the one hand, Sarkozy insisted on the continuity of his austerity-driven programme whereas Hollande called for a new anti-austerity direction focused on growth. Such differentiation meant that for the first time there was some political capital to be gained in both camps in making more of Europe as a key election theme.

Prior to 2012, the evasive approach of presidential candidates that had seen Europe pushed to the margins of campaign debates reflected the 'silent Europeanisation' experienced in France in spite of mounting fears, doubts and opposition (Rozenberg 2011a, 11). However, in the run-up to the 2012 campaign, a number of factors converged to ensure that any hope of Europe continuing as an unspoken issue would be impossible. The build-up in tension finally broke through as a result of the convergence between Sarkozy's Europeanised presidency and the onset of the financial crisis. The subsequent prioritisation of Europe and its now flagrant and undeniable importance to, and influence on, domestic French issues meant that it was no longer possible for it to be relegated to an issue of secondary importance.

Conclusion

The shift in election campaign coverage afforded to the issue of Europe in 2012 is important in signalling an irreversible change in how it will feature in future presidential elections, starting in 2017. With Europe now placed as a central concern for candidates, the proverbial cat has been let out of the bag and it is difficult to see how this can be undone. Furthermore, it was argued earlier that a number of convergent factors came together to essentially force candidates to move away from the evasive treatment of the European question that hitherto had been so dominant. Central to such concerns were the shifting contextual circumstances of the financial crisis that made it virtually impossible to push any consideration of Europe's influence or importance to the margins of the campaign debate. Given the events of the 2012–2017 period—the migrant crisis, the threat of terrorism, ongoing economic difficulties, the Brexit controversy, Hollande's failure to deliver on his anti-austerity rhetoric, and the growing support for the FN and its Eurosceptic stance—, it is obvious that Europe will remain an area of unavoidable and principal concern for all candidates in the 2017 presidential elections. One only has to consider the attention afforded to the European question in the all-important primaries on the left and the right as an early indicator of just how significant Europe has become and will continue to be.[38] The increased salience as dictated by recent contextual developments will not be without consequence on the priorities of the electorate. Whilst it is unlikely to bypass the traditional dominant concerns (unemployment, spending power and immigration), there is a distinct possibility that Europe as an explicit (as well as implicit) theme of concern will feature much more prominently in the list of priorities determining voters' choices in 2017. This will undoubtedly force candidates to afford Europe even more attention. Such a symbiotic process will see Europe progressively become increasingly important as an electoral issue, rendering its days as the 'elephant in the room' very much a thing of the past.

Notes

1. See for example Ipsos, Sondage sortie des urnes, April 23, 1995. http://www.ipsos.fr/ipsos-public-affairs/sondages/sondage-sortie-urnes-1; Ipsos, Sondage, sortie des urnes, May 7, 1995. http://www.ipsos.fr/sondages/sortie-urnes
2. Ipsos, 1er Tour Présidentielle 2002, April 21, 2002. http://www.ipsos.fr/sondages/1er-tour-presidentielle-2002comprendre-vote-francais-qui-vote-quoi-mot; Ipsos, Second Tour Présidentielle 2002, May 5, 2002. http://www.ipsos.fr/sondages/second-tour-presidentielle-2002-comprendre-vote-francais
3. Ipsos, 1er Tour Présidentielle 2007, April 22, 2007. http://www.ipsos.fr/presidentielle-2007/pdf/ssu.pdf
4. https://www.agitateur.org/IMG/pdf/Sarkozy2012.pdf
5. See for example campaign speeches in Annecy, February 16, 2012; Marseilles, February 19, 2012; Lille, February 23, 2012; Villepinte, March 11, 2012; Récy, March 15, 2012; Rueil-Malmaison, March 24, 2012. The following website is a useful resource for tracking down transcripts of such speeches: http://www.vie-publique.fr/
6. Nicolas Sarkozy, Récy, March 15, 2012.
7. http://www.ps29.org/IMG/pdf/Projet_FH2012.pdf
8. See for example campaign speeches in Toulon, January 24, 2012; Le Bourget, January 22, 2012; Le Mans, February 23, 2012; Lyon, March 1, 2012; Valence, March 13, 2012; Marseilles, March 14, 2012; Paris, March 17, 2012. The following website is a useful resource for tracking down transcripts of such speeches: http://www.vie-publique.fr/. See also http://www.les-crises.fr/documents/2012/discours-de-campagne-hollande-2012.pdf
9. François Hollande, Paris, March 17, 2012.
10. http://www.frontnational.com/pdf/projet_mlp2012.pdf
11. See for example campaign speeches in Rouen, January 15, 2012; Toulouse, February 5, 2012; Châteauroux, February 26, 2012; Marseilles, March 4, 2012; Paris, March 8, 2012; Toulouse-Blagnac, March 12, 2012. The following website is a useful resource for tracking down transcripts of such speeches: http://www.vie-publique.fr/
12. Marine Le Pen, Paris, March 8, 2012.
13. http://www.jean-luc-melenchon.fr/brochures/humain_dabord.pdf
14. See for example campaign speeches in Paris, January 4, 2012; Besancon, January 24, 2012; Lille, March 27, 2012; Toulouse, April 5, 2012; Paris, April 22, 2012. The following website is a useful resource for tracking down transcripts of such speeches: http://www.vie-publique.fr/. Alternatively see http://www.jean-luc-melenchon.fr/videotheque/
15. Jean-Luc Melenchon, Paris, March 18, 2012.
16. http://www.mouvementdemocrate.fr/media/PDF/lafrancesolidaire.pdf
17. See for example campaign speeches in Dunkirk, January 19, 2012; Strasbourg, March 6, 2012; Perpignan, March 29, 2012; Rennes, April 10, 2012; Tours, April 13, 2012; Lyon, April 16, 2012. The following website is a useful resource for tracking down transcripts of such speeches: http://www.vie-publique.fr/
18. François Bayrou, March 6, 2012.
19. Opinionway, le baromètre de la présidentielle 2012, March 14–15, 2012. http://www.opinion-way.com/pdf/opinionway-fiducial_pour_le_figaro_et_lci_le_barometre_de_la_presidentielle_2012_-_v5.pdf
20. Ipsos, 1er tour présidentielle 2012. Comprendre le vote des Français, April 19–21, 2012. http://www.ipsos.fr/decrypter-societe/2012-04-22-comprendre-vote-francais
21. CSA, élection présidentielle 2012. Sondage jour du vote premier tour, April 22, 2012. http://csa.eu/multimedia/data/sondages/data2012/opi20120422-sondage-jour-du-vote-premier-tour-election-presidentielle-2012-raisons-du-choix-et-profil-des-electorats.pdf
22. TNS Sofres, Le premier tour de l'élection présidentielle 2012. Sondage jour du vote, April 22, 2012. http://www.tns-sofres.com/etudes-et-points-de-vue/presidentielle-2012-tour-1-sondage-jour-du-vote#

23. Harris Interactive, Sondage jour du vote: Motivations de vote et d'abstention au premier tour de l'élection présidentielle de 2012. April 22, 2012. http://harris-interactive.fr/wp-content/uploads/sites/6/2015/09/Results_HIFR_Jourduvote_22042012.pdf
24. François Hollande, Quimper, April 23, 2012.
25. Nicolas Sarkozy, Saint-Cyr-sur-Loire, April 23, 2012.
26. *Des paroles et des actes*, France 2, April 26, 2012.
27. François Hollande, Nevers, May 1, 2012.
28. Nicolas Sarkozy, Paris, May 1, 2012.
29. Débat présidentielle, TF1/France 2, May 2, 2012. https://www.youtube.com/watch?v=Fhv1VVCRrJY
30. Nicolas Sarkozy, Toulon, May 3, 2012.
31. François Hollande, Toulouse, May 3, 2012.
32. Harris Interactive, Sondage Jour du vote: Motivations de vote et d'abstention au second tour de l'élection présidentielle de 2012, May 6, 2012. http://harris-interactive.fr/wp-content/uploads/sites/6/2015/09/Results_HIFR_Jourduvote_06052012.pdf
33. Opinonway, Sondage jour du vote 2nd tour de l'élection présidentielle du 6 mai 2012, May 6, 2012. http://opinionlab.opinion-way.com/dokumenty/Sondage_jour_du_vote_2nd_tour_de_l%C3%A9lection%20pr%C3%A9sidentielle_du_6_mai_2012_13.pdf
34. TNS Sofres, Le second tour de l'élection présidentielle 2012. Sondage Jour du Vote, May 6, 2012. http://www.tns-sofres.com/publications/presidentielle-2012-tour-2-sondage-jour-du-vote#
35. Ipsos, Présidoscope, Vague 10, April 27–30, 2012. https://issuu.com/cheurfa/docs/rapport_presidoscopie_vague10/2?e=2141223/5343041
36. See for example the FN reaction to the crisis: http://www.frontnational.com/dossier-special-crise-monetaire/
37. See for example Jean-Luc Melenchon's April 2012 declaration: http://www.humanite.fr/politique/avec-le-front-de-gauche-une-autre-europe-une-autre-mondialisation-494330
38. See for example http://www.lefigaro.fr/politique/le-scan/citations/2016/06/27/25002-20160627ARTFIG00108-projet-europeen-les-candidats-a-la-primaire-de-la-droite-tentent-de-se-demarquer.php; http://www.lexpress.fr/actualite/politique/primaire-ps-comment-benoit-hamon-tente-de-se-demarquer-d-arnaud-montebourg_1824989.html

Disclosure statement

No potential conflict of interest was reported by the author.

References

Belot, Céline, and Bruno Cautrès. 2004. « L'Europe, invisible mais omniprésente. » In *Le nouveau désordre électoral*, edited by Bruno Cautrès and Nonna Mayer, 119–144. Paris: Presses de Sciences Po.

Bickerton, Christopher J., Dermot Hodson, and Uwe Puetter. 2015. "The New Intergovernmentalism: European Integration in the Post-Maastricht Era." *Journal of Common Market Studies* 53 (4): 703–722.

Boussat, Gérard. 2006. *Faire l'Europe sans défaire la France. 60 ans de politique d'unité européenne des gouvernements et des présidents de la République française (1943-2003)*. Brussels: Peter Lang.

Cautrès, Bruno. 2007. "Les enjeux européens." *CEVIPOF. Baromètre politique français. Elections 2007*. http://www.cevipof.com/bpf/analyses/Cautres_EnjeuxEuropens.pdf.

Cole, Alistair. 2012. "The Fast Presidency? Nicolas Sarkozy and the Political Institutions of the Fifth Republic." *Contemporary French and Francophone Studies* 16 (3): 311–321.

Cole, Alisatair, Patrick Le Galès, and Jonah, Levy. 2008. *Developments in French Politics*. Hampshire: Palgrave Macmillan.

De la Brosse, Julie. 2009. "Le gouvernement s'est-il converti au 'modèle social français?" *L'Express*, 15/05/2009.

Dehousse, Renaud, and Anand Menon. 2009. "The French Presidency." *Journal of Common Market Studies* 47: 99–111.

Dehousse, Renaud, and Angela Tacea. 2012. "The French 2012 Presidential Election. A Europeanised Contest." *Les Cahiers Européens de Sciences Po*. 02/20012.

Dehousse, Renaud, and Angela Tacea. 2015. "Europe in the 2012 French Presidential Election." In *France After 2012*, edited by Goodliffe Gabriel and Brizzi Riccardo, 152–166. New York: Berghahn Books.

Dimitrakopoulos, D., A. Menon, and A. Passas. 2009. "France and the EU Under Sarkozy: Between European Ambitions and National Objectives?" *Modern & Contemporary France* 17 (4): 454–465.

Drake, Helen. 2003. "Europe in the 2002 French Elections." Paper presented for the 8th EUSA Biennial International Conference, March 27-29, 2003, Nashville, Tennessee, USA. http://aei.pitt.edu/6482/1/001502_1.PDF.

Drake, Helen. 2008. "The European Fifth Republic." *Contemporary French and Francophone Studies* 12 (2) 193–201.

Drake, Helen. 2013. "Everywhere and Nowhere: Europe and the World in the French 2012 Elections." *Parliamentary Affairs* 66: 124–141.

Dulphy, Ann, and Christine Manigand. 2006. "Le referendum du 29 mai 2005." *RSPB* 289 (1) 2006 22–46.

Flood, Chris. 2005. "French Euroscepticism and the Politics of Indifference." In *French Relations with The European Union*, edited by Helen Drake, 42–63. Abingdon: Routledge.

Gaffney, John. 2012a. "Leadership and Style in the French Fifth Republic: Nicolas Sarkozy's Presidency in Historical and Cultural Perspective." *French Politics* 10 (4): 345–363.

Gaffney, John. 2012b. *Political Leadership in France. From de Gaulle to Nicolas Sarkozy*. Hampshire: Palgrave Macmillan.

Hewlett, Nick. 2007. "Nicolas Sarkozy and the Legacy of Bonapartism. The French Presidential and Parliamentary Elections of 2007." *Modern and Contemporary France* 15 (4): 402–422.

Hewlett, Nick. 2012. "Voting in the Shadow of the Crisis. The French Presidential and Parliamentary Elections of 2012." *Modern and Contemporary France* 20 (4): 403–420.

Hooghe, Liesber, and Gary Marks. 2008. "A Postfunctionalist Theory of European Integration: From Permissive Consensus to Constraining Dissensus." *British Journal of Political Science* 39: 1–23.

Hurrelmann, Achim. 2007. "European Democracy, the 'Permissive Consensus' and the Collapse of the EU Constitution." *European Law Journal* 13 (3) 343–359.

Johnson, Douglas. 1997. "Foreign Policy Issues and the Election." In *French Presidentialism and the Election of 1995*, edited by John Gaffney and Lorna Milne, 259–271. Aldershot: Ashgate.

Kramer, Steven Philip. 2006. "The End of French Europe." *Foreign Affairs* 85 (4): 126–138.

Kuhn, Raymond. 2013. "The French Presidential and Parliamentary Elections, 2012." *Representation* 49 (1): 97–114.

Lequesne, Christian. 2012. « L'externe et l'européen dans la campagne présidentielle de 2012. » *Les Dossiers du CERI*. http://www.sciencespo.fr/ceri/fr/content/lexterne-et-leuropeen-dans-la-campagne-presidentielle-de-2012.

Leveque, Emilie. 2012. "La polémique sue la 'fête du travail' en 5 points." *L'express*, 24/04.

Lewis-Beck, Michael S., Richard Nadeau, and Eric Bélanger. 2012. *French Presidential Elections*. Hampshire: Palgrave Macmillan.

Lindberg, Leon A., and Stuart A. Scheingold. 1970. *Europe's Would-be Polity: Patterns of Change in the European Community*. Hemel Hempstead: Prentice-Hall.

Mazey, Sonia. 1995. "The Issue Agenda in Perspective." In *Electing the French President. The 1995 Presidential Election*, edited by Robert Elgie, 123–148. Hampshire: Macmillan.

Milner, Susan. 2000. "Euroscepticism in France and Changing State-Society Relations." *European Integration* 22 (1): 35–58.

Ross, George. 2000. "Europe Becomes French Domestic Politics." In *How France Votes*, edited by Michael S., Lewis-Beck, 87–114. New York: Chatham House Publishers.

Rowdybush, Brinton, and Patrick Chamorel. 2011. "Aspirations and reality: French Foreign Policy and the 2012 Elections." *The Washington Quarterly* 35 (1): 163–177.

Rozenberg, Olivier. 2011a. "Monnet for Nothing? France's Mixed Europeanisation." *Les Cahiers Européens de Sciences Po* 04/2011.

Rozenberg, Olivier. 2011b. "Debating about Europe at the French National Assembly: The Failure of the Rhetoric of Unanimity." In *What form of government for the European Union and the Eurozone?*, edited by Fabbrini Frederico, Ballini Ernst Hirsch, and Somsen Han, 145–165. Oxford: Hart Publishing.

Rozenberg, Olivier. 2015. "France in Quest of a European Narrative." *Foundation Robert Schuman* 345: 1–7.

Schmidt, Vivien A. 2007. "Trapped by their Ideas: French elites' Discourses of European Integration and Globalsization." *Journal of European Public Policy* 14 (7): 992–1009.

Tiersky, Ronald. 1995. "Mitterrand's Legacies." *Foreign Affairs* 74 (1): 112–121.

From 'la petite Europe vaticane' to the Club Med: the French Socialist Party and the challenges of European integration

David Hanley

ABSTRACT

Studies of the relationship of political parties to the European Community/Union (EC/EU) increasingly use the perspective of 'Europeanisation' to measure such relationships. There is also a case, however, for looking at Europe from the perhaps narrower but no less necessary point of view of intra-party dynamics: in particular, what kinds of challenge does 'Europe' represent to party managers and how do they deal with it? By analysing the relationship of the Socialist Party to the EC/EU at three key moments in the history of European integration, the author identifies some common tropisms which continue to operate even as the effects of 'Europeanisation' increase.

RÉSUMÉ

L'analyse du rapport des partis politiques à la Communauté européenne/Union européenne part habituellement du concept d'européanisation afin de saisir la mesure desdits rapports. On est cependant fondé à postuler la nécessité de saisir l'Europe également à travers le prisme, sans doute plus étroit mais non moins nécessaire, de la dynamique interne de parti : à savoir, quel genre de défi l'Europe pose-t-elle aux gestionnaires de parti et comment ces derniers y répondent-ils ? L'analyse du rapport entre la SFIO/PS et l'instance européenne tel qu'il existait à trois moments-clé du processus d'intégration européenne nous permet d'isoler quelques tropismes communs qui continuent à produire leurs effets alors même que s'approfondissent les conséquences de l'européanisation.

L'UE ne se serait pas faite sans les socialistes, mais elle s'est toujours faite sans, voire contre, une partie d'eux.

G. Finchelstein

It is now clear that the democratic states of the capitalist world have not one sovereign, but two: their people below and the international 'markets' above.

W. Streeck

***   ***   ***   ***

There is no shortage of work on the French Socialist Party (Parti socialiste, PS) in the context of European integration. Most scholarship tends to measure the party's input into the integration

---

I am grateful to Dr Graeme Garrard and the two anonymous referees for their helpful comments.

process, pivoting on its role as a governing party at certain decisive stages (Cerny and Schain 1984; Featherstone 1988; Marlière 2010; Newman 1983). Alongside this 'bottom-up' approach are works that look at the party within the context of the Europeanisation debate (Cole 2001; Goetz and Hix 2001; Kühlaci 2012; Ladrech 2000) and attempt to measure the extent to which the party may have become 'Europeanised' over the years as a direct result of its involvement in European Union-level politics (Ladrech 2002). This article lies within the second category, with the nuance, however, that it is less concerned with measuring degrees of Europeanisation than with discovering recurrent patterns of party behaviour in the face of pressure generated by European questions; we seek to plot permanence as much as change. The PS is, on the face of it, an attractive candidate for such an approach. In its incarnation as SFIO (Section française de l'Internationale ouvrière) it headed the government that signed the Rome Treaty; nearly six decades on, the party finds itself again in charge of France, as the EU struggles to emerge from recession and cope with pressures on its Southern periphery.

The focus of this study, then, is on the PS *as a party*. Parties have their own logics, and demand to be studied in their own right; our analysis lies firmly within the terrain of party scholarship. It is a constant of political history that parties are affected by some types of issue rather than others; we would place questions of international policy, including defence, very high on the list of potential disrupters of party unity, basically because they ask fundamental questions about the identity of parties and how they see their modes of operation. Among such issues of 'high policy', Europe is a particularly rich and challenging area, which should yield much insight into how the party functions.

As for method, we have chosen, rather than linear historical analysis, a number of key periods or 'moments' in the integration process which all demanded a response from the party. The periods chosen are:

(i) joining the European Economic Community (EEC) and its immediate aftermath;
(ii) the first Mitterrand presidency and the U-turn of 1983;
(iii) the Hollande presidency, the eurozone and the Greek crisis.

Others could no doubt have been chosen, but these seem to us to provide enough evidence to test our basic assumption that PS behaviour shows a high degree of continuity. Each moment presented a particular set of challenges to the party, but it seems to have responded to these with behaviour that demonstrates strong underlying continuity. An alternative approach might have been to concentrate exclusively on the present situation of the party in order to show the effects of Europeanisation. Such an approach might have enabled a fuller treatment of the present but it would—unless one used numerous 'flashbacks'— rule out any historical dimension; and our aim is precisely to capture the permanent features of the party's dilemma across different periods.

In each moment, several recurrent variables require consideration. What is the general political context, that is, how do the European questions at issue relate to other concerns? When the party has to choose, does it behave as a unitary actor, in particular in the light of possible tensions between the party-in-government or parliament (*les élus*), the party-in-the-country (voters) and the party as an organisation, to use Avril's triptych borrowed from US party scholarship (Avril 1990, 71–75)? Where there is opposition (as there usually is), what are its logics? Is it simply a left/right polarity, or are there more complex patterns? The question of factionalism, endemic to the PS, will be relevant here. What is the influence (direct or more distant) of allies within the left? Other factors, perhaps less important, might include the role of its allies in other states and/or in European Union (EU) institutions—in particular, perhaps, the European Parliament (EP) and its groups, or the transnational parties.

Not all of these variables will be equally important in each of our chosen periods. We will therefore review selectively such of these variables as seem appropriate, in hope of determining consistent patterns of behaviour.

EEC membership and its aftermath

Momentous in retrospect, the decision of the French government headed by SFIO leader Guy Mollet to sign the Rome Treaty in March 1957 was overshadowed at the time by other issues. The Algerian War was the most obvious, but the overall political context was dominated by the Cold War, which had frozen the French partisan landscape and with it many of SFIO's political options. For nearly a decade SFIO had been a key part of the so-called Third Force—an alliance of parties from the centre of the party system (the Catholic reformists of the MRP [Mouvement républicain populaire], the Radicals and smaller groups of the centre right)—which sought to preserve the finely balanced Republican system of coalition government against threats from strong nationalism on the right (the Gaullist Rassemblement du peuple français, RPF) and, on the left, the Parti communiste français (PCF), now cast firmly into the wilderness as the Cold War set in and in consequence unable to play more than an occasional wrecking role. Before 1948, the party apparatus under Secretary General Mollet (though not the great majority of its deputies) had favoured an alliance with the PCF, as had been the case in the immediate post-war period of *tripartisme*, when the two left parties had governed with the MRP. But communist takeovers in Eastern Europe and the eviction of the PCF from government in May 1947 had closed off this option (Graham 1994, 366–383).

These external pressures had also resolved (temporarily, but none the less conveniently) the party's perennial existential dilemma: whether to participate in government or not (Bergounioux and Grunberg 2005, 46–60). The history of this is well known. In 1905 SFIO was formed by a merger of a number of small socialist factions. From the outset, the dominant Guesdist faction imposed a purist doctrine of government. The party was only supposed to assume power when conditions for genuine revolutionary change were present; it was not its job, in the meantime, to 'manage capitalism'. Clearly not all of the party agreed, and a succession of leaders from Jaurès through to Blum managed to inflect the doctrine. Thus it was deemed possible to take office either when the Republic was threatened or when it might be possible to secure significant social reforms (even the more pragmatic socialists like Jaurès saw such reforms as incremental and probably irreversible; Jaurès would have agreed with Keith Joseph about the 'ratchet effect' of socialism). Such logic justified SFIO's heading the Popular Front government of 1936 (theorised by Blum as the 'occupation' of power rather than its 'exercise') and its participation in the social and economic reconstruction of the immediate post-war years. Leaving aside such doctrinal subtleties, SFIO's role in this period seems similar to that of its social democratic cousins across Western Europe: like them, it strove with some success to promote economic growth, raise wages and benefits for workers and create welfare infrastructure. But French socialism is, even more than its counterparts elsewhere, obsessed with doctrine. Hence there was never any generalised acceptance that SFIO was just another reformist party, maybe a little more ambitious than some, but without any idea of revolutionary transformation. Large parts of the party clung to the idea that its true objective was revolution, not management or mere reform; calls could still be heard after

1945 for the 'dictatorship of the proletariat' (Graham 1994, 378). Even today, there are still traces of this purist nostalgia, which marks the party out as an outrider (perhaps alongside the Walloon PS) among European socialists.

But for a decade after 1948, the party was to an extent freed from its power complex. The realities of the Cold War and the Third Force locked it into the reformist bloc which protected Republican democracy. Whether SFIO's leaders liked it or not, whether many of the militants realised it or not, it was by the late 1940s a key instrument of French governance. Accordingly, the party could at its congress divide over policy motions; but when in government, it mostly delivered a united response. Factional life tended to pivot on a polarity between revolutionaries and more or less avowed reformers; this polarity tended also to be expressed in a tension between deputies and activists and to an extent between federations which jockeyed for power at congress. But usually compromise was the order of the day; congress would vote for transformatory policies, while the party in government would try to secure reforms. Few worried about the gulf between rhetoric and action.

This situation made handling of European issues easier. Alongside its Third Force partners, and heavily influenced by Blum and the advocacy of André Philip, the most outspoken of the reformists (Marlière 2010, 54–56), SFIO voted for the Marshall Plan and the Atlantic Alliance, then for the Schuman Plan and the Coal and Steel Community. All these measures could be sold to members and voters as part of a strategy to promote growth and peace, plus security against communism. Significantly, these decisions involved little loss of sovereignty; the one supranational commitment that did, namely the proposal to join the European Defence Community (EDC) (effectively putting French forces under supranational command and rearming Germany in the process), provoked a massive split across the whole political spectrum which drove right through the middle of SFIO (Quilliot 1972, 476–502; Williams 1964, 100 ff.). After the sobering experience of seeing the EDC vote lost, the party split and the Germans rearmed anyway, SFIO would be open for modest doses of integration, but no more.

The EEC as first mooted was suitably modest; it was little more than a trading bloc with a common external tariff, a slow winding-down of domestic tariffs, and some weak and untried common institutions (Commission and Assembly). As French agriculture and industry were predicted to benefit rapidly, joining did not seem that big a risk to most of the party; Drake (2010, 191) shows that the socialists had negotiated good terms on key issues such as agriculture and workers' rights. The general drift of socialist economic policy during the Fourth Republic was, notwithstanding the rhetorical flourishes alluded to above, increasingly away from the planning and nationalisation doctrines that had prevailed in the 1930s and towards the market economy, albeit a mixed economy (Fulla 2016, 68–124). Coalition with the centre right aided this shift, as did the party's anti-communist and Atlanticist line. So too did the influence of experts from the trade union Force Ouvrière (FO) on the party's parliamentary economics committee; most deputies (though not activists) shared FO's enthusiasm for the practical achievements of social democracy elsewhere in Europe, particularly Attlee's government. SFIO programmes tended thus to concentrate on bread-and-butter issues such as increasing purchasing power, improving welfare protection and pensions. The 1956 Mollet government invested heavily in such measures, overspending and provoking an inflationary spiral which necessitated tax hikes in order to be corrected; the party would leave office with a spendthrift reputation. Thus in practice the party was moving away from its proclaimed Marxism; unfortunately it never performed an ideological *aggiorniamento* to this effect. Keynes, the theorist who inspired most of the young *énarques* who were striving to modernise the French economy, seems never to have even been discussed in party conclaves. Fulla believes that the old discourse of collective ownership was used to tie in party loyalists disappointed by the lack of results, but the result was 'un parti sclérosé, incapable de penser les mutations du capitalisme moderne' (2016, 90).

So far as EEC membership goes, Mollet thus came well prepared; he was used to working in a liberal economic framework alongside non-socialist allies. Even so, there was boldness about the way in which he overrode objections from much of the *patronat*, half of the political class and the technocracy in order to sign France up; clearly for him the long-term political benefits (tying Germany into the democratic order, the possibility of bringing in the UK) made this risk worthwhile. Economically too, as was stated, SFIO was confident that France would not lose out. Thus, objections to the EEC came not from within SFIO but from the Gaullist right on what today are called sovereignist grounds; the RPF saw international agreements of this type as implying progressive loss of autonomy for national states. The PCF opposed membership of what it saw as a capitalist club, directed, like NATO, against the USSR.

Some aspects of party ideology also made the handling of this dossier easier. The highly visible Christian Democrat input into the founding of the EU (Kaiser 2007) caused some misgivings among socialists raised on a culture of anti-clericalism (cf. Mollet's joke about the EEC being 'la petite Europe vaticane'), but these could easily be set aside on grounds of the pragmatism which the party practised in office. After all, if SFIO collaborated regularly with the French variant of political Catholicism at home, it should not have any difficulty in working with other EEC governments, which were mostly based on similar partnerships of confessional and secularist parties. A further ideological justification lay in the notion of internationalism. Socialists everywhere have always been committed to internationalism, a concept with considerable mobilising power but little foundation in reality, given the socialist family's singular historic failures to achieve anything more than information-sharing and common voting or campaigning in supranational institutions such as the EP (Hanley 2008, 2014). This is unsurprising because parties are first and foremost national organisations whose natural sphere of activity is the national territory. SFIO was a perfect illustration of this; it functioned as a Jacobin party, believing firmly in an indivisible, secular Republic which was a locus of strong public action, hence its natural sphere of operation which it could even present as an antechamber to socialism. This was its real identity, and the party's internationalist discourse (based on class solidarity as opposed to national feeling) sat rather uneasily alongside it; potential contradictions were seldom explored. Rhetoric about transnational cooperation was and is useful, providing it does not bring any policy implications. Early French engagement with the EEC was loose enough to allow this kind of rhetoric to flourish. Over the years, 'Europe' would become a desirable goal, on a par with 'socialism'; politicians wishing to sound progressive could demand 'more Europe' without being too specific about what that entailed.

By the end of the Fourth Republic, Europe had proved useful as an item to cement party unity, always the leadership's priority. The Cold War had overridden (in practice, if not at congress) the division between reformists and revolutionaries, deputies and party bureaucrats. The party was engaged in reformist politics, and Europe could be easily fitted into this, not least because any political consequences of EEC membership effects were barely beginning to be felt. Mainstream allies were in agreement, as were like-minded parties in neighbouring states; even if the *frère ennemi* of the PCF was not, the Cold War made it mostly irrelevant anyway. Cynics might also believe that focus on Europe helped to an extent to deflect attention from the main disaster area of Third Force policy, namely the Algerian War. The SFIO's involvement in government through 1956–1957 saw the worst escalation and laid the foundations for the end of the Fourth Republic. It also dealt heavy blows to party unity, with the departure of such as Édouard Depreux and Michel Rocard to form what would eventually become the Parti socialiste unifié (PSU), for a while a serious rival to SFIO. Compared with the fallout from Algeria, Europe was a minor management problem (Newman 1983, 37). Overall, what this episode shows is that whereas 'Europe' is usually presented as a constraint on party action, it can in certain circumstances be turned into an active resource; a threat (though the EEC could hardly be called that in 1958) can become an opportunity. We move ahead now to another significant period of European integration to see how much of the above still held true.

The Mitterrand presidency and the turning of 1983–1984

A quarter-century later, the Socialist Party faced a very different situation, at home and abroad. The PS, as it now was since 1971, was in an unheard-of position. Clearly the dominant party of a now united left, it had in 1981 won presidential and legislative elections handsomely, following years of steady gains in local government. It could now apply an ambitious programme of economic and social change—a 'rupture with capitalism'. This was a very different situation from the 1950s when an SFIO with under 20% of the vote had to bargain with potential coalition partners as awkward as Radicals or Catholics. Nor could the party be seriously obstructed by the PCF, with whom it had resurrected the post-war partnership. The PCF had dipped sharply to some 15%, well below the socialists, and was glad to accept four modest posts in government. The 1981 win crowned 20 years of socialist reconstruction. Initially, SFIO had incurred much of the dissatisfaction with the Fourth Republic's failures and was a major victim of the swing to Gaullism after 1958, slumping close to extinction through the 1960s. Belatedly the party had renewed its personnel, its thinking and its strategy. By 1971 it had elected the charismatic François Mitterrand as leader (Short 2014, 261–297); he rapidly implemented a strategy of alliance with the PCF on the basis of a joint programme of government, judging correctly that in an all-left alliance the more moderate pole would in the long run have greater appeal to voters ready for a change from the right. His gambit reflected a fundamental change that had occurred within the party system. The success of Gaullism had unified much of the centre right under its banner, including much of the Catholic vote; so much so that the MRP was wound up by 1967, leaving Catholic activists with a choice between rallying to the General or soldiering on in the increasingly narrow space of 'centrist' politics which persists to this day. Now, if the right was mostly unified, this put real pressure on the left to respond and thus complete the bi-polarisation of French politics into left and right blocs. Mitterrand understood this quickly and sought alliance with the PCF, confident, as we remarked above, that the more reassuring PS would soon dominate the alliance. But even its candidate's 110 propositions still contained radical measures; the key idea was to reflate the French economy by a mixture of Keynesian demand management and economic planning, thereby securing strong durable growth. The presidency was thus to deploy the might of the Jacobin state.

This much is known to everyone, as is the disappointing outcome of the strategy (it was by no means a complete failure, in terms of growth, redistribution or even employment; Hall 1984, 100; Machin and Wright 1985). The basic problem for the socialists was that they were trying to reflate when the rest of the world economy was beginning to contract. Within two years, the government therefore faced problems of inflation and foreign trade balances which led to pressure on the franc, which was devalued three times. Faced with such clear signals from the international markets that 'Keynesianism in one country' was not working, the government changed tack, calling for an initial 'pause' in reform and increasing taxes to rein back consumption and strengthen the franc. This would not be a temporary tactic but can in retrospect be seen as the beginning of a firm commitment by the PS to a liberal market economy. One recent commentator sees this reversal of the policies on which Mitterrand was elected two years previously as bringing about ' the end of the economic and social model of the *trente glorieuses*' and 'hastening the victory of liberalism' (Sarlat 2015, 19).

This section aims not to analyse in detail the Mitterrand experiment, as this has been amply done (Maclean 1998; Short 2014), but to show within that process the role played by the European Community (EC). For Europe was central to the outcome. By now it was a much more developed community than in 1958, having enlarged its membership and developed a number of common policies (agriculture, social and regional funds) and a number of ongoing agendas, particularly the goal of economic and monetary union. The European Monetary System, engineered by Helmut Schmidt and Valéry Giscard d'Estaing, was an anticipation of this, obliging member states to keep the value of their currency within agreed parameters; clearly this was a major constraint on the monetary and fiscal policies of states. European decision-making was now, moreover, a more complex affair, with a more assertive Commission counterbalanced by the European Council (again, a heavily Giscardian initiative), which sought to restore the weight of sovereign states against unelected technocrats. Within the supranational institutions, however, there was one new factor which perhaps overdid all the others, namely the Franco-German connexion. Bred of de Gaulle's and Adenauer's 1963 treaty, with its provisions for regular consultation between heads of government, the partnership was by now widely seen as the motor behind any aspect of European integration. Mitterrand had inherited this policy instrument which offered possibilities but also constraints. At the time it was possible to see it as a deal between equals (German economic strength plus French military and diplomatic prowess); to see the two as equals today requires a leap of the imagination.

Mitterrand's own party was also a different animal (in some respects) from the old SFIO. The 'new' party of 1971 combined SFIO with various other fragments of the 'non-communist left', as commentators still felt compelled to call it. One of these would join slightly later, namely the PSU of Rocard. Another, which existed within SFIO prior to 1971 but now became increasingly autonomous, was the CERES (Centre d'études, de recherches et d'éducation socialistes) of Jean-Pierre Chevènement (Hanley 1986). These two groups soon came to polarise debate within the socialist family. The 1970s were the golden age of party factionalism, when genuine ideological communities, with bases across all levels of the party, confronted each other over the direction which the party should take; today's mini-factions of followers lining up behind a presidential hopeful are a very diminished version. On the one hand were advocates of a decentralised, bottom-up socialism, aspiring to worker control of workplaces and borrowing freely from French and other liberal writers; on the other, more in tune with the traditional SFIO ethos, were neo-Marxist champions of state socialism, using the full weight of the Jacobin state, including its strong patriotic grounding (this nationalist tone, audible but not dominant in the 1970s, would grow apace after 1981). Add to this a clear personal rivalry between the two leaders (both saw themselves as Mitterrand's successor), plus some deep-lying cultural antipathies (many Rocardians had a Catholic background), and the stage was set for factional battles of rare intensity. This would go beyond the relatively mild 'jeu des tendances' of the old SFIO (Graham 1982). Crucially, from the point of view of this essay, European integration would prove a key marker between the factions; CERES was increasingly sceptical about the possibility of moving towards socialism within the existing EEC, while the Rocardians, after brief initial scepticism (one of Rocard's first works was entitled *Le Marché commun contre l'Europe* [Jaumont, Lenègre, and Rocard 1973]) soon came to see, especially through the influence of Jacques Delors, that the European space was the best arena for action (Drake 2000; Featherstone 1988, 81 ff.). If this made party management harder for Mitterrand, there was one consolation, namely the decline of the PCF. It seemed apparent even as of 1981 that it would never recover its previous strength; its blackmail potential over the actions of the socialist government (which it left in July 1984) remained thus limited. Mitterrand also had one immense advantage, namely his hold on the presidency; over 20 years of office by the right had established it as the major source of authority and decision-making. Elected by universal suffrage and usually able to rely on a party majority elected 'on his coat-tails', a Fifth Republic president enjoyed vastly greater power than a Fourth Republic prime minister, head of a small party and condemned to constant deals and compromises. Even if he were not nominally head of the party, the president was its real boss.

Such, then, were the international and domestic contexts of the fateful decision of 1983. The party's liberal turn did not save it from defeat in 1986, though Mitterrand retained the presidency comfortably enough in 1988. In the short term, it seemed as if the party had mostly achieved the key objective of unity despite the problems encountered in government, even if that unity could only now be kept by excluding some elements.

The consequence of this exclusion proved serious, albeit with some delay. Chevènement's initial opposition to austerity saw him dropped from government before being recalled as education minister to conduct a fire-fighting operation following the fury provoked by Mitterrand's abortive attempt to 'integrate' Catholic schools into the state system. This gave him a certain weight within government which he would use to the maximum; yet he was unable to shift the main policy lines to any real degree. Increasingly he would speak for the Jacobin, sovereignist tendency within the party that found the sound-money, pro-monetary integration, Germanophile and generally pro-integration line of Mitterrand and the majority ever harder to stomach. By 1993, he felt that there was no chance of progress, so left the party and set up the Mouvement républicain et citoyen (Chevènement 1992). Deep-lying motifs in his thinking now rose to the surface, as he called for a return to Republican values (Chabal 2015), central to which was a strong, independent foreign policy. A series of works, self-promotional as well as politically challenging, inveighed against PS orthodoxy on Europe (Chevènement 2002, 2011). His critiques also went beyond mere words. Although he had served in the Jospin government of 1997–2002 as interior minister, he competed against Jospin in the first round of the 2002 presidential election. The 6% which he won sealed Jospin's fate, as the latter was narrowly denied access to the second round by Le Pen. By effectively handing victory to Chirac (more in tune with Chevènement's views on high policy), the veteran sovereignist had demonstrated peerlessly how a small party can use its blackmail potential. Yet this party had been forced out of its original home in the PS. Thus some of the fallout from the 'turn' of 1983 took time to land, but when it did the effects were devastating.

Featherstone is correct to claim (1988, 133) that 'the experience of government had left the party more strongly committed to action via the Community'. But this experience came with a price. Overall, party leadership was able to keep most members on board, even as it took decisions which went against the platform on which it was elected. The marginalisation and later departure of the Chevènement group suggests another pattern, however. In every 'European' crisis, there is likely to be a part of the party which finds the latest pro-integration move a step too far. In terms of the celebrated triptych, they show loyalty at first, then give increasing voice and finally exit. Party managers will see this as a loss of talent and energy, but which can be endured in the longer scheme of things. The dissidents' view might, however, be less sanguine. They have ended up in a crowded space on the left of the PS battling with the remains of the PCF, Greens and other small groups for the right to be heard. Their message on Europe has, moreover, not been that clear. While the populist Front national (FN) has called for a French exit from the euro and even EU (albeit trimming rapidly as the regional elections of 2015 approached), the Chevènementists have never gone that far, criticising French policy towards it but with decreasing effect; it is hard to imagine them pulling off another version of 2002 in a future presidential contest. One could wonder whether their trade-off of increased freedom to criticise from without against closeness to the leadership from within was actually worth it. This is a question that can also be asked of future departures from the party.

Hollande, stagnation and the crisis of the eurozone

When François Hollande won the presidency in May 2012, socialist commitment to European integration was beyond doubt; this had long been the case for most other socialists in Europe, as Scharpf pointed out quite early on (1991). The later Mitterrand years had seen implementation of the Single Market, and France had entered the single currency in the first wave. It is true that on his surprise accession to Matignon following the snap election of 1997, which Chirac called and lost, Lionel Jospin had threatened briefly to delay French accession to the euro (on the grounds that it was purely an anti-inflation instrument whose structures were too inflexible to promote growth); but a few weeks of office were enough to show that this was largely an electoral ploy. Jospin duly signed up, accepting that the EU probably still represented the best protection for a French social model whose high-tax, high-spend logic was beginning to run foul of the growing neo-liberal orthodoxy. Potentially more worrying was the referendum on the European Constitutional Treaty (ECT) of 2005, rejected at the polls not just by voters angry at losing sovereignty but also in part by socialist voters leaving the pro-European bloc in fear of the consequences of globalisation (Schmidt 2007). First Secretary Hollande had got the party to back a yes vote via an internal poll, but some figures from the party's left argued against; crucially they were backed by a mainstream figure in Laurent Fabius, ex-prime minister and holder of numerous offices (Crespy 2008; Wagner 2008). There was more than a hint of opportunism about Fabius' move, as this intending candidate for the 2007 presidential elections was hoping to pick up disaffected voters ready to blame the EU for various problems (Perrineau 2005). In the event, the voters' no did not lead to an immediate split; the left enjoyed a rare victory, while the rest of the party simply waited until the new president, Sarkozy, pushed the Lisbon Treaty (which contained most of what the ECT backers wanted) through the route of parliamentary ratification. For some on the left, it was too much, however. Jean-Luc Mélenchon and his supporters left to form a new Parti de gauche (PG). Offering a radical programme of social and economic change, it was firmly Eurosceptic and anti-German; in the EP it allied not with the Party of European Socialists but with the mainly ex-communists of the Party of the European Left (Mélenchon 2015). Despite Mélenchon's brave showing in the 2012 presidential contest (11%), his new party struggled to find room in the increasingly crowded Bermuda triangle that constitutes the space to the left of the PS.

Hollande's party thus took office in 2012 fairly well united, but in a very different context from previous spells in government. Integration was much further advanced. The euro was established, and despite growing evidence of its fundamental design faults (Marsh 2013, 36–41; Stiglitz 2016, 85–170), eurozone governments were determined not to let it fail. From a French point of view, the main problems lay in the Stability and Growth Pact, which set statutory limits to public debts and budget deficits. Although both French and German governments had overridden these early in the twenty-first century and France had actually succeeded in loosening some of the terms of the pact (Howarth 2007), the Harz reforms undertaken by Germany meant that, well before 2012, this system of constraints had come to suit Germany very well; but France, long addicted to deficit financing, was much less comfortable. As Germany's revived economy, built on sound money, low wages and strong exports, forged ahead, German leaders could impose this *Ordoliberalismus* as the dominant paradigm within the eurozone. France and some Southern states in particular, which needed more flexible budgetary arrangements, were constantly having to argue against the dominant partner. For this is another change which had set in firmly; in 1964 or even 1984 it was possible for French leaders to present themselves as having equal weight in the Franco-German relationship. But since reunification, successive German leaders clearly were setting initiatives which the French were following.

In terms of public presentation, also, Europe offered further difficulties. Barely an issue at the time of Mollet, presented by Mitterrand as some kind of silver bullet that took care of his economic failures, Europe had become highly politicised since at least the time of the Maastricht Treaty of 1992. Gone were the years of 'permissive consensus', when senior functionaries and political elites, not necessarily out-and-out federalists but ready for substantial degrees of integration in various policy areas, did deals on European governance and presented them to the wider public without too many problems in an era of generally steady prosperity. Henceforth every new step in integration, starting with the controversial new currency, would be argued about in member states much more openly and angrily than before; the consequences of such moves on everyday life were that much more visible. Symptomatic of this was the steady rise of sovereignist movements, not all extremist, who sought to blame the EU for a variety of problems ranging from economic and social grievances to, increasingly, questions of national identity. These forces pointed up, with some plausibility, the growing gulf between a political class happy with the system of behind-the-scenes elite bargaining and 'the people', unhappy victims of such a system.

The partisan context had changed too. While politics remained broadly polarised between left and right, the FN grew steadily, even if the electoral system prevented it from achieving representation in proportion to its strength (Perrineau 2014). It nevertheless narrowed the space in which the mainstream parties could operate. Among these, the PS was now clearly pre-eminent in the left camp; but it had become, more than ever, a 'notabilised' party, dominated by local office-holders who bossed their party branches (Lefebvre and Sawicki 2006); this immersion in sub-national governance during the party's long exile from national office is, according to Juhem (2006), the main reason why an increasing number of party elites were managerial and pragmatic in outlook, with only modest ambition for change. A further complication ensued within the left bloc. Although the PCF had declined relentlessly, it could still just raise a parliamentary group in 2012; the French Greens meanwhile had broken though to the extent that their latest incarnation, EELV (Europe-Écologie Les Verts, EELV), polled strongly enough at secondary elections to persuade the PS to offer them a deal, including enough deputies to make a parliamentary group. Add to this the persistence of small groups (Radicals, Chevènement's Mouvement des Citoyens, etc.), and it is clear that although the PS was the biggest fish in the left pond, it would have to work very hard to maintain overall leadership. The 'plural left' put together by Jean-Christophe Cambadélis in 1997 to support Jospin's government showed how such a coalition can work but also how it can fail (Cambadélis 1999).

It is important also to remember that Hollande won the presidency largely by default. Voters' disappointment with five years of Nicolas Sarkozy, who constantly talked big changes but achieved very little, plus an active dislike of the incumbent's flashy style, seem to have been enough to move votes, rather than the very general and quite cautious promises that Hollande made on the economy (Perrineau 2013).

The context of Hollande's presidency was firmly set from the start, when he signed the treaty on Stability, Co-ordination and Governance, which reinforced the neo-liberal orthodoxy of previous financial agreements in the eurozone (Duflot 2014, 81 ff.). This commitment to market discipline would not stop him, he hoped, from securing significant growth needed to reduce the high unemployment rate in France, notably among the under-25s. His main tactic was to build confidence among employers and potential investors by means of generous fiscal policy; under the main programme CICE (Crédit d'Impôt pour la Compétitivité et l'Emploi) some 20 billion euros of tax were transferred from employers to general taxation (i.e. households), while savings of 50 billion euros were to be made on general government expenditure. The other prong of his strategy was so-called reform of labour legislation, i.e. removing legal protection from dismissal for workers and generally extending working hours and the number of years spent at work; this is a form of 'internal devaluation' in order to increase competitiveness. His abrasive young minister Emmanuel Macron, not a PS member and recruited from private sector finance, was one figurehead of this drive; the other was prime minister Manuel Valls, from the right of the party and an economic liberal. None of the above measures were apparent from Hollande's electoral programme or speeches, but, as Duflot remarked, his main fault was never saying what he actually thought (2014, 219). Suffice it to say that by 2015 the policy did not seem to be working well, as firms pocketed the new cash, paid down some debt and sat on their hands, waiting for a change of government in 2017.

Predictably, this approach caused difficulty for party and allies. By 2014, Arnaud Montebourg, minister for industrial revival, had been dropped from government with some of his cabinet allies. Articulate, ambitious and a skilled media performer, he had come to stand for a more Colbertist approach to economic revival, using state muscle to promote an active industrial policy (cf. his 'made in France' campaign), gain tighter control over foreign investment and even not rule out some protectionism. The closure of the Florange steelworks, which he had fought hard to preserve, marked a key stage of his disillusion with prevailing policy. Prior to that there had emerged a sort of proto-faction within government, to the extent that Montebourg, Christiane Taubira, Benoît Hamon and Cécile Duflot met regularly to try and find ways of changing the government's line (Duflot 2014, 101 ff.); little seems to have come of this, and all were eventually forced out of government (Fressoz 2015, 197 ff.). In autumn 2016 Montebourg, a challenger for the 2012 presidential nomination and someone who had led a sizeable faction (le Nouveau Parti socialiste) during the PS's opposition years, announced his intention to run in 2017 from a leftish, Republican-socialist position, effectively replicating Chevènement's gambit. From early in the presidency, the executive was also confronted with a permanent rebellion of some 30–40 backbenchers. These *frondeurs* included none of the big beasts of the PS, but some consistent and incisive critics such as Emmanuel Maurel and Marie-Noëlle Lienemann. None of them quit the party, even though their critiques always fell on deaf ears. Nonetheless, by late 2015 the press was full of reports about the demoralisation and impotence of the MPs, grimly awaiting their comeuppance in 2017. Silence was the main contribution also from one important personality, former First Secretary Martine Aubry. Passed over for the presidential nomination in favour of Hollande, she refused to join the government, staying in her Lille *mairie*; she also refused, however, to head up a faction, signing the main motion at the 2015 Poitiers Congress, though her critique of policy and advocacy of a more interventionist style became less muted as the government struggled in the polls (*Le Monde*, September 25, 2015). Her future intentions as to 2017 and beyond remained unclear, but she was clearly not throwing all her support behind Hollande. In an attempt to keep the party onside, Hollande had replaced the inept careerist Harlem Désir at the head of the PS with the veteran fixer Cambadélis; but even his legendary brokerage skills could not disguise the party's impotence in the face of the executive. Scholars of 'party government' would recognise a familiar truth here. In modern parties, the party-in-office usually controls the party machine, hence to a large extent the party-in-the-country; and in presidential systems, the president controls the party-in-office. Roberto Michels' 'iron law of oligarchy' was thus verified again. What was clear from all this was that Hollande had tied the PS to a line that was liberal and business-friendly in economics and strongly repressive in terms of civil liberties (in the name of the 'war against terror'); any alternative from the left was simply ignored or marginalised. Ambitious strategists like Valls and Macron had long ago calculated that this was a winning electoral formula; they had finally won Hollande, famous for his ability to broker compromise between left and right tendencies inside the party, over to their viewpoint. Little of this conflict surfaced in official party pronouncements on Europe, needless to say; for example, the resolution from the 2012 congress spoke of the need to maintain a 'Europe sociale et protectrice', pleaded for growth-oriented policies and generally blamed the right for the persistence of austerity. Among such bromides nothing was said about Hollande's endorsement of austerity in practice (PS 2012).

Disillusion with Hollande's policies was not confined to his own ranks. The most savage critiques came from allies. EELV leader Cécile Duflot quit as housing minister in summer 2014; lack of serious investment in her sector was one reason, but the main one was European policy. Duflot identified the alignment with *Ordoliberalismus* as the source of all PS policy failings; she demanded that France confront Angela Merkel head-on in an attempt to move EU policy in a more growth-oriented and less deficit-fixated direction (Duflot 2014, 81–89). Just how this was to be achieved, other than by repeated and ineffectual attempts by Hollande and Finance Minister Michel Sapin to persuade the Germans, remained vague. Ideas of France's taking the leadership of some Mediterranean bloc of debtor countries (sarcastically dubbed the 'Club Med' by Germans and PIIGS by the British) were clearly a non-starter so far as Hollande was concerned; the best he could extract from Berlin was some indulgence towards continuing French inability to meet her deficit-reduction targets. Merkel certainly showed no interest in the latest French version of that Loch Ness monster known as 'economic government of the eurozone', particularly the French proposal that the zone should have its own budget (code for mutualising national sovereign debts; see *Le Monde*, September 12 and October 8, 2015). Duflot wanted Hollande to lead the debtor states in a campaign to reopen the terms of the Treaty on Stability, Co-ordination and Governance which France signed shortly after Hollande's victory. This idea of a Southern bloc of progressive states, seen as a counterpart to the domination of the 'Anglo Saxon' North, is in fact an old CERES shibboleth, dating back at least to the 1970s; then as now it belongs more to political mythology than to practical politics. Mélenchon's polemics were even harsher, evoking a total German domination of European policy-making which the author did not hesitate to compare, none too subtly, to the Nazi era; he too touted the idea of a Southern bloc (naturally under French leadership) which would rebuild a 'free union of nations' (Mélenchon 2015, 200–204). Readers could guess whether this meant leaving the euro or even the EU. In autumn 2015 the various parties of the left—PS, PG, PCF and Greens—fought the regional elections in disarray, with disastrous results. The plural left was well and truly finished, and the PS's European line had done much to kill it.

No better example exists of PS acceptance of the new European order than policy towards Greece. The sources of the Greek problem are well known; entry to the euro on the basis of false macro-economic information (much of it supplied, apparently, by Goldman Sachs operatives) enabled successive governments of left or right to borrow generously and spend much of the money in clientelistic fashion, at the cost of productive investment, eschewing reform of the Greek state in general and its tax system in particular. That such transfers (from North to South effectively) helped fuel the German export boom is sometimes forgotten by those quick to criticise Greece for its profligacy (Streeck 2012, 65). The financial crash of 2008 led to the end of easy credit, as horrified creditors realised the extent of Greek public debt and the consequent unlikelihood of their ever being repaid very much of their outlay. One EU rescue plan succeeded another, and by 2015, if most of the private creditors had been forced to take a sizeable 'haircut' on what was owed them and the remaining debt was now largely public (a mixture of EU, European Central Bank, IMF and various national banks), the debt continued to rise. The deal concluded with the radical left Syriza government in the summer of 2015 (after Greek voters had rejected a first deal by referendum) was worse than what had been refused. Greece ended up with more severe terms than ever, amounting in the view of commentators like Larry Elliot or Joseph Stiglitz to a severe curtailment of national sovereignty, as all major economic decisions were to be subject to oversight by the EU/IMF 'troika' and vast amounts of public assets were to be sold off (Stiglitz 2016, 177–236). Greece faced an endless tunnel of austerity, with little prospect of the growth needed even to begin paying off the debt mountain. On the one hand, Northern, particularly German, opposition to further reduction of the debt was insurmountable; on the other, even the radical left Syriza, allied to the PG in France, would not countenance the 'Kirchner option' (after the Argentine president who defaulted in 2003 and painfully reconstructed the national economy) of defaulting on the debt and thus leaving the euro. Erstwhile Finance Minister Yannis Varoufakis and some of the Syriza left canvassed this move, but it was never a serious runner. The role of France in all this is revealing.

Those to the left of the PS were unequivocal in their condemnation of the EU's treatment of Greece; Mélenchon denounced what he saw as German brutality in no uncertain terms, showing little sympathy for Northern taxpayers asked to sponge up others' debts (2015, 166–170). Duflot was also much kinder towards the Greeks, seen as victims of the markets (2014, 85–86). Hollande's position was more nuanced (*Le Monde*, October 23, 2015). On the one hand there was a certain sympathy for a Mediterranean state which some have seen in geo-political terms (shoring up the South against Northern domination); also, French banks were heavily exposed in Greece. The main consideration was, however, as always, to hang in with German positions, which were not so clear-cut as some thought. If Finance Minister Wolfgang Schäuble made clear his preference for a Grexit (if need be temporary), Merkel's position was that Greece must be kept in at all costs, lest the whole structure of the single currency unravel. Bailouts must continue, while at the same time imposing the severest conditions possible on the Greeks (hence the sell-off of assets tacked on to the latest agreement) in the hope of getting some debt back. This is essentially what Hollande went along with, despite talking of the need for some debt relief and trying to make political capital from his role in the last-minute shuttle-diplomacy that accompanied the eventual capitulation of the Prime Minister Alexis Tsipras. It is worth remembering here that France, heavily exposed in Greece, stood in a good position along with Germany to benefit from the fire-sale forced on the Greeks (*Le Monde, Économie et Entreprise*, October 24, 2015). Overall, then, acceptance of German leadership and policy prevailed over any other considerations, though naturally this was painted in glowing Europhile colours; Greece had been saved for Europe.

The main policy tension throughout Hollande's presidency would thus seem to lie between on the left, Keynesians and deficit financers, and on the right, advocates of a balanced budget putting their faith in supply-side measures. At the heart of this polarity lies of course European policy. Hollande and his team were firmly committed to the disciplines of the monetary union, which set strict limits to budget and spending deficits; such disciplines virtually outlaw any counter-cyclical measures. Finance Minister Michel Sapin had to obtain exemptions, or at least the absence of sanctions, from the EU Commission in order to continue with the modest French deficits that existed, promising to run them down progressively. More clearly than ever before, then, Europe emerged at the heart of basic economic policy; by sticking to the rules, French governments deprived themselves of major policy tools. In liberal economic theory, if deficits are eliminated and budgets balanced, the economy is supposed to perform optimally in the end. Unfortunately the eventual return to equilibrium is usually at the price of years of lost growth. But such are the beliefs which inform the single currency, and they are highly constraining for member states.

To be sure, France continued to argue for a looser approach to deficits and for a more positive commitment to growth from the European Central Bank (which the ECB President Mario Draghi has done his best to promote, at the cost of some rule-bending), but her voice made little impression on the major player, Germany.

Conclusion

From the point of view of party managers, then, it is clear that 'Europe' has always remained a mixture of threat and opportunity. PS responses to the challenges of European integration obey a consistent pattern. Leaders' main concern has been to preserve party unity, but not at any price; indeed, as integration has progressed over time and constrained policy options, it has become harder to maintain unity and there has been regular jettisoning of dissidents.

In the early days, Europe was a new opportunity, with few apparent constraints; the general aim of integration seemed quite compatible with the party's traditional supranational rhetoric. Hence it was easy to keep most of a weak, coalition-dependent party on board; those who left did so mostly because of Algeria. Anyone with doubts about Europe could easily be referred to the Cold War situation; in the light of the Soviet threat, refusal of greater transnational cooperation was not, it could be argued, a real option.

By the time of the Mitterrand years, Europe had assumed a much greater saliency, and its direct effects on economic policy, the most important area for social democratic parties, could be seen more easily. The party leadership, personalised by Mitterrand in full presidential mode, chose clearly sticking with the EC and moving towards eventual monetary integration rather than pursuing an ambitious demand-led strategy in one country and possibly building alliances with like-minded states. The increasingly important German connexion and the desire to stay a part of this leadership duo prevailed over other considerations. Already, though, there was a price; a key section of the party, believing in the power of the Jacobin state to implement significant change, could not endorse the European option. It would duly leave and campaign, with little success, against further integration; its influence would be at best negative (cf. 2002), strangely reminiscent of the PCF's longstanding obstructionism under the previous Republic. This pattern of disgruntled activists leaving would be repeated over the years (Mélenchon, Montebourg etc.). Most of the party stayed with the pro-Europe line, not least because many provincial activists were more concerned with local matters.

Nothing that has happened under Hollande suggests a fundamental break in this pattern. The leadership sticks to the dominant EU policy strand of neo-liberalism, increasingly imposed by a Germany that is France's equal partner in name only. Some activists depart, to compete for space on the left with former allies who are by now too weak to have much influence; the *frondeurs* who stay within the fold continue to argue the case for more reflationary policy, but no decider listens. The decreasing number that remain await their electoral fate in 2017.

Europe is thus a litmus paper which separates out those within the PS who believe in some kind of change through committed public action from those who believe themselves to be realists, letting markets ultimately lay down policy and hoping, when the austerity pays off and growth returns, to do some modest good unnoticed. This is what commitment to 'Europe' now amounts to. Commentators on France often like to cite examples of 'French exceptionalism', but they would be hard put to place the PS in this category. Its experiences and its dilemmas are, unfortunately, precisely those of every socialist or progressive party in the global economy of today.

Disclosure statement

No potential conflict of interest was reported by the author.

References

Avril, Pierre. 1990. *Essai sur les partis politiques*. Paris: Payot.
Bergounioux, Alain, and Gérard Grunberg. 2005. *L'ambition et le remords: les socialistes français et le pouvoir, 1905–2005*. Paris: Fayard.
Cambadélis, Jean-Christophe. 1999. *L'avenir de la gauche plurielle*. Paris: Plon.
Cerny, Philip, and Martin Schain. 1984. *Socialism, the State and Public Policy in France*. London: Pinter.

Chabal, Emile. 2015. *A Divided Republic: Nation, State and Citizenship in Contemporary France*. Cambridge: CUP.

Chevènement, Jean-Pierre. 1992. *Une certaine idée de la République m'amène à....* Paris: Albin Michel.

Chevènement, Jean-Pierre. 2002. *Le courage de décider*. Paris: R. Laffont.

Chevènement, Jean-Pierre. 2011. *La France est-elle finie?* Paris: Fayard.

Cole, Alistair. 2001. "National and Partisan Contexts of Europeanisation: The Case of the French Socialists." *Journal of Common Market Studies* 39 (1): 15–36.

Crespy, Amandine. 2008. "Dissent over the European Constitutional Treatry within the French Socialist Party." *French Politics* 6: 23–44.

Drake, Helen. 2000. *Jacques Delors; Perspectives on a European Leader*. London: Routledge.

Drake, Helen. 2010. "France, Europe and the Limits of French Exceptionalism." In *The End of the French Exception?*, edited by T. Chafer and E. Godin, 187–202. Palgrave: Basingstoke.

Duflot, Cécile. 2014. *De l'intérieur: voyage au pays de la désillusion*. Paris: Fayard.

Featherstone, Kevin. 1988. *Socialist Parties and European Integration: A Comparative History*. Manchester, NH: MUP.

Fressoz, Françoise. 2015. *Le Stage est fini*. Paris: Albin Michel.

Fulla, Mathieu. 2016. *Les socialistes français et l'économie, 1944–81*. Paris: Sciences Po, Les Presses.

Goetz, Klaus, and Simon Hix. 2001. *Europeanised Politics? European Integration and National Political Systems*. London: Cass.

Graham, Bruce. 1982. "The Play of Tendencies: Internal Politics in SFIO before and after the Second World War." In *Contemporary French Political Parties*, edited by D. Bell and E. Shaw, 138–164. London: Croom Helm.

Graham, Bruce. 1994. *Choice and Democratic Order: The French Socialist Party, 1937–50*. Cambridge: CUP.

Hall, Peter. 1984. "Socialism in One Country: Mitterrand and the Struggle to define a New Economic Policy for France." In *Socialism, the State and Public Policy in France, 81–107*, edited by P. Cerny and M. Schain, 81–107. London: Pinter.

Hanley, David. 1986. *Keeping Left? CERES and the French Socialist Party*. Manchester, NH: MUP.

Hanley, David. 2008. *Beyond the Nation-State: Parties in the Era of European Integration*. Basingstoke: Palgrave.

Hanley, David. 2014. "Outside their Comfort Zone? National parties, European Parliament Groups and Transnational Parties." In *Routledge Handbook of European Politics, 590–608*, edited by J. Magone, 590–608. London: Routledge.

Howarth, David. 2007. "'Making and Breaking the Rules: French Policy on Europe and 'gouvernement économique'." *Journal of European Public Policy* 14 (7): 1061–1078.

Jaumont, Bernard, Daniel Lenègre, and Michel Rocard. 1973. *Le Marché commun contre l'Europe*. Paris: Seuil.

Juhem, Philippe. 2006. "La production notabiliaire du militantisme au PS." *Revue française de science politique* 56 (6): 909–942.

Kaiser, Wolfram. 2007. *Christian Democracy and the Origins of European Union*. Cambridge: CUP.

Kühlaci, Erol, ed. 2012. *Europeanisation and Party Politics*. Colchester: ECPR Press.

Ladrech, Robert. 2000. *Social Democracy and the Challenge of the European Union*. Boulder, CO: Lynne Riener.

Ladrech, Robert, ed. 2002. "The Europeanisation of Party Politics." Special issue of *Party Politics* 8 (4).

Lefebvre, Rémi, and Frederic Sawicki. 2006. *La société des socialistes: le PS aujourd'hui*. Bellecombe-en-Bauges: Edns du Croquant.

Machin, Howard, and Vincent Wright. 1985. *Economic Policy and Policymaking under the Mitterrand Presidency, 1981–84*. London: Pinter.

Maclean, Mairi, ed. 1998. *The Mitterrand Years*. Basingstoke: Macmillan.

Marlière, Philippe. 2010. "The French Socialist Party and European Integration: Faltering Europeanism." In *Social Democracy and European Integration*, edited by D. Dimitrakopoulos, 51–82. London: Routledge.

Marsh, David. 2013. *Europe's Deadlock: How the Eurocrisis could be Solved and Why it Won't Happen*. New Haven and London: Yale UP.

Mélenchon, Jean-Luc. 2015. *Le Hareng de Bismarck (le poison allemand)*. Paris: Plon.

Newman, Michael. 1983. *Socialism and European Unity: The Dilemma of the left in Britain and France*. London: Junction Books.

Perrineau, Pascal. 2005. "Le référendum français du 29 mai 2005: l'irrésistible nationalisation d'un vote européen." In *Le vote européen 2004–5: de l'élargissement au référendum français*, edited by P. Perrineau, 229–244. Paris: FNSP.

Perrineau, Pascal, ed. 2013. *La Décision électoral en 2012*. Paris: Colin.

Perrineau, Pascal. 2014. *La France au Front*. Paris: Fayard.

PS. 2012. *Résolution Europe Congrès du PS à Poitiers*. See PS website www.parti-socialiste.fr/le-PS

Quilliot, Roger. 1972. *La SFIO et l'exercice du pouvoir, 1944–58*. Paris: Fayard.

Sarlat, Guillaume. 2015. *En finir avec le libéralisme à la française*. Paris: Albin Michel.

Scharpf, Fritz. 1991. *Crisis and Choice in European Social Democracy*. Ithaca: Cornell UP.

Schmidt, Vivien. 2007. "Trapped by their Ideas: French elites' Discourses of European Integration and Globalisation." *Journal of European Public Policy* 14 (7): 992–1009.

Short, Philip. 2014. *A Taste for Intrigue: the Multiple Lives of François Mitterrand*. New York: Henry Holt.

Stiglitz, Joseph. 2016. *The Euro and Its Threat to the Future of Europe*. London: Allen Lane.

Streeck, Wolfgang. 2012. "Markets and Peoples: Democratic Capitalism and European Integration." *New Left Review* 73: 63–71.

Wagner, Markus. 2008. "Debating Europe in the French Socialist Parrty: The 2004 Internal Referendum." *French Politics* 6: 257–279.

Williams, Philip. 1964. *Crisis and Compromise: Politics in the Fourth Republic*. London: Longmans.

Between Euro-Federalism, Euro-Pragmatism and Euro-Populism: the Gaullist movement divided over Europe

Benjamin Leruth ⓘ and Nicholas Startin

ABSTRACT

Since the creation of the European Community, the Gaullist movement has never been united over the question of European integration. De Gaulle's intergovernmental vision of the European project has largely been the dominant discourse. At times however, this narrative has been questioned—on the one hand by more supranational notions of European integration; and on the other by a more pro-sovereignty Eurosceptic discourse. Subsequently, in its various modern-day guises the Gaullist movement has faced a series of major internal divisions with regard to its position on 'Europe'. This uncertainty has also manifested itself at the highest level as demonstrated by the changing discourse advocated by former French presidents Jacques Chirac and Nicolas Sarkozy. This paper analyses the internal tensions over the European issue within the Gaullist movement at elite level. It determines that despite Chirac's and Sarkozy's attempts to unite the party throughout their presidencies the Gaullist movement is far from having moved towards a united European stance. Accordingly, the authors identify that over the past three decades, it is possible to identify three distinct, and at times conflicting, Gaullist stances on European integration with which the party's elites have vacillated, namely Euro-Federalism, Euro-Pragmatism and Euro-Populism.

RÉSUMÉ

Depuis la création de la Communauté européenne, le mouvement gaulliste n'a jamais adopté une vision commune en ce qui concerne l'intégration européenne. La vision intergouvernementale du projet européen telle que préconisée par de Gaulle a dominé l'histoire du mouvement. Cependant, cette vision a été remise en cause, d'une part par un soutien pour les valeurs fédéralistes, et d'autre part par un discours plus eurosceptique et souverainiste. Plus récemment, le mouvement gaulliste a dû faire face à une série de divisions internes majeures en raison de l'absence de compromis sur la question européenne. Ces divisions se sont également manifestées au plus haut niveau du pouvoir, comme en témoigne l'évolution des positions prises par Jacques Chirac et Nicolas Sarkozy. Cet article analyse les tensions internes relatives à la question européenne au sein du mouvement gaulliste. Malgré les tentatives de Jacques Chirac et de Nicolas Sarkozy d'unir le parti durant leurs présidences, le mouvement gaulliste est loin d'avoir adopté une position européenne commune. Les auteurs déterminent donc qu'au cours des trois dernières décennies, il est possible de définir trois positions gaullistes distinctes et parfois contradictoires relatives à l'intégration européenne, à savoir l'Euro-fédéralisme, l'Euro-pragmatisme et l'Euro-populisme.

Introduction

European integration has always been a difficult issue to manage for French political parties, on both the left and the right of the political spectrum. Throughout the history of the Fifth Republic, right-wing parties in particular have struggled to manage the European question, with Charles de Gaulle's historical legacy maintaining a significant impact on the debate. Accordingly, from de Gaulle's intergovernmental 'France First' interpretation of the European project to Nicolas Sarkozy's most recent opposition to Schengen, the mainstream French Right has been divided over the issue. Gaullist leaders post-de Gaulle have wrestled with how to carry the movement forward in terms of its outlook towards the European integration process. Pompidou softened de Gaulle's stance on the United Kingdom's entry to the European Union (EU); Chirac moved from his Eurosceptic 'appel de Cochin' position in 1978 drawing on a traditional Gaullist interpretation of Europe, before performing a volte-face towards a pro-integrationist stance as he closed in on the presidency in the early 1990s.

The former Union pour un mouvement populaire (UMP), a merger of several centre-right parties founded in 2002, and rebranded in 2015 as Les Républicains (LR), is the most recent heir of the Gaullist movement. However, and in contrast to a strict interpretation of Gaullism, the UMP (and more recently the LR), despite concerns about political sovereignty raised in the Maastricht Treaty, have adopted in policy terms a pro-European stance from the 1990s onwards greatly influenced by the impulse of French president Jacques Chirac. Yet, in the 13 years of its existence, the UMP suffered from major internal divisions over the European question between its various political movements, from the souverainiste 'Droite populaire' to the Euro-Federalist 'France moderne et humaniste'. These divisions have become more apparent recently in the LR, reinforced by a rise in the prominence of Euroscepticism in political discourse as evidenced by the European election results in 2014, where Marine Le Pen's Front national came first in the plebiscite for the European Parliament.

Based on a qualitative discourse and manifesto analysis, this paper analyses the internal tensions over the European issue within the Gaullist movement at elite level. It determines that, despite Jacques Chirac's and Nicolas Sarkozy's attempts to unite the party throughout their presidencies, the Gaullist movement is far from having moved towards a united European stance, and that internal divisions remain salient in the aftermath of the 2014 European elections. Accordingly, we identify that over the past three decades, it is possible to identify three distinct, and at times conflicting, Gaullist stances on European integration with which the party's elites have vacillated, namely Euro-Federalism, Euro-Pragmatism and Euro-Populism.

This paper begins by drawing on the history of the Gaullist movement in France, and what constitutes the European dimension of Gaullism. It then highlights the troubled evolution of the European discourse within the Gaullist movement since the post-de Gaulle era. The third section briefly analyses Nicolas Sarkozy's stance on Europe during his presidency, as this is a particularly significant turning point in the debate. Section four constitutes the core of this paper and reflects on some of the most recent developments within the

Box 1. List of major Gaullist political parties, 1947–2015.

Rassemblement du peuple français (1947–1955)
Union pour la nouvelle République (1958–1967)
Union démocratique du travail (1956–1967)
Union des démocrates pour la (Cinquième) République (1967–1976)
Rassemblement pour la République (1976–2002)
Union pour la majorité présidentielle/Union pour un mouvement populaire (2002–2015)
Les Républicains (2015–)

Gaullist movement, by focusing on the UMP's institutionalised factions following the 2012 presidential election defeat, and the attempt to unify the movement under a new party name. Finally, the conclusion suggests that while the Gaullist movement has often struggled to adopt a common stance on European integration, most recent developments ahead of the 2017 presidential election, as illustrated by the row between candidates during the centre-right primary election campaign, suggest that such divisions over Europe are likely to last, and that the Gaullist movement's stance on Europe will continue to fluctuate primarily between a Euro-Pragmatic and Euro-Populist stance.

Euro-Federalism, Euro-Pragmatism and Euro-Populism: the European dimension of Gaullism as an ideology

Existing studies on party opposition to European integration tend to focus on Taggart and Szczerbiak's (2008, 240) much-cited soft/hard Eurosceptic dichotomy, 'with attitude towards a country's membership of the EU being viewed as the ultimate litmus test of whether one fell into the first or second camp'. However, even though such two-dimensional conceptualisation paved the way towards a clearer conceptualisation of the phenomenon, it is sometimes considered as too finite (see e.g. Kopecký and Mudde 2002; Leruth 2015) and does not offer an accurate tool on which to reflect on the Gaullist movement's stance on Europe. Indeed, even though prominent Gaullists have often been critical of the European Union, they have never argued in favour of its disintegration or for a French withdrawal. Accordingly, we decided to deploy a tri-dimensional conceptualisation to portray outlooks on the process of European integration, using the notions of Euro-Federalism, Euro-Pragmatism and Euro-Populism.

The notions of 'federalism', 'populism' and 'pragmatism' have been widely used in the existing literature on European integration. In fact, the literature is characterised by a lack of consensus over widely accepted definitions of each concept. Firstly, *Euro-Federalism* is a notion used by Schmitter (2003), for example, and while it does not necessarily mean the creation of a 'United States of Europe', it favours a strong European Union with further competences transferred to the European level, thus calling for a strengthening of supranational institutions (see also Jeffery and Paterson 2003). Secondly, populism is defined by Mudde (2004, 543) as 'an ideology that considers society to be ultimately separated into two homogenous and antagonistic groups—"the pure people" versus the "corrupt elite", and which argues that politics should be an expression of the volonté générale (general will) of the people' (543). In the context of European integration, *Euro-Populism* is often linked to the notion of Euroscepticism, as the European Union is often portrayed as the 'corrupt elite' acting against the sovereign state. Finally, *Euro-Pragmatism* can be defined as contingent support for the European Union combined with a certain reluctance towards the principles of closer integration. Accordingly, Kopecký and Mudde (2002, 303) defined Euro-Pragmatist political parties as parties that 'do not hold a firm ideological opinion on European integration, and on the basis of pragmatic (often utilitarian) considerations decide to assess the EU positively because they deem it profitable for their own country or constituency'.

The dominant narrative on the question of European integration within the Gaullist movement has undoubtedly been a Euro-Pragmatist, 'France First' stance which emanates from de Gaulle and his legacy. This narrative, built around contingent support for an intergovernmental Europe with France at its core, has been at the forefront of the Gaullist party's outlook in its various guises in the post-de Gaulle era. This vision has, however, been challenged from within both the Left and the Right of the party: firstly, on the Left by a more Euro-Federal approach which has taken its inspiration largely from the Christian Democrat vision of its coalition partner as epitomised by the Union pour la démocratie française (UDF) founded in 1974; secondly, on the Right of the party, by a more *souverainiste* Eurosceptic and populist vision inspired by the Front national's negative stance on the European Union, which has at key moments from the Maastricht era onwards gained increasing traction within the Gaullist movement. The interplay between these three different visions of the EU has ensured that the issue of European integration has caused, and continues to cause, major tensions with the modern-day Gaullist movement.

The notion of Gaullism as an ideology and well-established political movement is widely accepted in French politics. Built around the grandeur of Charles de Gaulle, it is yet difficult to offer a definition of this ideology which encompasses all of its dimensions. Knapp (1994, 4–6) distinguishes four principal tenets of Gaullism: firstly, the independence of France, implying a refusal to submit France and French policy to the authority of supranational organisations; secondly, the authority of the State, according to which the central State and its institutions constitute the ultimate source of power and thus implying a strong core executive often considered as *dirigiste*; thirdly, the unity of the French, referring to de Gaulle's willingness to 'rally the French beyond the confines of political parties', beyond right and left ideologies (a claim nowadays used by most contemporary French leaders); and finally, the leadership of de Gaulle, perceived as a charismatic leader who is the founder of a new relationship between the State and its citizens.

The European dimension of Gaullism is expressed in the three former tenets of Gaullism. As noted by Startin (2005, 65), they 'raise fundamental questions about France's sovereignty and her role in Europe'. De Gaulle's vision of Europe was essentially pragmatic—intergovernmental in outlook, championing a 'Europe of nations' (or 'Europe des patries'), and using 'France First' as a guiding principle. This contrasted sharply with the Federal vision espoused by the centre-right, Christian Democrat Mouvement républicain populaire as championed by Robert Schuman. De Gaulle's rationale for closer European cooperation, although reluctant to embrace transnational European institutions and supranational authority, did nevertheless imply that France's destiny was as an active shaper of the European integration process. In the Gaullist era Gaullists generally believed European integration should be confined to economic matters, rejecting binding forms of political integration. The rejection of the Pleven Plan for a European Defence Community in 1954, through a combination of Gaullist and Communist votes in the French National Assembly, was a major victory for the Gaullist vision of Europe, defending a strong independent French foreign and security policy (Guyomarch, Machin, and Ritchie 1998). In the 1960s, the 'empty chair crisis' again demonstrated the influence of Charles de Gaulle in shaping the European integration process in an intergovernmental direction, as some other member states feared a potential withdrawal of France from the European project.

A cornerstone of the traditional Gaullist dimension of Europe is the predominance of the Common Agricultural Policy (CAP) as a tool to serve French farmers. As mentioned by Guyomarch, Machin, and Ritchie (1998, 141), de Gaulle and his ministers wanted an agricultural policy for the Community based on established French practices, anticipating that such a system would not only provide outlets for surplus French production, but also ensure that French farmers would benefit greatly from the guaranteed prices. In addition,'[d] e Gaulle not only established a firm pattern of defining joint European policies as "foreign" and French inputs as expression of national interest, he also contributed to ensuring that this approach would outlive his own political demise by its institutionalization within the CAP system' (141). In other words, the way the CAP was introduced in the framework of the European integration process reflected the Gaullist approach—that is, to use European institutions as a political asset for national interest—rather than emphasising the benefits of supranationalism and the Community method of integration.

De Gaulle's legacy on Europe was largely one of unity for the Gaullist movement in its successive guises as the Union pour la nouvelle République, the Union des démocrates pour la Ve République and the Union des démocrates pour la République. There are several explanations for this. Firstly, there is what Shields (1996, 86–109) describes as the 'highly personalised relationship of disciplined support which existed between the General and his *compagnons*'. A second factor is that traditionally Europe fell within the domain of foreign affairs and defence, which, according to de Gaulle's interpretation of the constitution, remained very much the president's prerogative. Finally, de Gaulle's 'France First' rhetoric commanded general support amongst a majority of the French public, who entrusted him to make the right choices for France within the Community framework. De Gaulle's popularity was never higher than during his defence of the National Veto and opposition to Qualified Majority Voting during the 1965 Empty Chair Crisis and subsequent Luxembourg Compromise of 1966 (Guyomarch, Machin, and Ritchie 1998, 86). Under de Gaulle, the party was able to steer a course between independence from and commitment to Europe, and it developed a preference for an intergovernmental Europe based primarily on economic trade with weak institutions, and decision-making power lying primarily with national governments.

Following Charles de Gaulle's death in 1970, the idea and interpretation of Gaullism as an ideology moved in several directions, a consequence of which would mean that, with regard to the issue of European integration, the Gaullist movement would never be as united in a post-Gaullian era. In terms of the evolution of the Gaullist movement with regard to its party structure, the movement as a whole has cohabitated within the confines of a broad right-wing political party which has undertaken various name changes (see Box 1).

The apparent unity implied by the broad structure of a one-party title has not disguised the various differences and factions which have evolved in the post-Gaullian era. Knapp and Wright (2006, 226) list five movements which materialised from the 1970s onwards:

1. *Gaullisme de Résistance*: a movement loyal above all to 'the man of 18 June 1940', i.e. the General, who played a major role during the Second World War;
2. *Gaullisme de Gauche*: a movement focusing on the social dimension of Gaullism, often linked to social democracy and characterised by Euro-Pragmatism;

3. *Gaullisme pompidolien*: a Euro-Pragmatic movement loyal to the legacy of Georges Pompidou, emphasising the need for France to adapt to an increasingly competitive world while preserving social peace;
4. *Gaullisme chiraquien de première génération*: a movement loyal to the original Euro-Populist argument advocated by Jacques Chirac in the late 1970s, characterised by a fierce opposition to European integration and the free market;
5. and the *Gaullisme chiraquien de deuxième génération*: a Euro-Pragmatic movement loyal to the aggressive pro-free market and pro-European rhetoric advocated by Chirac from the mid 1980s onwards.

Europe and the Gaullist movement post-de Gaulle: a troubled evolution

In order to reassess the European dimension of Gaullism and unravel why this issue continues to divide the movement as a whole, the next section provides some context by examining the evolution of the European question in the post-de Gaulle era. For the duration of the Pompidou presidency divisions did not surface in any significant way. Like his predecessor, Pompidou adopted a Euro-Pragmatic stance favouring a European Economic Community (EEC) of nation states based on mutual cooperation and placed French national interests before wider Community issues, but, unlike de Gaulle, Pompidou was in favour of the United Kingdom joining the Community. He had a certain suspicion of Germany and was closer in political outlook to the pro-European Conservative Edward Heath than the Social Democrat Helmut Schmidt (Frears 1981, 104). Pompidou recognised that the Franco-German axis was the key to political and diplomatic progress towards European integration but believed that it could not really function without the influence of British membership of the EEC. Pompidou's presidency was one of relative unity among Gaullists. His vision of the EEC was shared by the two prime ministers of his presidency, Jacques Chaban-Delmas and Pierre Messmer, and, apart from minority opposition from a wing of traditional Gaullists loyal to de Gaulle's opposition to British entry to the Community, the view that France continued to prosper economically within the EEC framework predominated.

In reality, it was the election of the pro-EU, centre-right and Christian Democrat Valery Giscard d'Estaing as president in 1974 which increased tensions within the Gaullist movement around the issue of 'Europe'. Giscard's plans for the introduction of European elections and regular bilateral EU summits—today's European Council—were perceived as supranational in their intentions at odds with the vision of a Europe of nations still predominant in the Gaullist movement. Strands of the party became increasingly wary of Giscard's pro-integration stance, and with the launch of the Rassemblement pour la République (RPR) in 1976 and as Jacques Chirac became more influential among the traditional Gaullist Right, the party progressively distanced itself from the president's stance. In 1976, Chirac resigned as prime minister citing his opposition to Giscard d'Estaing over direct elections to the European Parliament as the reason for his decision (Guyomarch, Machin, and Ritchie 1998, 84).

The party was to enter a distinctly Euro-Populist phase in the late 1970s, publicly opposing the 1976 Tindemans Report, which proposed greater powers to the European Parliament and the Commission. The decade culminated in the nationalist and anti-integrationist campaign led by Chirac and de Gaulle's former prime minister Michel Debré in the 1979 European elections. As Shields (1996, 86–109) points out, these elections 'marked a critical point in the

RPR's attempt to define its position on Europe ten years on from the departure of de Gaulle'. The period leading up to the elections was one of sustained confrontation between Chirac and Giscard d'Estaing on the question of Europe. The conflict centred on the Spanish and Portuguese applications for membership of the Community and the role of the European Commission as well as the president's views on supranationalism. From his hospital bed in Paris in 1978 while recovering from a car accident prior to the 1979 election, Chirac issued his famous 'appel de Cochin', in which he berated the president and his newly formed UDF as the 'parti de l'étranger' (foreign party), ready to compromise French national interests in the market place of an enlarged, pro-American Europe:

> La politique européenne du gouvernement ne peut, en aucun cas, dispenser la France d'une politique étrangère qui lui soit propre. L'Europe ne peut servir à camoufler l'effacement d'une France qui n'aurait plus, sur le plan mondial, ni autorité, ni idée, ni message, ni visage. Nous récusons une politique étrangère qui cesse de répondre à la vocation d'une grande puissance, membre permanent du Conseil de sécurité des Nations unies et investie de ce fait de responsabilités particulières dans l'ordre international.

> C'est pourquoi nous disons NON.

> NON à la politique de la supranationalité.

> NON à l'asservissement économique.

> NON à l'effacement international de la France. (Chirac 1978, 227)

The RPR's campaign was essentially a failure, with the party polling a meagre 16%, apparently having misread the mood of the electorate. An estimated 39% of the Gaullist vote from the previous 1978 legislative elections deserted the party and voted for other lists, rejecting the RPR's overtly nationalist stance (SOFRES 1980). In addition, the 1979 European election caused the first real Europe-related fissures to emerge within the RPR with a group of members of the parliament led by Euro-Federalists Alain Peyrefitte and Michel Cointat criticising the Euro-Populist spirit of the Gaullist list and threatening to field a dissident list of pro-European Gaullists (SOFRES 1980). The 1979 elections marked a new phase for the Gaullist movement in its attempt to redefine its European outlook in the post-de Gaulle period. From this moment onwards, the divisions within the party hierarchy become increasingly open and difficult to reconcile.

The conversion of the majority of the RPR's hierarchy to economic liberalism in the early 1980s ensured that the party became a supporter of the legislative programme for the completion of the internal market. In 1983, the party's central committee all but abandoned its Euro-Populist stance, by performing a volte-face on Europe. The party now called for greater economic, monetary and defence cooperation without calling for Euro-Federalism, adopting a more Euro-Pragmatist stance. Following a series of poor electoral results, the party hierarchy was forced to take into account the need to extend both Chirac's and the party's appeal to the crucial middle ground so successfully occupied by Giscard d'Estaing. A changed policy on Europe was seen as part of that new appeal.

This was also the opportunity to push to prominence a generation of younger and more Euro-Pragmatic Gaullists such as Alain Juppé. During the 1984 European election campaign the RPR was to tread a careful line between its pragmatic support of Europe and its commitment to cooperation with the UDF. The joint UDF/RPR list polled 42.9% of the vote, which on the surface seemed a resounding success for Chirac and the RPR (Saint-Ouen 1987). However, the result of the election was as much a mid-term reflection on the

Mitterrand presidency as an endorsement of the RPR's conversion to a more pro-European, Euro-Pragmatic stance, which did nothing to resolve the problem of identity and direction within the Gaullist movement. The emergence of the Front national at the 1984 European elections only served to reinforce the problems facing the RPR in terms of where to position itself on the political spectrum. Despite the electoral success of the RPR–UDF coalition in the 1986 legislative elections, the meagre 19.9% polled by Chirac in the first round of the 1989 presidential election and his subsequent defeat in the second round only aggravated problems for the Gaullist movement (Fysh 1988). There were calls from modernisers such as Michel Noir and Nicolas Sarkozy for a merger with the UDF but this request was met with vehement opposition from traditional Gaullists such as Charles Pasqua and Philippe Séguin (Subileau 1999). Central to the debate was the question of Europe and in what direction the party should proceed. Existing divisions were tempered during the 1989 European election campaign with a joint RPR-UDF list asserting the need for a strong France within a strong Europe; the realisation of the single market; building a monetary union with a common currency; strengthening the existing EU institutions; and contributing to a more social Europe. The 28.87% of the vote obtained and 26 seats gained by the joint list was far from a convincing result for France's mainstream Right.

The ratification of the Maastricht Treaty, which paved the way towards a political union, triggered tensions within the Gaullist movement and was very damaging in terms of party unity. Senior members of the party leadership were in favour of its ratification but the majority of its members were opposed (Duhamel and Grunberg 1993). Hampered by the strength of the traditional *France d'abord* views of large swathes of the RPR's membership, the broadly pro-Maastricht leadership trio of Jacques Chirac, Édouard Balladur and Alain Juppé felt unable to fully endorse a 'Yes' vote to their members and supporters. In a special issue Maastricht edition of the RPR monthly, *La Lettre de la Nation*, party chairman Juppé (1992, 1), who was given the task of converting wavering supporters, in his editorial supported a free vote stating, '[t]he Gaullist movement has decided to accept its differences in opinion. We could have chosen, like some others, to impose a party line on our supporters but we preferred to play a more open game based on transparency and truth.' With one eye on the presidency Chirac, now converted to the European cause, summed up his overall pragmatic position: 'My conviction is that the need for Europe is greater than ever. Even though Maastricht is far from perfect, the treaty nevertheless represents a way forward that France cannot afford to reject'.

The RPR campaign against Maastricht was launched in July 1992 by Philippe Séguin and Charles Pasqua. Séguin was against Maastricht from the outset, predicting the end of the nation state in Europe and the beginning of a federal Europe. During the campaign he emerged 'as a forceful orator, championing the principle of national sovereignty in grand Gaullist tones' (Shields 1996, 86–109). Pasqua's decision to add weight to the 'No' movement was not apparent until the announcement by Mitterrand of the referendum. In line with most of the party hierarchy, Pasqua had been expected to support the Treaty with certain reservations. From the outset the *Rassemblement pour le Non* campaign stressed that it was not opposed to the construction of a united Europe but simply against the 'rampant federalism' of Maastricht itself. In a circular sent to RPR members Pasqua (1992) summarised his position as follows: 'I am not saying no to Maastricht to put an end to closer European cooperation but instead to put it back on a surer footing.' Accordingly, his Euro-Populist position can also be interpreted as an anti-Euro-Federalist one.

Thus, Maastricht, with its increased politicisation of the European project, ensured that the European Union was to become one of the most divisive issues within the mainstream Right as a whole. The cohabitation between Euro-Pragmatists and Euro-Populists was to become very fragile for the Gaullists, and led to the creation of three splinter parties in the 1990s: the relatively low-key 'Rassemblement pour la France', founded by Nicolas Stoquer in 1992 to oppose the Maastricht Treaty; Philippe de Villiers''Mouvement pour la France', founded in 1994 following the success of the 'Majorité pour l'autre Europe' list in the European elections; and Charles Pasqua's 'Rassemblement pour la France et l'indépendance de l'Europe', founded in 1999 to unite *souverainistes* defectors from the RPR. These Eurosceptic splinter parties were thus founded as a response to the Gaullisme chiraquien de deuxième génération, which became predominant within the Rassemblement pour la République: '[f]or Gaullist diehards, the transfers of sovereignty to which Chirac consented in the treaties of Maastricht and of Amsterdam were breaches of the essential Gaullist value of national independence' (Knapp and Wright 2006, 226–227). Jacques Chirac's subsequent decisions to support the processes of deepening and widening the European Union through the ratification of the Amsterdam, Nice as well as the short-lived (and unratified) 'Rome 2004' treaties, demonstrate an ideological U-turn. The discourse given by Chirac before the Bundestag in June 2000 illustrates this major switch:

> Nos nations sont la source de nos identités et de notre enracinement. La diversité de leurs traditions politiques, culturelles, linguistiques est une des forces de notre Union. Pour les peuples qui viennent, les nations resteront les premières références. Envisager leur extinction serait aussi absurde que de nier qu'elles ont déjà choisi d'exercer en commun une partie de leur souveraineté et qu'elles continueront de le faire, car tel est leur intérêt. (Chirac 2000, https://www.bundestag. de/parlament/geschichte/gastredner/chirac/chirac2/244736)

Yet the Gaullist movement remained strongly divided over the issue of Europe. Following Jean-Marie Le Pen's shock result in the first round of the presidential election, the UMP was founded in 2002, originally standing for 'Union pour la majorité présidentielle' but renamed 'Union pour un mouvement populaire'. This new political party combined both Gaullist and non-Gaullist movements (including most of the centrist UDF and Démocratie libérale [DL]), with the objective to consolidate Chirac's leadership.

Accordingly, the UMP was not the direct successor of the Gaullist movement, but a merger of various political parties aiming to become the largest right-wing movement on the French political landscape. With regards to its position on the European Union, while the bulk of its elites were broadly Euro-Pragmatic and pro-integrationist, the UMP activists still comprised some Euro-Populist *souverainistes* and traditional Gaullists.

Sarkozy and European integration: je t'aime, moi non plus?

In his emotional victory speech in the Salle Gaveau in Paris when elected President of France in 2007, Nicolas Sarkozy proclaimed himself a true European. He underlined this point by stating:

> Je veux lancer un appel à nos partenaires européens, auxquels notre destin est lié, pour leur dire que toute ma vie j'ai été européen, que je crois en la construction européenne et que ce soir la France est de retour en Europe. (Sarkozy 2007, http://www.touteleurope.eu/l-union-europeenne/acteurs-d-aujourd-hui/synthese/nicolas-sarkozy.html)

The tone of this proclamation marked him out as a new-generation Gaullist in contrast to the 'France First' rhetoric of de Gaulle, Pompidou and (to a lesser extent) Chirac. Following the 2005 'No' votes on the Constitutional Treaty in France and the Netherlands, Sarkozy was determined to stamp his authority on the European Union and kick-start the process of European integration while France held the presidency of the EU between July and December 2008. His vision of the EU as laid out in his manifesto *Mon Projet* was one with a developed Common Foreign and Security Policy; that does more to fight global terrorism and combat global warming; with a Common Energy Policy modelled on the Common Agricultural Policy; which opposes Turkish membership; where a Mediterranean Union (including Turkey) is set up as a trading block to work closely with (but not become part of) the EU. In a speech to the European Parliament in July 2008, Sarkozy set out his priorities for his six-month tenure of the EU presidency and highlighted the themes of energy, climate change, immigration and the need for Europe to develop a defence policy as areas requiring urgent action, as well as the need to find a way forward after the Irish 'No' vote on the Lisbon Treaty.

What is both interesting and consistent about Sarkozy's positioning on the EU is his clear recognition that the French nation state is no longer (in isolation) sufficiently influential to combat the negative aspects of economic and cultural globalisation in terms of protecting French firms from *délocalisations*, foreign takeovers and social dumping, or in terms of protecting the French language and culture from global dilution. Accordingly, his stance can be considered as a Euro-Pragmatic one. Sarkozy lays out his rationale in his November 2006 speech delivered in Saint-Étienne:

> Je veux une Europe qui protège les Européens comme tous les autres pays protègent leurs ressortissants. Car si l'Europe ne se protège pas assez, c'est le protectionnisme qui triomphera, les égoïsmes nationaux qui prévaudront, et le projet européen qui se délitera. L'Europe a besoin de protections même si je déteste l'idée du protectionnisme. (Saknozy 2006, http://discours. vie-publique.fr/notices/063003997.html)

His position was not a total break with tradition in France. Howarth (2008, 127) argues that economic governance at the EU level and more specifically the Economic and Monetary Union (EMU) project 'can be seen as mechanisms through which French governments have sought to manage both European and international constraints, in this way using Europe to keep the world at bay'. What is different about Sarkozy's approach though is that he became the first French president to fully recognise the futility of trying to respond to global economic developments from a uniquely French perspective and that a measure of protectionism is only feasible and effective at the EU level. Central to Sarkozy's outlook in the 2007 presidential election campaign, and in direct contrast to the Front national's increasingly Euromondialist outlook (see Lecoeur 2007), was his belief that the EU can soften the impact of some of the negative consequences of globalisation, and his portrayal of the EU as a 'pragmatic' go-between in the triangular relationship that is globalisation, the EU and the nation state:

> L'Europe est la seule entité capable d'encadrer la toute-puissance du marché. La seule capable de transformer la mondialisation de l'intérieur. La seule capable de se mesurer aux pays continents avides de puissance. La seule capable dans le cadre d'un dialogue transatlantique apaisé de pondérer la vision mondiale de notre allié américain. (Sarkozy 2006)

One of his first concrete actions on becoming president was to persuade his fellow leaders to drop the principle of 'free and undistorted competition' from Article 3 of the old Constitutional Treaty and to bury it in a protocol annexed to the treaties. In essence Sarkozy succeeded in persuading the EU to drop its commitment to the internal market with free and undistorted competition, a popular and symbolic move in terms of French public opinion, the Left and the bulk of the French media.

Unfortunately for Sarkozy, the onset of the crisis in the Eurozone and the global economic crisis were to ensure that his vision for changing Europe in grand architectural terms had to be put on hold as he was forced to wrestle with combatting the dire economic situation. This, combined with the negative outcome of the vote on the referendum on the Lisbon Treaty in Ireland in June 2008, turned the hostility of the world's media onto the EU right at the beginning of the French EU presidency, a setback in his efforts to reinvigorate his presidency. As Grunstein (2008) argues, Sarkozy was counting on using the parallel track of the EU presidency to re-inject some dynamism into his flagging first term in office. This did not materialise and the final year of his presidency began with a setback when in January 2012 the credit rating agency Standard and Poor's downgraded France's triple-A credit rating, blaming the country for not dealing with the debt crisis (Startin 2013). This was a blow for a president who had staked his reputation on his handling of the economic crisis within the context of the 'Merkozy' partnership and the Franco-German relationship (Startin 2013). Sarkozy finished his presidency by appearing to have performed something of a volte-face on Europe by proceeding in a Euro-Populist direction, especially on the issue of Schengen. At an election rally at Villepinte in March 2012 he claimed: '[l]es accords de Schengen ne permettent plus de répondre à la gravité de la situation, ils doivent être révisés. On ne peut pas laisser la gestion des flux migratoires aux seules mains des technocrates et des tribunaux (Trinquet 2015, 38).' As such, Sarkozy had appeared to perform something of a change of direction on Europe but in the opposite direction in comparison to Chirac. This switch to a more Euro-Populist position served to underline the divisions and uncertainty on the EU which pervade the modern-day Gaullist movement.

After 2012, the UMP and its factions: unity in diversity?

In order to defuse the various ideological differences within the UMP (not least with regard to the issue of European integration), the party leadership decided to introduce a model introduced by the Parti socialiste: namely the institutionalisation of political groups, or *mouvements*. These movements were effectively launched in May 2004 during the UMP's national committee meeting. In practice however, it was not until a nearly a decade later that these movements would become an integral part of the UMP's operational structure, in the aftermath of Nicolas Sarkozy's 2012 defeat against François Hollande in the second round of the presidential election. This was one of (then) party leader Jean-François Copé's initiatives in order to prevent defections prior to the subsequent legislative elections held in June 2012. Article 28 (formerly 15) of the UMP statutes defined the role of these movements within the party:

> Les Mouvements expriment la diversité des sensibilités politiques, historiques, philosophiques ou sociales qui animent la vie politique française et composent l'Union. Ils contribuent à la richesse du débat démocratique et intellectuel et à la représentation du plus grand nombre de Françaises et de Français au sein de l'Union.

In other words, the recognition of such movements within the UMP aimed to represent and legitimise the various 'school of thoughts', following a congressional vote in which each movement was required to register at least 10% of the vote. It remained to be seen whether this development would ease or exasperate the tensions surrounding the European question within the Gaullist movement as a whole.

On 18 November 2012, five movements (out of six) reached the 10% threshold and were thus officially recognised as part of the UMP: La Droite forte (27.77% of votes); La Droite sociale (21.69%); France moderne et humaniste (18.17% of votes); Gaullistes en mouvement (12.31%); and La Droite populaire (10.87%). La Boîte à idées, though being supported by some key leaders within the party (such as Alain Juppé and Édouard Balladur), only received 9.2% of votes (Le Monde 2012). The following sub-sections analyse the ideology and major political trends within each of the recognised movements, and more specifically their positions towards European integration in the context of the 2014 European elections.

La Droite forte

Proposed by Guillaume Peltier, who was one of Sarkozy's spokesmen during the 2012 presidential campaign and started his political career with the Front national, La Droite forte (originally named 'Génération Sarkozy') defends a right-wing populist line within the UMP (Knapp 2014). Rather than finding its roots in Gaullism, this movement followed the legacy of Nicolas Sarkozy's 2012 manifesto entitled 'La France Forte'. The raison d'être of this movement was defined as such: 'Rassembler politiquement tous ceux qui, dans la lignée de Nicolas Sarkozy, veulent construire une "France forte"; la Droite forte souhaite offrir une perspective d'espérance à travers une droite juste, forte, populaire et protectrice' (La Droite forte 2012).

This movement has been scrutinised for copying key aspects of the programme advocated by the Front national, and for promoting a strong 'droitisation' of the UMP. A study from Médiapart (2012) appeared to outline the 'copy-paste' character of its founding manifesto, especially with regards to issues such as secularism, fraud, trade unions and civil society.

With regards to its position on European integration, La Droite forte was a reformist movement defending the most recent political line promoted by Nicolas Sarkozy with regards to the Area of Freedom, Security and Justice, through the suppression of the Schengen Agreements and the introduction of a points-based system to control immigration within the borders of the European Union. The movement also drew on the Gaullist legacy by referring to the empty chair crisis, in case an agreement cannot be reached:

> … si nos partenaires rechignent, il faut faire comme Charles de Gaulle pour la politique agricole commune ou Margaret Thatcher pour la contribution financière du Royaume-Uni à l'Union européenne : la politique de la chaise vide afin de sauvegarder l'intérêt national. Cela demande du courage politique. Mais une majorité des Français nous donnera raison. (Peltier 2014)

Accordingly, La Droite forte advocated a strong Euro-Populist stance, building on Nicolas Sarkozy's 2012 manifesto.

La Droite sociale

La Droite sociale was initially launched as a think tank in 2010. It can be located towards the centre-left of the UMP. In contrast to La Droite forte, its supporters were a mix of Christian Democrats, Gaullistes de Gauche and Centrists around a project. Initially, European integration did not feature as a high-salience issue addressed by this movement. However, ahead of the 2014 European elections, the movement's leader, Laurent Wauquiez, campaigned on the grounds that 'l'Europe ne marche plus ; ... il faut tout changer' (Zagdoun 2014), and advocated a series of reforms for the European Union, from France's withdrawal of Schengen to the creation of a hard core of the six founding member states within the Union. Several representatives of La Droite sociale and the Gaullistes en mouvement co-signed an opinion column in *Le Figaro* (2014), calling for a reform of the European project:

> La libre circulation poussée à l'excès qui interdit tout contrôle des déplacements de populations à l'intérieur de l'Europe pouvant mettre en péril la cohésion de nos sociétés et qui va jusqu'à mettre en concurrence, sur notre sol, nos salariés avec des salariés qui supportent trois fois moins de charges sociales, ça ne peut plus durer. Le dumping fiscal et social à l'intérieur de l'Europe, ça ne peut plus durer. Les frontières extérieures de l'Espace Schengen qui laissent passer des flux d'immigration incontrôlés, ça ne peut plus durer. L'élargissement sans fin, ça ne peut plus durer. (*Le Figaro* 2014)

In sum, La Droite sociale (mostly through its leader) adopted a Euro-Populist discourse throughout the 2014 election campaign, criticising the current state of European integration, especially with regards to the Area of Freedom, Security and Justice.

France moderne et humaniste

Led by two tenors of the UMP, former prime minister Jean-Pierre Raffarin and Luc Chatel, France moderne et humaniste was a moderate centrist movement within the UMP. It is mostly composed of former members of the UDF and DL, before these two parties merged with the RPR in 2002. Although the UDF and DL were non-Gaullist parties, France moderne et humaniste was also composed of some Gaullistes de Gauche, and it defended a social, liberal and European humanism.

Unlike La Droite forte, France moderne et humaniste promoted a stronger, Euro-Federalist vision of the European Union. Its outlook is summarised as such:

> L'Union européenne doit peser davantage sur la scène internationale et être capable de protéger ses frontières ainsi que son activité économique en imposant le principe de réciprocité. Nous sommes partisans d'une Europe fédérée, qui n'a pas peur d'élargir les domaines de souveraineté partagée, ni d'ériger une Union budgétaire, fiscale et sociale. Cela suppose une impulsion démocratique forte avec la création d'un gouvernement de l'Union et le renforcement du rôle des parlements nationaux et européen. (France moderne et humaniste 2012)

The movement's vision of Europe was closer to the one which was advocated by Centrists in the 1970s, under the presidency of Valéry Giscard d'Estaing. It was not opposed to the current principles of European integration and even calls for extending the competences of the European Union. No reference to a 'Europe des patries', a key concept of the various (Euro-Populist) forms of Gaullism, features. Of the current movements officially recognised within the UMP, France moderne et humaniste was the most pro-European and Euro-Federalist, reflecting its centrist and Christian Democrat historical legacy.

Gaullistes en mouvement

Founded in September 2012 by Michèle Alliot-Marie, Roger Karoutchi, Henri Guaino and Patrick Ollier, les Gaullistes en mouvement was the main movement representing the heirs and defenders of Gaullism within the UMP. The four dimensions of Gaullism (the independence of France, the authority of the state, the unity of the French and the grandeur of de Gaulle) were key values constituting the main *raison d'être* of this movement:

> Nous avons la conviction, qui était celle du Général de Gaulle, que la politique peut et doit encore influencer le cours de l'Histoire et qu'elle ne doit pas suivre l'économie et la finance mais les précéder. ... Nous aspirons à la restauration de l'autorité d'un État centré sur ses compétences régaliennes, à l'ardente obligation de défendre les valeurs républicaines de réussite, de travail, d'effort et de promotion au mérite. (Gaullistes en mouvement 2012)

As far as the 'Europe' issue is concerned, which caused internal divisions within the Gaullist party from the 1990s onwards, the Gaullistes en mouvement defended an intergovernmental, Euro-Pragmatic vision, based on de Gaulle's 'Europe des patries' and opposing any forms of federalism at the European level. Some of its members (including Henri Guaino) wanted to put an end to the Schengen area, thus promoting a form of disintegration in the Area of Freedom, Security and Justice. Yet, some important differences with de Gaulle's vision of Europe were evident. Firstly, and in sharp contrast with de Gaulle's opposition to the Pleven Plan in the 1950s, the movement was in favour of a European Defence Community, and favoured the current Common Foreign and Security Policy. Secondly, it did not oppose enlargement per se, but advocated a full assessment of the European institutions before resuming this process. Thirdly, and also in contrast with the position defended by La Droite forte, the movement did not advocate the empty chair as a solution to defend national interest, but instead favoured consensus at the European level.

La Droite populaire

The last movement that reached the 10% threshold in 2012 was La Droite populaire, founded in 2010 by former minister Thierry Mariani. This movement was ideologically close to La Droite forte, located towards the right wing of the UMP, and called for a broader 'droitisation' of the party line. It has also been criticised in the media and within the party for copying aspects of the programme defended by the Front national, though to a lesser extent than La Droite forte (*Le Monde* 2011). The legacy of de Gaulle was also claimed by this movement, as indicated in the motion presented before the party's congress: 'Aujourd'hui, la Droite Populaire entend poursuivre sa lutte contre la Gauche et faire prévaloir, au sein de l'UMP, la priorité de l'intérêt national, dans la continuité des principes légués par le général de Gaulle' (Droite populaire 2012).

The movement defended a Euro-Pragmatic vision of European integration based on de Gaulle's objectives:

> Fidèle à l'héritage du général de Gaulle, la Droite Populaire défendra l'idée d'une Europe des Nations, seule capable de relever les défis de la mondialisation. ... Nous croyons en la France indépendante, maîtresse de ses décisions, puissance d'équilibre aux yeux du monde et en une Europe forte, fondée sur les peuples. (Droit populaire 2012)

> As such, it advocated reforms of the European institutions, with stricter border controls and tougher regulations, and it favoured economic above political integration.

The emergence of these five movements within the mainstream Right (as represented by the UMP) and their divergent views on European integration clearly demonstrate that in recent years, the Gaullist movement has been increasingly divided. It also shows that between Euro-Federalism, Euro-Pragmatism and Euro-Populism, as defined at the beginning of this paper, there are various 'shades' of opposition to European integration within these movements. In particular, the Area of Freedom, Security and Justice (and more particularly Schengen) appeared to be a key policy area criticised by Euro-Pragmatist and Euro-Populists alike.

Following Nicolas Sarkozy's comeback in politics as UMP leader, the party rebranded itself as Les Républicains in May 2015. In an attempt to unify the party, the institutional role of the movements disappeared from the LR's institutional structure. However, the ideological divisions within the Gaullist movement over the issue of European integration remain prominent within the party. This is demonstrated by current debates over the nomination of the centre-right candidate for the 2017 presidential election. Nicolas Sarkozy and Alain Juppé were quickly designated as the two favourites by the media and French commentators. However, former prime minister François Fillon eventually won the contest over Juppé in the second round of this primary election, with 66.5% of the votes. During the campaign, the three aforementioned candidates held diverging views on European integration. While Sarkozy appeared as a candidate close to the ideas advocated by La Droite forte, Juppé's campaign was more in line with the heritage of the ideals of the Gaulliste chiraquien de deuxième génération. Fillon started rising in opinion polls a week before the first round of the election, and adopted a Euro-Pragmatic approach which is reflected in his manifesto. Six EU-related priorities are advocated by Fillon: reforming and strengthening Schengen, including by tripling the European Border and Coast Guard Agency's budget; strengthening EU cooperation in terms of security and defence including with the United Kingdom post-Brexit; strengthening the EMU by creating an intergovernmental 'Euro-board'; a form of European protectionism, but combined with the opportunity for France to veto any EU decisions that would go against the country's own interest (such as economic sanctions on Russia); reforming the role of the European Commission and restoring the principle of subsidiarity; and finally, boosting European innovation and technology through stronger cooperation between member states (Fillon 2017).In sum, while Fillon advocates more cooperation and integration in the Area of Freedom, Security and Justice as well as in the EMU, he also favours a more intergovernmental Union where national sovereignty and the principle of subsidiarity would prevail.

Conclusion: towards an ever more divided house?

The issue of European integration has been dividing the Gaullist movement since its creation. From de Gaulle's presidency to the Gaullist nomination for the 2017 elections, the movement has failed to forge a coherent, common stance on Europe. This led to the creation of significant splinter movements at various stages from the Maastricht era onwards, which have been particularly successful in European elections held in the 1990s. The creation of the UMP in 2002 offered an opportunity for the Gaullist movement to perhaps bury its equivocal stance towards Europe, to come to terms with its past and to lay to rest the Eurosceptic influences within the party. This has not proved to be the case and the creation of the now-defunct mouvements really only served to divide (rather than unite) the party further on this issue. This paper has also demonstrated that between Euro-Federalism, Euro-Pragmatism and Euro-Populism, the Gaullist stance on European integration has been very much a 'moving target', sometimes focusing on opposition to supranationalism as a whole, and sometimes highlighting the problems of specific policies or policy areas. In its current guise as the LR, the Gaullists remain divided, reopening the wounds that have divided it on the issue of European integration. In the context of the Front national's victory at the 2014 European elections and following the recent British vote to leave the European Union, these divisions look set to intensify within the movement as a whole. As Fillon attempts to find a middle ground through his suggested Euro-Pragmatic manifesto, Les Républicains face a series of important challenges in the build-up to the 2017 presidential elections. Whether these divisions intensify to the extent that they have within the British Conservative Party remains to be seen. Whatever the future holds, there is no doubt that the populist, *souverainiste* flame remains very much alight within the modern-day Gaullist movement.

Disclosure statement

No potential conflict of interest was reported by the author.

ORCID

Benjamin Leruth (iD) http://orcid.org/0000-0002-1999-918X

References

Chirac, J. 1978. *Discours pour la France à l'heure du choix*. Paris: Stock.

Chirac, J. 2000. *Notre Europe: Discours prononcé par Monsieur Jacques Chirac devant le Bundestag Allemand*. Berlin: Deutscher Bundestag.

Droite populaire. 2012. *Motion: L'appel de la Droite Populaire: Maîtriser notre destin et réaffirmer le pacte républicain* [online] Accessed March 25, 2015. http://ladroitepopulaire.com/motion-lappelde-la-droite-populaire-maitriser-notre-destin-et-reaffirmer-le-pacte-republicain/

Duhamel, O., and G. Grunberg. 1993. "Referendum: les dix France." In *L'Etat de l'opinion*, edited by O. Duhamel, and J. Jaffré, 79–85. Paris: SOFRES.

Fillon, F. 2017. *Une France Souveraine dans une Europe Respectueuse des Nations* [online] Accessed January 12, 2017. https://www.fillon2017.fr/europe/

France moderne et humaniste. 2012. La motion [online] Accessed March 25, 2015. http://www.fmhump.fr/la-motion/

Frears, J. R. 1981. *France in the Giscard Presidency*. London: Allen & Unwin.

Fysh, P. 1988. "Defeat and Reconstruction: the RPR in 1988." *Modern and Contemporary France* 35: 15–25.

Gaullistes en mouvement. 2012. Le Gaullisme, voie d'avenir pour la France ! [online] Accessed March 25, 2015. http://gaullistesenmouvement.org/?page_id=300

Grunstein, J. 2008 "Sarkozy the European: France's EU Presidency". *World Politics Review* [online] Accessed March 25, 2015. http://www.worldpoliticsreview.com/article.aspx?id=2361

Guyomarch, A., H. Machin, and E. Ritchie. 1998. *France in the European Union*. Basingstoke: Palgrave Macmillan.

Howarth, D. 2008. "Using Europe to Keep the World at Bay: French Policy on EU Economic Governance", In *France and the World Stage: Nation State Strategies in the Global Era*, edited by M. Maclean, and J. Szarka, 127–143, Basingstoke: Palgrave Macmillan.

Jeffery, C., and W. Paterson. 2003. "Germany and European Integration: A Shifting of Tectonic Plates." *West European Politics* 26 (4): 59–75.

Juppé, A. April 1992. "La Traité de Maastricht." *Lettre de la Nation*. Paris: Rassemblement pour la République.

Knapp, A. 1994. *Gaullism since de Gaulle*. Aldershot: Dartmouth Publishing.

Knapp, A. 2014. "En Attendant Sarko? France's Mainstream Right and Centre, 2012–14." *Modern & Contemporary France* 22 (4): 473–489.

Knapp, A., and V. Wright. 2006. *The Government and Politics of France*. 5th ed. Abingdon: Routledge.

Kopecký, P., and C. Mudde. 2002. "The Two Sides of Euroscepticism: Party Positions on European Integration in East Central Europe." *European Union Politics* 3 (3): 297–326.

La Droite Forte. 2012. "Notre motion." Accessed 25 March 2015. http://www.ladroiteforte.com/actualites/article/notre-motion

Le Figaro. 2014 "L'appel de 40 parlementaires pour changer l'Europe." [online] Accessed March 25, 2015. http://www.lefigaro.fr/vox/politique/2014/04/25/31001-20140425ARTFIG00081-henriguainolaurent-wauquiez-il-est-temps-de-tout-changer-en-europe.php

Le Monde. 2011 "La Droite populaire rejoint en partie le programme du FN." [online] Accessed March 25, 2015. http://www.lemonde.fr/politique/article/2011/09/28/la-droite-populaire-rejointen-partie-le-programme-du-fn_1578638_823448.html

Le Monde. 2012. "La Droite forte grande gagnante des motions de l'UMP." Accessed March 25, 2015. http://www.lemonde.fr/politique/article/2012/11/20/la-droite-forte-grande-gagnante-des-motions-de-l-ump_1793301_823448.html

Lecoeur, E. 2007. *Dictionnaire de l'Extreme Droite*. Paris: Larousse.

Leruth, B. 2015. "Operationalizing National Preferences on Europe and Differentiated Integration." *Journal of European Public Policy* 22 (6): 816–835.

Médiapart. 2012 « La "Droite Forte", un copier-coller du FN.» [online] Accessed March 25, 2015. http://www.mediapart.fr/journal/france/111012/la-droite-forte-un-copier-coller-du-fn

Mudde, C. 2004. "The Populist Zeitgeist." *Government and Opposition* 39 (4): 542–563.

Pasqua, C. 1992. "Chacun et son âme et conscience." *Supplément à la Lettre de La Nation* 24 April 1992. Paris: Rassemblement pour la République.

Peltier, B. 2014. «Votation Suisse sur l'immigration: un exemple à imiter.» *Le Figaro* [online] Accessed March 25, 2015. http://ladroiteforte.fr/actualites/article/votation-suisse-sur-limmigration

Saint-Ouen, F. 1987. "Les partis politiques français et l'Europe." *Revue française de science politique* 37: 205–226.

Sarkozy, N. 2006. « Déclaration de M. Nicolas Sarkozy, ministre de l'aménagement du territoire et président de l'UMP, sur la France dans la mondialisation, Saint-Etienne le 9 novembre 2006.» [online] Accessed March 25, 2015. http://discours.vie-publique.fr/notices/063003997.html.

Sarkozy, N. 2007 « Déclaration de M. Nicolas Sarkozy, président de l'UMP, à l'annonce de son élection comme président de la République.» Paris, 6 May 2007. Accessed on March 25, 2015. http://discours.vie-publique.fr/notices/073001681.html

Schmitter, P. C. 2003. "Democracy in Europe and Europe's Democratization." *Journal of Democracy* 14 (4): 71–85.

Shields, J. G. 1996. "The French Faullists." In *Political Parties and the European Union*, edited by J. Gaffney, 86–109. London: Routledge.

SOFRES. 1980. *Les Elections Européennes: Enquête Post-Electorale*. Paris: SOFRES.

Startin, N. 2005. "Maastricht, Amsterdam and Beyond: The Troubled Evolution of the French Right." In *French Relations with the European Union*, edited by H. Drake, 64–85. Abdingdon: Routledge.

Startin, N. 2013. "France." *European Journal of Political Research Political Data Yearbook* 52 (1): 70–82.

Subileau, F. 1999. "France: crise dans la participation." *Revue politique et parlementaire* 1001: 16–22.

Taggart, P., and A. Szczerbiak. 2008. "Theorizing Party-based Euroscepticism: Problems of Definition, Measurement, and Causality." In *Opposing Europe? The Comparative Party Politics of Euroscepticism Volume 2: Comparative and Theoretical Perspectives*, edited by P. Taggart, and A. Szczerbiak, 238–262. Oxford: Oxford University Press.

Trinquet, M. 2015. *ABCD'R du Sarkozysme: Nicolas Sarkozy en 26 discours*. Paris: Books on Demand.

Zagdoun, B. 2014 « Laurent Wauquiez et l'Europe: un changement de ton radical.» *France Télévisions Info* [online] Accessed March 25, 2015. http://www.francetvinfo.fr/elections/europeennes/video-laurent-wauquiez-et-l-europe-unchangement-%20de-ton-radical_595545.html

France and European macroeconomic policy coordination: from the Treaty of Rome to the euro area sovereign debt crisis

David Howarth and Joachim Schild

ABSTRACT

French support for European (EC/EU)-level macroeconomic policy coordination has been driven by remarkably consistent preferences since the 1950s. With the exception of the de Gaulle decade (1958–1968), French governments have sought European-level mechanisms for balance of payments support. This article sets out to explain these remarkably stable French preferences on European-level macroeconomic policy coordination over time through a combination of an interest-based analysis referring to structural and competitive weaknesses of the French economy and an ideational explanatory analysis focused upon French Keynesian thinking on symmetrical adjustment of both deficit and surplus countries. French preferences align largely with the concept of 'embedded liberalism'. This article also interprets a number of developments in EU-level economic governance in response to the banking and sovereign debt crises that provided a policy window for France to move European-level mechanisms and institutions towards long-held French preferences.

RÉSUMÉ

La politique française en faveur de la coordination des politiques macro-économiques à l'échelle européenne est dirigée par les préférences remarquablement constantes depuis les années 1950. À l'exception de la décennie de Gaulle (1958–1968), les gouvernements français ont cherché des mécanismes au niveau européen pour soutenir la balance des paiements nationale. Cet article vise à expliquer ces préférences françaises consistantes au fil du temps à l'aide d'une analyse basée sur les intérêts économiques se référant à des faiblesses structurelles et la compétitivité de l'économie française combinée avec une analyse idéationnelle focalisée sur la pensée keynésienne en faveur d'un ajustement symétrique des pays déficitaires et excédentaires. Ces préférences françaises s'alignent largement avec le concept de « libéralisme enchâssé ». Cet article interprète également un certain nombre de développements en matière de gouvernance économique au niveau de l'UE/la zone euro en réponse à la crise de la dette souveraine qui a fourni à la France une ouverture politique de transformer les mécanismes et des institutions au niveau européen.

Introduction

French support for European (EC/EU)-level macroeconomic policy coordination has been driven by remarkably consistent preferences since the 1950s. With the exception of the de Gaulle decade (1958–1968), French governments have sought European-level mechanisms for balance of payments support. French proposals came in the form of a European Reserve Fund (ERF) (conceived by the Belgian American economist Robert Triffin); the creation of a balance of payments support mechanism in 1969; monetary support for weak currencies in the Werner Plan, the Snake mechanism and the Exchange Rate Mechanism (ERM) of the European Monetary System (EMS); and—since the outbreak of the euro area sovereign debt crisis—financial support for the purchase of sovereign debt on primary and secondary markets, with the aim of breaking the sovereign debt/bank doom loop that risks undermining the solvency of both sovereigns and banks in the euro area periphery and, through contagion, undermine international confidence in French sovereign debt. French support for the creation of the Macroeconomic Imbalance Procedure, agreed in 2010, should also be seen in terms of French preferences on mutual adjustment. In the negotiations on Banking Union (from 2012), the French Socialist-led government supported the use of European-level funds to prop up ailing banks and the Europeanisation (and thus mutualisation) of national deposit guarantee schemes and resolution funds. Fears of moral hazard—of great importance in German government and ordoliberal thinking and discourse on European-level support mechanisms—rarely appeared in French government discourse.

This article sets out to explain these stable French preferences on European-level macroeconomic policy coordination over time through a combination of an interest-based analysis referring to structural and competitive weaknesses of the French economy and an ideational explanatory analysis focused upon French Keynesian thinking on symmetrical adjustment of both deficit and surplus countries. We argue that this consistency is remarkable and puzzling notably because other important features of French political economy, its model of capitalism and its macroeconomic policies, experienced profound changes from the 1980s (Boyer 1996; Levy 1999; Schmidt 2002; Vail 2010). French preferences align largely with the concept of 'embedded liberalism'. This article also interprets a number of developments in EU-level economic governance in response to the banking and sovereign debt crises that provided a policy window for France to move European-level mechanisms and institutions towards long-held French preferences.

The ideas behind French preferences: 'embedded liberalism', 'embedded currency area theory' and Keynesianism

The concept of 'embedded liberalism' has likely never been explicitly adopted by French policy-makers. Nonetheless, it describes effectively French preferences on European integration generally, and European-level macroeconomic policy coordination specifically, and provides an analytical framework through which to understand these preferences. 'Embedded liberalism' has also inspired the concept of 'embedded currency area' (McNamara 2015), which is relevant to our examination of French preferences on macroeconomic policy coordination in the context of the euro area. John Ruggie's concept of 'embedded liberalism' (1982) describes the post-war Bretton Woods monetary and trade regime of gradual liberalisation and largely fixed exchange rates, designed to prevent participating countries from engaging in competitive devaluations. The founding provisions of the monetary system included a temporary escape clause for participating countries facing a situation of 'fundamental disequilibrium'—a condition in which a country faced a significant balance of payments deficit (not specifically defined) and downward pressure on its currency—allowing a national government to adjust its currency (devaluation) and introduce temporary capital controls. Balance of payments support (both precautionary and in the context of crisis) was provided notably through the International Monetary Fund. Ruggie describes embedded liberalism in the Bretton Woods regime as one of 'intergovernmental collaboration to facilitate balance-of-payments equilibrium, in an international environment of multilateralism and a domestic context of full employment' (1982, 394–395). This was an economic order that encouraged liberalisation (opening of countries to international trade) but also allowed for national interventionism to achieve domestic macroeconomic stabilisation which was assigned legitimate social purpose. The concept of 'embedded liberalism' is based on an older concept first developed by Karl Polanyi (1944) of 'embedded versus disembedded economic orders'.

It is important for the purposes of our article to point out that the bulk of the burden of readjustment of the 'embedded liberalism' of the Bretton Woods system rested with the deficit countries. This reflected US government preferences at the time of the 1944 negotiations establishing the regime. However, many government participants in and observers of the Bretton Woods negotiations (notably John Maynard Keynes, the British government representative) sought the introduction of provisions ensuring the obligation of mutual readjustment for both creditor and debtor countries (Skidelsky 2000). Keynes furthermore wanted a clearer definition of the point at which mutual readjustment should have to take place: he suggested a surplus or deficit of 3%. Keynes sought to highlight the pernicious influence of the gold standard as it had operated in the interwar years. He argued that trying to achieve internal balance by deflating in response to a loss of reserves was not only harmful for the country itself but also had the external effect of depressing economic activity in other countries, leading to the race to the bottom seen in the Great Depression (Skidelsky 2000; Vines 2003). Keynes wanted surplus countries to be required to curtail their imbalances in more or less the same way that deficit countries were obliged to curtail their imbalances under the gold standard. In his Clearing Union proposal developed during the Second World War, Keynes sought to impose taxes and sanctions on chronic surplus countries (Eichengreen and Temin 2010). Burdens upon creditor countries were, however, avoided owing to US government opposition. However, of particular relevance for future discussions on monetary cooperation and integration in Europe, Keynes insisted that an exchange rate system created obligations on both sides of the exchange rate relationship to contribute to its stability and smooth operation. The actions of surplus as well as deficit countries had systemic implications. Their actions mattered for the stability and smooth operation of the international system; they could not realistically assign all responsibility for adjustment to their deficit counterparts.

Keynesian thinking had strong currency in France after the Second World War, especially among the modernising technocratic elites, and it was firmly anchored in the French *grandes écoles*, where most of the political, administrative and economic elites were trained.[1] French policy-makers could easily find arguments provided by Keynes when asking for a more symmetrical approach to macroeconomic imbalances in the global and European currency systems. Of course, the general importance of Keynesian thinking for French economic policy-making changed over time. Starting with the 1970s stagflation and the Barre adjustment plan in 1976, and later with the Socialist-led government's policy U-turn of 1983 towards a policy of 'competitive disinflation', Keynesian ideas lost currency in France as in other wealthy industrialised countries (Hall 1986; Uterwedde 1988). In the aftermath of the international financial and euro area crisis, when Keynesian economic ideas gained renewed attention, both the centre-right president Nicolas Sarkozy and the centre-left president François Hollande made only selective use of Keynesian ideas and instruments to reflate the economy (Clift 2012, 2014). However, little change can be observed over time with regard to French preferences for sharing the burden of adjustment between current account deficit and surplus countries in order to reduce macroeconomic imbalances and the French pursuit of European support mechanisms. In this respect, Keynesian thinking never lost its appeal. Indeed, Prime Minister Raymond Barre, who eschewed Keynesianism in his domestic economic policy, was very much in favour of the creation of a more symmetrical exchange rate mechanism and an ERF in order to help make domestic adjustment easier to manage economically and politically (Howarth 2016).

The economic interests behind French preferences: tackling French deficits and challenging unilateral adjustment

French support for sharing the burden of adjustment between deficit and surplus countries was not only anchored in economic ideas but also in economic interests. With only occasional exceptions, from the last third of the nineteenth century through to the start of Stage Three of Economic and Monetary Union (EMU) in 1999, France faced overall trade deficits. France faced significant current account problems in the 1950s, 1970s and 1980s and again from the mid 2000s (Figure 1). France enjoyed an improving current account position in the 1990s, with a record surplus at the start of Stage Three of EMU in 1999, but this owed largely to the

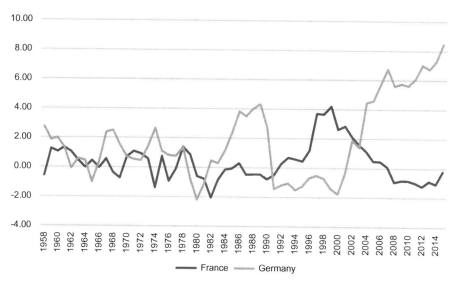

Figure 1. France and Germany, current account, 1958–2015 (in % of GDP). Sources: 1958–1979: Banque de France and Deutsche Bundesbank; 1980–2015: International Monetary Fund, World Economic Outlook Database, October 2016.

success of the French policy of competitive disinflation, with record high real-interest rates, and the negative then slow French GDP growth.

Prior to EMU, current account deficits combined with periodic inflationary pressures to make the French economy vulnerable to currency crises and speculative attacks, especially as international capital movements gained in importance from the 1970s. Frequent devaluations of the franc or revaluations of stronger European currencies such as the Deutschmark and the Dutch florin against the franc served only as temporarily measures to cope with imbalances. Despite a gradual weakening of the franc versus the Deutschmark from the 1950s (Figure 2), France never enjoyed an annual trade surplus with Germany. From limited amounts in the 1950s and 1960s, the French trade deficit with Germany increased significantly in the 1970s and 1980s. Even in the 1990s, despite the improving French current account position, the trade deficit with Germany only stabilised prior to ballooning from the late 1990s and reaching a peak of 39 billion euros in 2012 (Figure 3). From 1999, declining French wage competitiveness in relation to Germany (see Figure 4) contributed to both the deteriorating French trade deficit with Germany and French current account deficits.

Macroeconomic interests directed French preferences in favour of support mechanisms for weaker currencies in the Bretton Woods system, in the European Snake and the ERM of the EMS. More recently, these interests drove French preferences in favour of support mechanisms for sovereign debt. Economic interests also encouraged French governments to push for more symmetry in the operation of currency systems in which the franc took part, with more obligations for surplus countries in addition to support mechanisms. These consistent preferences in regard to European macroeconomic policy coordination were driven by the search for greater room to manoeuvre in the pursuit of domestic macroeconomic policies aimed at reducing unemployment.

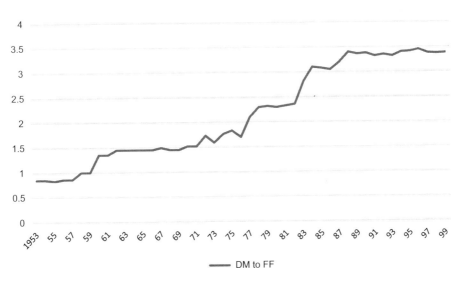

Figure 2. German Deutschmark to French franc, exchange rate, 1953–1999. Source: FXTOP (http://fxtop.com/).

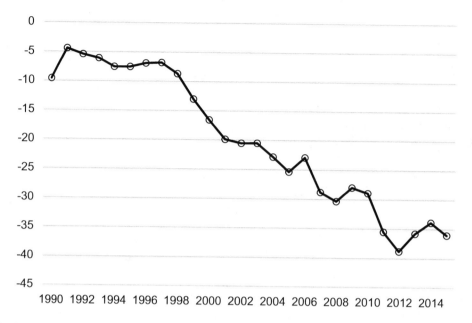

Figure 3. French bilateral trade balance with Germany, 1990–2015 (in bn €, not adjusted). Source: Federal Statistical Office of Germany.

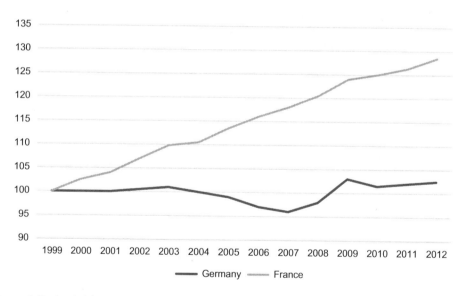

Figure 4. Real unit labour costs, France and Germany, 1999–2012 (1999 = 100). Source: OECD (stats.oecd.org).

The decline of 'embedded liberalism'

It is widely acknowledged that the Bretton Woods system worked thanks to the United States, which assumed the central burdens of the system, opening its markets to the goods of a number of Western European and East Asian countries, and providing liquidity. The United States also enjoyed the exorbitant privilege of being able to print unlimited quantities of dollars without fear of devaluation in relation to gold. The Triffin dilemma eventually brought down the Bretton Woods system, whereby the central currency of the system—the dollar—which was needed to provide liquidity in the system was also subject to inflationary pressure and thus devaluation in relation to other currencies in the system. A dollar overhang was created as other countries exporting to the USA ended up holding large quantities of devaluing dollars. The French, under de Gaulle in particular, had issues with the dominant position of the United States and its exorbitant privilege in the Bretton Woods system. De Gaulle sought to replace dollars with gold.

The decline and then collapse of the Bretton Woods system has been widely discussed in the literature. For some, this decline and collapse reflects the relative decline of the American hegemon, and its decreased willingness to assume the main burdens in the system (Keohane 1984). This collapse of the 'embedded liberalism' rooted in the Bretton Woods system was followed by the rise of the 'Washington Consensus' with structural adjustment programmes inspired by neo-classical economics imposed by the IMF on governments facing large current account deficits and in need of emergency finance.

Features of 'embedded liberalism' can also be identified in a range of EC (and then EU) policies, reflecting French (and other) government caution with regard to trade liberalisation (Krotz and Schild 2013; Lynch 1997). Thus trade liberalisation was very gradual, starting with manufactured items first and extending to labour, some services and capital only later. Regional policy was inserted into the Treaty of Rome officially condoning government assistance to disadvantaged regions of the Community—assistance that might otherwise contradict European Competition Policy. European-level structural funds were created to help these regions. The Common Agricultural Policy (CAP) created a significant carve-out to European rules on market integration and government assistance. Yet there were clear limits to the 'embedded liberalism' of the European Community. For French governments, reinforced EC/EU macroeconomic policy cooperation and coordination was meant to supplement the Bretton Woods system and then replace it (as much as possible).

Some scholars have also pointed to the EMU project—designed in large part by European central bank governors and reflecting German government preferences—in terms of creating a euro area that must be seen as '"disembedded" from the broader social institutions needed for adjustment when a currency is removed from national control' (McNamara 2015, 22). According to McNamara's (2015, 26) 'embedded currency area' approach, four elements constitute the 'minimum, rather than an optimal foundation for monetary union': a 'legitimated generator of market confidence and liquidity'; 'mechanisms for fiscal redistribution and economic adjustment'; 'regulation of financial risk and uncertainty'; and 'political solidarity'. This vision—implying a Fiscal Union that includes fiscal distribution and sovereign debt pooling—aligns largely with the economic ideas held by French decision-makers (Krotz and Schild 2013).

Neglected European macroeconomic policy coordination in the Treaty of Rome

The European Community (and then Union) provided minimal balance of payments support. This absence initially reflected the existence of the Bretton Woods system. Furthermore, the current account position of the EC member state with the largest economy (Germany) was the reverse of the situation within the Bretton Woods system. The US government supported Bretton Woods by providing liquidity (dollar overhang) and by running a large current account deficit. Germany was in a very different position, with its almost constant trade surplus in relation to other EC/EU member states from the 1950s and, from the early 2000s, massive overall trade and current account surpluses and large surpluses in relation to all but a few euro area member states. German governments consistently rejected a greater role for fiscal policy either at the national level—through reflation—or European level—through transfer mechanisms beyond the limited funds provided through European policies. Therefore, during the EC's first decade, there was a near absence of macroeconomic policy coordination and the complete absence of mechanisms to assist member states needing to adjust, not to mention mutual adjustment mechanisms.

This state of affairs existed despite explicit French preferences expressed in the discussions and negotiations leading to the Treaty of Rome (Kaplan and Schleiminger 1989; Lynch 1997). In the context of a difficult French balance of payments situation in the final years of the Fourth Republic, the French government explicitly endorsed Robert Triffin's 1956 proposal for a European current account fund (Triffin 1957). Triffin, inspired by Keynes, called for the creation of a fund to which all EC member states would be required to contribute. Triffin called for mutual commitment to the system which would in effect have posed obligatory burdens upon surplus countries to support those with deficits (Bussière and Maes 2016; Maes and Buyst 2004). The Mollet government at the time—a coalition of socialists, Christian democrats and centrists—supported Triffin's proposal and shared the economist's concerns on the need to prolong the European Payments Union (EPU) (Lynch 1997; Triffin 1954). The Mollet government saw an ERF as a vital mechanism to achieve the consolidation and permanence of the EPU because it ensured that, in the event of an economic crisis in the United States and a return to US protectionism, an ERF would protect Europe from the asymmetric effects of a dollar shortage and resulting intra-European tensions. The French (like Triffin) queried the usefulness of international mechanisms and looked to a regional 'amortisseur des chocs' where 'strong economic interdependence and a proximity of interests would facilitate political economy compromises' (Triffin 1954, 360). Few in the French government shared Triffin's federalist vision of economic and monetary coordination. However, the French government did support Triffin's ERF proposal, which would have worked to prolong the EPU through a regional mechanism responsible for transfers among participating European countries.

Leading members of the Mollet government also shared many of Triffin's concerns with regard to the limited scope of balance of payments support mechanisms created in the context of the European Monetary Agreement (EMA) signed in 1955, which was to come into effect after the dissolution of the EPU (Bussière and Maes, 2016). According to the EMA, a European fund provided EMU members access to non-automatic credit facilities in case of temporary balance of payments difficulties, and a Mutual System of Settlements created to encourage the settlement of international payments through the foreign exchange markets, rather than through central banks as had often previously been the case. The Mollet government found that these EMA arrangements were not ambitious enough (Kaplan and Schleiminger 1989). The French advocated the transformation of EPU into what Triffin called a European Clearing House that would also pool a certain percentage—Triffin had recommended 20%—of the total gold and foreign exchange reserves held by European central banks. The European Clearing House would use these reserves to intervene in international exchange markets, approximating the open market operations performed by national central banks in their domestic markets. Therefore, this clearing mechanism could have been a powerful collective European instrument to fight against speculative currency movements (Kaplan and Schleiminger 1989). For Triffin—a view not shared by the French government or by a significant number of French government officials—the European Clearing House would have been a predecessor to a European Monetary Authority (Triffin 1957).

Upon its creation, the European Commission was preoccupied by the French balance of payments crisis in 1958, the weak franc and the potential for French economic difficulties to undermine European economic integration (Bussière and Maes, 2016). Moreover, with the dissolution of the EPU imminent, the return to convertibility of European currencies and the creation of the CAP, many in the Commission feared the impact of currency instability. Robert Marjolin, the Keynesian French head of DG II (Economic and Monetary Affairs), sought greater balance of payments and currency support at the European level (see Seidel 2016).[2] As both a former junior minister for economic reconstruction in France and the first head of the Organisation for European Economic Co-operation from 1948, Marjolin was very knowledgeable on both the difficult situation of the French economy and the importance of the EPU. Marjolin was convinced that the clearing and credit facilities of the EPU contributed to the liberalisation of trade among European countries, strengthening them both economically and thus (in a period of intensifying Cold War) politically (Seidel 2016). In May 1958, Marjolin presented his first Memorandum to the Commission, focusing on the need for coordination of national economic policies (Seidel 2016; see Annexes 4 to 8 in Ferrant and Sloover 2010). Marjolin started from the observation that the Treaty of the European Economic Community (EEC) provided for the basic principles of the coordination of economic policies, but that the details of this coordination needed to be supplemented and made more explicit. To put into practice economic policy coordination, Marjolin proposed to undertake regular critical surveys of member state economies. Moreover, he proposed that the Community institutions could formulate policy recommendations. In Marjolin's view, the weight of these recommendations would be stronger if the Community had at its disposal resources to facilitate financial solidarity, although he did not initially clarify the structure of this facility (Bussière and Maes, 2016).

Marjolin envisaged balance of payments support as an inherent part of the move to 'European Monetary Union' (Seidel 2016). In the first of three stages, member states would benefit from financial solidarity if they followed a code of good conduct. In the second phase, member state governments would be obliged to follow the recommendations by the Council, taken by qualified majority voting. All member states would be required to make available a certain percentage of their currency and gold reserves to provide credits to those member states with balance of payments difficulties. This could eventually, in a worst-case scenario, be extended to a 'total' solidarity in which member states would use larger parts of their reserves to support a member state in need. This 'total' solidarity reflected Keynesian thinking on mutual obligations for both deficit and surplus countries. By the end of Stage Two (duration left unspecified), Marjolin considered member states would be in a 'state of monetary union'. His Stage Three was not spelled out.

In his second memorandum of 7 November 1958, written with the assistance of Triffin, who had become his advisor in DG II, Marjolin was more explicit and detailed about the structure of the ERF. However, he was also more cautious on supranationalism than in his May memoranda, and Commission policy recommendations were no longer to be binding for member state governments. Financial solidarity was still on the agenda but the situation in

France had improved and was less threatening so Marjolin placed less emphasis on this issue. Each member state would pay into the ERF a minimum of 10% of national foreign reserves. The fund would have numerous functions and its reserves could be used for all settlements between the central banks of the member states as well as with EPU members and the rest of the world. The memorandum also proposed to use a unit of account for managing the fund, as suggested by Triffin.

The Commission discussed Marjolin's proposals at its meeting of 20 November 1958. The Commissioners agreed in principle with the need for balance of payments support, but postponed the discussion of the specific details to a future meeting (Bussière and Maes, 2016). The proposals were subsequently pushed aside. National central banks were sceptical about the unit of account and the design of the ERF, and the German government did not approve of the potential support obligations imposed on surplus countries (Bussière 2007, 394). Most importantly, the French political context had changed with Prime Minister and then President de Gaulle pushing through a devaluation of the franc, austerity reforms and a broader liberalisation of the French economy through the Pinay–Rueff Plan. EPU member countries subsequently restored the external convertibility of their currencies in the framework of the Bretton Woods system. The need for an ERF became less pressing, and was downplayed or absent in Marjolin's subsequent proposals on European macroeconomic policy coordination. While Triffin served as an *éminence grise* at the European Commission throughout the 1960s, his influence was limited (Bussière and Maes 2016; Seidel 2016).

With the Bretton Woods system nearing collapse, in 1969 the EC member states agreed to a regulation 'Establishing a facility providing medium-term financial assistance for Member States' balances of payments' (1969/88). The adoption of this regulation also reflected the influence of the leading French economist Raymond Barre, the new Commissioner responsible for economic and financial affairs, who was aligned with neither Marjolin nor Triffin on the need for macroeconomic policy coordination and mutual readjustment involving obligations for both deficit and surplus countries (Howarth 2016). Barre nonetheless recognised that balance of payments support mechanisms were crucial for some member states (notably France and Italy) to accept more trade liberalisation, and notably the liberalisation of short-term capital movements. In response to French concerns, a below-market interest rate was to be attached to loans provided through the mechanism and no conditionality was to be applied. However, the financial assistance facility agreed by the member states only had a limited loan ceiling which in 1988 was set at 16 billion European Currency Units (ECUs) and Community loans were to be financed exclusively with funds raised on the capital markets and not by other member states. Prior to the 2000s, no member state made use of the mechanism. In 2002, the member states adopted a new regulation (332/2002) applying balance of payments support only to non-euro area member states, reflecting the view that balance of payments problems would cease to be relevant for euro area member states (see below). The 2002 regulation also lowered the loan ceiling from 16 billion to 12 billion euros. Subsequently, Hungary and Latvia received balance of payments of support from the facility.

Macroeconomic imbalances in the first EMU discussions from 1969

Until the final collapse of Bretton Woods in 1973, French calls for a closer European-level coordination of monetary policies served the primary purpose of stabilising and reforming the 'embedded liberal' order of the International Monetary System which provided room for domestic economic policy autonomy, economic interventionism and the pursuit of domestic stability goals (Howarth 2001). In the dominant French view, steps towards European monetary cooperation had to deal with two asymmetries. First, they should reduce or set an end to the 'exorbitant privilege' of the dollar as the world's leading reserve currency (see Bordo, Simar, and White 1993; Howarth 2001). Second—of greater relevance to our discussion—French governments saw European monetary cooperation as a mechanism to serve the purpose of symmetrically sharing the burden of adjustment between EC member states with weak and strong currencies in case of balance of payments and currency crises induced by huge dollar fluctuations. The end of the Bretton Woods system then led to a shift in French attention away from reform of the International Monetary System towards renewed interest in European monetary integration.

An 'embedded liberal' European monetary order suiting French interests and reflecting its economic ideas would have comprised the following four core elements: fixed, but adjustable exchange rates between EC currencies providing for monetary stability; a coordination of national monetary policies in order to give France a say over German policy and shielding it from the negative impact of unilateral German decisions; mutual support mechanisms to handle balance of payments and currency crises, to provide for a symmetric distribution of the burdens of adjustment and to avoid deflationary domestic adjustment in France; and a common European exchange rate policy towards the US dollar, reducing the power asymmetries in the International Monetary System. For French governments, mutual support mechanisms were a key prerequisite for the creation and maintenance of any regime of fixed but adjustable exchange rates. French governments advocated mutual financial support and symmetrical obligations to intervene in the markets to support exchange rate parities. At The Hague European summit in December 1969, President Georges Pompidou advocated he creation of a European Monetary Union. His main immediate goal was to set up what the French labelled a European Reserve Fund that pooled member state central bank foreign reserves as 'a means of achieving concerted action in relation to the US dollar' (Dyson and Featherstone 1999, 106) and was to be used for short-term support measures as part of a first stage of monetary cooperation. The then German Chancellor, Willy Brandt, supported the idea of pooling reserves in an ERF, but only after an initial period of economic convergence. This German 'economist' approach prevailed over the French 'monetarist' approach: The Hague Summit's conclusions envisaged the creation of an ERF only after a period of significant economic policy convergence.

In January 1970, the ECOFIN Council reached a formal agreement on the system of short-term monetary support. Through this facility, the participating central banks provided each other unconditional, 'quasi-automatic' credits for up to three months in situations of balance of payments deficits, renewable for an additional three months (Ungerer 1997, 90). In April 1973, the member states agreed to establish the European Monetary Cooperation Fund to coordinate Community monetary policies and manage existing short-term and very short-term financing mechanisms created to support the exchange rate parities of weaker Community currencies.

Regarding the maintenance of fixed exchange rates inside the EC, the turbulent fields of international monetary relations after the demise of Bretton Woods only allowed for the abortive experience of the Snake mechanism, which began operation in April 1972. This system of exchange rate parities allowed only half the fluctuation margins permitted in the International Monetary System, thus the so-called Snake in the Tunnel. From March 1973, with German government refusal to stem the appreciation of the Deutschmark in relation to the dollar, the Snake floated free of its tunnel. Asymmetry characterised the Snake, the Deutschmark serving as its anchor currency. The burden of economic adjustment lay fully with the deficit/weak currency countries, and all participants—save Germany—had to sacrifice their monetary autonomy in order to maintain their currencies within the mechanism. France proved neither willing nor able to do so and the franc was forced to withdraw from the Snake twice, in January 1974 and in March 1976. France sought to shield Community member states from international monetary instability by defining narrow margins of fluctuation between their currencies. To achieve this goal, both reliable European-level monetary support mechanisms and the convergence of economic policies and inflation rates were necessary. France advocated the former but refused the latter because concerted economic policy convergence would have necessarily limited the autonomy of French macroeconomic policy-making.

In September 1974, the French Finance Minister Jean-Pierre Fourcade came up with the 'most important French proposal on European monetary reform prior to the Balladur Memorandum of 1988' (Dyson and Featherstone 1999, 113). The Fourcade plan's main goal was to address the issue of asymmetry and to 'spread the burden of intervention more fairly' (Dyson 1994, 88). The plan called for a concerted float of the Community currencies, joint interventions in the exchange markets including intra-marginal interventions to underpin an exchange rate system and the extension of Community credit facilities as well as the issuing of Community loans (Howarth 2001, 28). Although this proposal was quickly blocked owing to German and Dutch objections, it served as a blueprint for later French ideas and proposals for the design of the EMS. The French government thus persisted with the Keynesian objective of imposing readjustments on both deficit and surplus countries with the aim of achieving a more durable exchange rate regime, while allowing for continued margin of manoeuvre in national macroeconomic policy.

The European Monetary System: bold plans, modest outcomes

In the negotiations leading to the creation of the EMS in 1979, the French sought to eliminate the asymmetry of the Snake through several mechanisms. First, the French wanted the new system to be built around a currency basket, with the ECU serving as pivot and a means of settlement between EEC monetary authorities. Second, the French wanted unlimited intra-marginal interventions by strong currency central banks once a weak currency crossed a 'divergence threshold' (Howarth 2001, 40–41). Third, the French sought the creation of a European Monetary Fund, pooling the foreign reserves of participating member states, to replace the existing European Monetary Cooperation Fund (Ludlow 1982, 165).[3]

At the insistence of the Bundesbank and the Federal Ministry of Finance, the EMS design that was finally adopted turned out to be much less symmetrical than envisaged by French authorities (Kaltenthaler 1998, 53–54). A bilateral parity grid system along the lines of the Snake was finally adopted and the Deutschmark once again performed the function of an anchor currency—as in the Snake (James 2012). Central banks were only required to intervene in situations when their own currency reached the upper or lower ceiling of the fluctuation band. Central banks of surplus countries were not legally bound to intra-marginal interventions which were necessary to nip currency crises in the bud. Indeed, in the EMS, the German Bundesbank's interventions to defend currency parities turned out to be limited (Giavazzi and Giovannini 1988). Furthermore, the European Monetary Fund was never created. As in the Snake, France was forced to follow the monetary policy choices of Germany or risk the forced departure of the franc from the ERM. From its economic policy U-turn in 1983, the French Socialist government adopted its strategy of the strong franc (*franc fort*) and competitive disinflation, becoming ever more determined to avoid the devaluation of the franc. Ultimately though, the asymmetric functioning of the EMS and the dominant role of the Bundesbank led to renewed French interest in EMU from 1988.

The French made several attempts to address the asymmetry of the EMS and improve macroeconomic policy coordination, notably the Basel–Nyborg Accords of 1987 and the creation of the Franco-German Economic and Financial Council in 1988. The limited success or failure of these efforts increased French interest in a bold move towards EMU. So too did the liberalisation of short-term capital movements. The Commission made the removal of capital controls a core element of its 1992 Single Market Programme and the German government was strongly in favour of capital liberalisation. However, removing capital controls meant dis-embedding markets. Under the condition of free capital movements, the only option to combine fixed exchange rates and some French influence on monetary policy appeared to be the irrevocable fixing of exchange rates and a centralisation of monetary policy, delegated to a supranational central bank—Mundell's (1961) 'Unholy Trinity'. In the early 1970s, French governments had advocated the use of capital controls to stabilise exchange rates and preserve national monetary and macroeconomic policy-making autonomy (Howarth 2001, 32). In the late 1980s, French governments made a different choice.

The move towards EMU and macroeconomic coordination as fiscal consolidation

The January 1988 memorandum of the French Minister of Finance, Édouard Balladur, was unusually explicit in expressing key French concerns regarding EMS asymmetry: 'It must be avoided that one single country [i.e. Germany] has, de facto, the responsibility to fix the objectives of the economic and monetary policy of the entire system' (Balladur 1988, 18 and 20). The memorandum advocated a two-track approach: short-term EMS reforms combined with reflections on further steps in monetary integration to create 'a single currency', 'a common central institution' and 'federal banks in the individual countries'. Balladur saw these steps as being the logical consequence of the liberalisation of capital markets, making the status quo untenable (Balladur 1988, 18 and 20; see also James 2012, 228).

In the Delors Committee, tasked by the Hanover European Council in June 1988 to report on monetary union, the Governor of the Bank of France, Jacques de Larosière, raised the issue of balance of payment problems. In his comment annexed to the report, he called for a European Reserve Fund with significant powers to intervene in exchange markets to be established during the transition to monetary union (de Larosière, interview, June 1995). This was not adopted. The dominant view in the Committee was that balance of payments problems would cease to exist with the economic convergence required during the second stage of the EMU project (Klaus Regling, interview, April 2014; Nils Thygessen, interview, March 2015). In their draft treaty on monetary union, the French continued to push the idea of a European fund intervening in international exchange markets in the transition to the single currency (Palayret 2009, 207–211). Prime Minister Pierre Bérégovoy also insisted on embedding the single currency in a political framework: the creation of a European economic government as a political counterweight to the European Central Bank and as an institution able to coordinate an appropriate policy mix between monetary and fiscal policies with the ECB (Howarth 2001, 2007, 1067; Palayret 2009, 207). This French preference for *ex ante* policy coordination that is prior to central bank monetary policy decisions ran counter to the German approach. In the German view, governments' fiscal policies and social partners' wage-setting had to take the ECB's stability-oriented single monetary policy as 'given', which would 'lead to *implicitly* coordinated policy outcomes *ex post*' (Issing 2002, 346; emphasis in the original).[4]

The problem of European macroeconomic imbalances and coordination, and mutual support mechanisms, lost the attention of policy-makers following the start of EMU's Stage Three in 1999. Currency crises were effectively ended inside the common currency area and current account imbalances in the euro area only built up over time and were disguised by the Target II Payments system. However, with the euro area crisis—a case of 'rapid unwinding of economic imbalances' (Baldwin and Giavazzi 2015, 19)—the issues of both macroeconomic imbalances and mutual support mechanisms for members states made a forceful comeback.

The banking and sovereign debt crises: a window of opportunity for France on macroeconomic policy coordination?

From the start of the euro area's sovereign debt crisis in 2009, familiar topics returned to the European agenda. French preferences on the stabilisation of the euro area and reforms of its governance framework displayed a number of similarities with its preferences during the 1950s (prior to de Gaulle), 1970s and 1980s when the focus was the stabilisation of international and European exchange rates. Just as the French wanted support mechanisms to undermine disruptive speculative attacks against the franc and other weak European currencies back in the 1970s and 1980s, they now advocated the creation of instruments to discourage speculation on euro area periphery sovereign debt and to reduce bond yields, with the fear of contagion to France. As in the pre-EMU past, French governments tried to find ways to avoid an economic policy convergence towards German 'austerity' policies, thus leaving room for French national policy autonomy and fiscal policy discretion. French governments thus, yet again, sought mechanisms to bring about a symmetrical adjustment of both surplus and deficit member states, instead of the asymmetrical adjustment of deficit countries, the deflationary macroeconomic effects of which French governments feared. France also tried to avoid, now as in the 1970s and 1980s, the growing power asymmetry inside Europe in favour of Germany, the macroeconomic policy choices of which it was unable to influence, putting France in a situation of a 'policy taker' suffering from the negative economic consequences of Germany's unilateral decisions. Nonetheless, the French also proved more successful than in the past in achieving reforms to economic governance which in effect softened the asymmetry of economic relations in the euro area and created more macroeconomic policy margin of manoeuvre for deficit countries.

The focusing event of the twin banking and sovereign debt crises opened a window of opportunity for French governments. It enabled them to advocate successfully a number of steps towards the construction of an 'embedded currency area' as defined by McNamara (2015). Euro area member states agreed new policy instruments and institutions to coordinate fiscal support for illiquid or insolvent member states and to prevent banking crises from fuelling sovereign debt crises, thus breaking the sovereign debt/bank doom loop.

The successive French presidents Nicolas Sarkozy and François Hollande actively advocated strong euro area support mechanisms, the preventive set-up of financial facilities (rescue funds) and their purchase of sovereign debt to ward off speculative pressures. They followed what the German economist Hans-Werner Sinn called the 'money-in-the-display-window theory' (Sinn 2014, 5), signalling to investors and speculators that the euro area governments were able to mobilise huge amounts of money and guarantees to counter speculative attacks.

Throughout the crisis, French governments, of the right and then left, displayed a clear preference for vigorous and decisive crisis management action, including rescue schemes for Greece and, later, Ireland and Portugal, to prevent contagion to Spain, Italy and ultimately to France. In May 2010, in addition to a bilateral loan facility for Greece, the EU member states agreed upon the establishment of the European Financial Stability Facility (EFSF) and the European Financial Stabilisation Mechanism (EFSM) backed by the Union's budget. Together with the IMF, they were able to mobilise up to €750 billion to purchase sovereign debt on primary markets (IMF: €250 bn, EFSF: €440bn, EFSM: €60bn). The French government (and others) argued that this amount was far from sufficient, as the crisis deepened in 2011. In calling for ever more fiscal and monetary 'firepower', the French government found itself aligned with the Commission, the IMF and the ECB, the Troika institutions. As part of their Deauville compromise of October 2010, the French and German governments jointly promoted the establishment of a permanent lending facility, the European Stability Mechanism (ESM), which was inaugurated in October 2012.[5] President Sarkozy also supported assigning to the EFSF a banking licence and hence unlimited access to ECB funds (Le Monde 2011), an idea shared by his successor, François Hollande, who called for a banking licence for the ESM, the permanent successor to the EFSF (Spiegel online international 2012). Moreover, President Hollande was a fervent advocate of a European Banking Union to sever the link between banking and sovereign debt crises (Howarth and Quaglia 2013). This involved, notably, the creation of the Single Resolution Fund, which supranationalised financial support for the resolution of banks (Howarth and Quaglia 2016). However, Germany was able to set limits to these rescue funds and operations; on the EFSF and ESM see Krotz and Maher (2016); on the Banking Union see Howarth and Quaglia (2016).

Finally, French governments actively promoted and then supported all the nonconventional monetary policies adopted by the ECB to tackle the banking and sovereign debt crises, thus compensating in part for the inadequacy of the support mechanisms agreed by the member states. Indeed, the clearest changes to the economic constitution of the euro area away from German preferences involved the effective violation of the 'no-bail-out' logic of the Maastricht Treaty—most clearly symbolised by the ECB President Mario Draghi's promise in July 2012 to do 'whatever it takes to preserve the euro'—and the de facto violation of Treaty provisions prohibiting the monetisation of public debt, through the range of nonconventional monetary policies adopted.

There is a strong parallel between French preferences since the outbreak of the sovereign debt crisis and the French 'monetarist' approach during the first half of the 1970s. At that time, France pursued the goal of increasing monetary stability without sacrificing domestic macroeconomic policy autonomy to German 'economist' demands for convergence. During the twin sovereign debt and banking crises, France pursued the goal of improved stability of banks and sovereigns without economic policy convergence towards the macroeconomic policy preferences of surplus and creditor states (notably Germany). Hence the repeated French government calls for more symmetrical obligations for both deficit and surplus countries and, specifically, reflation by surplus member states in the euro area and for stronger elements of mutual support, embedding the euro area in a new set of political institutions and policies.

One politically significant, albeit ultimately limited, success of French efforts to achieve greater symmetry in macroeconomic policy coordination was the adoption in 2011 of the Macroeconomic Imbalance Procedure (MIP), part of the so-called 'Six Pack' legislation (EU Regulation No 1176/2011). Through the MIP, current account imbalances, *both* huge deficits and surpluses, trigger an in-depth review by the Commission and could ultimately lead to sanctions. However, the German government succeeded in watering down initial Commission proposals regarding the level at which a surplus triggered the Commission's review. The Germans successfully insisted on setting the surplus threshold indicator at 6% of GDP (averaged over three years)—well in excess of the 3% recommended by Keynes to trigger mutual adjustment—while the deficit threshold was set at 4%.

In 2016, the institutional framework and macroeconomic policies of the euro area were still a far cry from the 'embedded currency area' approach and from French preferences. The full mutualisation of risks, seen by French policy-makers as crucial, was not (yet) in place. There remained strong constraints on the use of ESM funds to recapitalise ailing sovereigns and banks, and the Single Resolution Mechanism for banks was to have limited funds. The German government remained firmly hostile to the establishment of a European Deposit Insurance Scheme and Commission plans to eventually replace national schemes (Howarth and Quaglia 2016). During his presidential election campaign and immediately after entering office in 2012, François Hollande called for the mutualisation of public debt through the introduction of Eurobonds. However, such proposals, keenly supported by euro periphery member states, were stillborn in the face of German hostility. Other ideas aired by the French government to promote a fiscal union and a common macroeconomic stabilisation function[6] that might take the form of a specifically euro area 'fiscal capacity' (Gabriel and Macron 2015) or a European-level unemployment insurance scheme,[7] found support in principle from the Commission and the *Five Presidents' Report on the Future of EMU* (European Commission 2015), but not from the German government. Despite the new MIP, Germany accumulated ever higher current account surpluses (8% of GDP in 2015), and rather than using its room for countercyclical fiscal policy, it achieved a surplus of €12 billion in its 2015 federal budget (Handelsblatt 2016).

The German reluctance to make more symmetric the burdens of adjustment (Bulmer and Paterson 2013) cannot only be explained by a material interest. This reluctance was also deeply rooted in ideas of ordoliberal inspiration. The German government emphasised the close association between private risk-taking and private liability, advocated the role of market pressure to reduce the moral hazard both of states and financial market actors thanks to market pressures[8] and sought institutional reforms to impose strict and enforceable rules upon member state fiscal policies. In French discourse on EU/euro area economic governance, moral hazard arguments, so central to German thinking and preference formation, were almost inaudible. In effect, French governments wanted Germany to undertake the heavy lifting in providing support for member states with high public or current account deficits. However, French governments also repeatedly refused or sought to undermine the fiscal and macroeconomic policy terms that the Germans attached to the provision of their support. For French governments, short-term crisis management considerations and the reduction of contagion risks through both fiscal support mechanisms and the ECB's nonconventional monetary policies prevailed over considerations of the destabilising potential of these fire-fighting measures.

Conclusion

French preferences in favour of European-level balance of payments and currency/sovereign debt support proved remarkably stable from the negotiations leading to the Treaty of Rome to the sovereign debt crisis, with the exception of the decade of the de Gaulle presidency. In addition to the flexibility and support offered through the Bretton Woods form of 'embedded liberalism', French governments sought to impose support obligations upon surplus countries and even readjustment. French governments sought to avoid the huge currency fluctuations that would result from trade and capital liberalisation, while also preserving a degree of autonomy in domestic macroeconomic policy. In line with these preferences, French governments of both the right and left responded to the euro area crisis that erupted in late 2009 by advocating the creation of new support instruments in order to avoid transnational contagion, the deflation of austerity policies and, ultimately, euro area disintegration. We explain the stability of these French preferences on European macroeconomic policy coordination in terms of the lasting influence of Keynesian economic thinking in French policy-making circles and the long-term economic interests of a country with almost constant trade and current account deficits, and—through to the early 1990s—difficult-to-master inflationary pressures and repeated experience with currency crises and devaluation.

French governments failed to bring about a more symmetric International Monetary System. They only achieved limited success in creating more symmetric forms of European monetary and macroeconomic policy coordination. The euro area crisis provided a window of opportunity and French governments succeeded to some extent in moving European-level mechanisms and institutions towards long-held French preferences with the creation of rescue funds (notably the EFSF and the ESM), core elements of Banking Union and the MIP put into place. The French were vocal supporters of ECB nonconventional monetary policy. The French also resisted greater German influence in shaping the design of the euro area, blocking German government efforts to create a revised EMU architecture (Maastricht 2.0) which involved both limiting common liabilities and shifting control to the European level where some common European liabilities for risk were accepted.[9] French governments failed, however, to build a strong framework of 'embedded liberalism' in euro area macroeconomic policy coordination, failing to gain German support on crucial elements of an 'embedded currency area' approach, including the mutualisation of euro area member state liabilities.

Establishing institutions of monetary cooperation without sufficient economic convergence and without the political will to create generous support mechanisms at the European level proved an unstable solution in the Snake mechanism, the EMS framework and, it turned out, EMU. Following the outbreak of the euro area sovereign debt crisis, France pushed for another uneasy combination of ever more joint European liabilities without the corresponding shift of control to the European level, as national budgetary autonomy remained jealously guarded. The erosion of the main pillars of the original EMU project, French unwillingness to accept the supranational implications of the German proposed Maastricht 2.0, combined with only some watered-down elements of an 'embedded currency area', left the euro area in a dangerous in-between-territory. 'Any half-baked implementation of this option, however, with substantial national control remaining vis-à-vis joint liability, would be the worst of all worlds' (Feld et al. 2016, 3).

Notes

1. Rosanvallon (1987) retraces the history of Keynesian ideas in France. For a comparative view on the impact of Keynesian ideas on economic policies, see Hall (1989).
2. Robert Marjolin was 'the first French economist who can really be called a Keynesian' and wrote a doctoral thesis on Keynes' theory in 1940 (Rosanvallon 1987, 30, our translation).
3. Cf. Conclusions of the Presidency of the European Council on 6 and 7 July 1978, Bremen, July 18, 1978 (final version).
4. Issing was serving as the ECB's chief economist when he published this article.
5. For an overview of the Franco-German bilateralism during this crisis, see Schild (2011, 2013).
6. The French and Italian Ministers of Finance, Michel Sapin and Pier Carlo Padoan, called for a European-level fiscal instrument for anti-cyclical macroeconomic stabilisation (see their joint statement at the occasion of the 33th Franco-Italian summit in Venice on 8 March 2016: http://www.economie.gouv.fr/files/files/PDF/33e-sommet-italie-france2016.pdf, accessed March 10, 2016. In September 2015, the French Economics Minister Emmanuel Macron called for a permanent transfer mechanism that provided funding in exchange for real member state commitments to reform (*Financial Times*, September 24, 2015). Macron proposed that member states contribute part of their VAT tax receipts and unemployment insurance to fund these transfers.
7. This idea was aired by the Direction du Trésor of the French Ministry of Finance. For an overview of the debate, see Assemblée nationale (2016).
8. The 'no-bail-out' clause was an example in kind; as was the orderly sovereign default procedure advocated by Germany.
9. For an in-depth elaboration of this argument, see the approach developed by the German Council of Economic Experts (2012, 37–43).

Disclosure statement

No potential conflict of interest was reported by the authors.

References

Assemblée nationale. 2016. *Rapport d'information déposé par la commission des affaires européennes sur l'assurance chômage européenne*, présenté par M. Jean-Patrick Gille, Député. Paris. (19 janvier 2016 AN, No 3420).

Baldwin, Richard, and Francesco Giavazzi. 2015. "Introduction." In *The Eurozone Crisis. A Consensus View of the Causes and a Few Possible Remedies*, edited by Baldwin/Gavazzi, 18–60. London: CEPR Press.

Balladur, Edouard. 1988. "Mémorandum sur la construction monétaire européenne." *Ecu, revue trimestrielle* 3: 17–20.

Bordo, Michael, Dominique Simar, and Eugène White. 1993. "La France et le système monétaire de Bretton Woods." *Revue d'économie financière, No* 26: 249–286.

Boyer, Robert. 1996. "Le capitalisme étatique à la française à la croisée des chemins." In *Les capitalismes en Europe*, edited by Colin Crouch and Wolfgang Streeck, 97–137. Paris: Éd. La Découverte.

Bulmer, Simon, and William Paterson. 2013. "Germany as the EU's Reluctant Hegemon? of Economic Strength and Political Constraints." *Journal of European Public Policy* 20 (10): 1387–1405.

Bussière, Eric. 2007. "Moves Towards an Economic and Monetary Policy." In *The European Commission, 1958–72: History and Memories*, 391–410. Luxembourg: Office for Official Publications.

Bussière, Eric, and Ivo Maes. 2016. "Robert Triffin: A Hedgehog for European Monetary Integration." In *The Architects of the Euro*, edited by K. Dysonand I. Maes, 30–50. Oxford: OUP.

Clift, Ben. 2012. "Les politiques économiques sous Sarkozy. Un patriotisme économique néolibéral?" In *Les politiques publiques sous Sarkozy*, edited by Jacques Maillard, 299–320. Paris: Presses de Sciences Po (Domaine gouvernances; 3).

Clift, Ben. 2014. *The Hollande Presidency, the Eurozone Crisis and the Politics of Fiscal Rectitude*. Sheffield: Sheffield Political Economy Research Institute. (SPERI Paper, 10)

Dyson, Kenneth. 1994. *Elusive Union. The Process of Economic and Monteary Union in Europe*. London and New York: Longman.

Dyson, Kenneth, and Kevin Featherstone. 1999. *The Road to Maastricht: Negotiating Economic and Monetary Union*. Oxford: Oxford University Press.

Eichengreen, Barry, and Peter Temin. 2010. "Fetters of Gold and Paper." NBER Working Paper, No. 16202, July. Accessed February 1, 2016. http://www.nber.org/papers/w16202

European Commission. 2015. "Completing Europe's Economic and Montary Union. Report by Jean-Claude Juncker in close collaboration with Donald Tusk, Jeroen Dijsselbloem, Mario Draghi and Martin Schulz." Brussels. https://ec.europa.eu/priorities/sites/beta-political/files/5-presidents-report_en.pdf.

Feld, Lars. P., Christian Schmidt, Isabelle Schnabel, Volker Wieland. 2016. "Maastricht 2.0: Safeguarding the Future of the Eurozone, in: voxeu.org (CEPR's Policy Portal)." Accessed February 12, 2016 URL: http://www.voxeu.org/article/maastricht-20-safeguarding-future-eurozone

Ferrant, Catherine, and Jean Sloover. 2010. *Robert Triffin: Conseiller des Princes*. Témoignage et Documents, Bruxelles: PIE-Peter Lang.

Gabriel, Sigmar, and Emmanuel Macron. 2015. "Europe Cannot Wait Any Longer: France and Germany Must Drive Ahead." *The Guardian.com*, 3 June 2015. Accessed. March 15, 2016 URL: http://www.theguardian.com/commentisfree/2015/jun/03/europe-france-germany-eu-eurozone-future-integrate

German Council of Economic Experts. 2012. "Annual Economic Report, Wiesbaden." November 2012 URL: http://www.sachverstaendigenrat-wirtschaft.de/fileadmin/dateiablage/Sonstiges/chaptertwo2012.pdf

Giavazzi Francesco, and Alberto Giovannini. 1988. "Modèles du SME: l'Europe n'est-elle qu'une zone deutsche mark?" *Revue économique* 39 (3): 641–666.

Hall, Peter A. 1986. *Governing the Economy*. The Politics of State Intervention in Britain and France. Cambridge: Polity Press.

Hall, Peter A. 1989. *The Political Power of Economic Ideas. Keynesianism Across Nations*. Princeton, N.J.: Princeton University Press.

Handelsblatt. 2016. *Etat-Plus von 12,1 Milliarden für 2015*, 13 January 2016.

Howarth, David J. 2001. *The French Road to European Monetary Union*. Basingstoke, Hampshire: Palgrave.

Howarth, David J. 2007. "Making and Breaking the Rules: French Policy on EU 'gouvernement économique'." *Journal of European Public Policy* 14 (7): 1061–1078.

Howarth, David J. 2016. "Raymond Barre: Modernising France through European Monetary Integration." In *The Architects of the Euro*, edited by K. Dyson and I. Maes, 75–92. Oxford: OUP.

Howarth, David, and Lucia Quaglia. 2013. "Banking Union as Holy Grail: Rebuilding the Single Market in Financial Services, Stabilizing Europe's Banks and "Completing" Economic and Monetary Union." *Journal of Common Market Studies* 51 (s1): 103–123.

Howarth, David, and Lucia Quaglia. 2016. *The Political Economy of European Banking Union*. Oxford: Oxford University Press.

Issing, Otmar. 2002. "On Macroeconomic Policy Co-ordination in EMU." *Journal of Common Market Studies* 40 (2): 345–358.

James, Harold. 2012. *Making the European Montary Union. The Role of the Committee of Central Bank Governors and the Origins of the European Central Bank*. Cambridge, Massachusetts and London: The Belknap Press of Harvard University Press.

Kaltenthaler, Karl. 1998. *Germany and the Politics of Europe's Money*. Durham: Duke University Press.

Kaplan, Jacob J., and Gunther Schleiminger. 1989. *The European Payments Union: Financial Diplomacy in the 1950s*. Oxford: Clarendon Press, Oxford.

Keohane, Robert O. 1984. *After Hegemony. Cooperation and Discord in the World Political Economy*. Princeton, N.J.: Princeton University Press.

Krotz, Ulrich, and Richard Maher. 2016. "Europe's Crises and the EU's 'Big Three.'" *West European Politics* 39 (5): 1053–1072.

Krotz, Ulrich, and Joachim Schild. 2013. *Shaping Europe France, Germany, and Embedded Bilateralism from the Elysée Treaty to Twenty-First Century Politics*. Oxford: OUP.

Le Monde. 2011. *Du clash de Francfort au sommet de Bruxelles, la folle semaine de l'Europe*, 28 October 2011.

Levy, Jonah D. 1999. *Tocqueville's Revenge. State, Society, and Economy in Contemporary France*. Cambridge, Mass.: Harvard Univ. Press.

Ludlow, Peter. 1982. *The Making of the European Monetary System: A Case Study of the Politics of the European Community*. London: Butterworth.

Lynch, Francis. 1997. *France and the International Economy*. London: Routledge.

Maes, I., and E. Buyst. 2004. "Triffin, the European Commission and the Project of a European Reserve Fund." In *Réseaux Economiques et Construction Européenne*, edited by M. Dumoulin, 431–444. Bern: P.I.E. - Peter Lang.

McNamara, Kathleen R. 2015. The Forgotten Problem of Embeddedness. In *The Future of the Euro*, edited by Matthias Matthijs, and Mark Blyth, 21–43. Oxford and New York: Oxford University Press.

Mundell, Robert. 1961. "Theory of Optimum Currency Areas." *American Economic Review* 51: 509–517.

Palayret, Jean-Marie. 2009. "La voie française vers l'Union économique et monétaire durant la négocation du traité de Maastricht (1988-1992)." In *L'Europe au cœur. Études pour Marie-Thérèse Bitsch*, edited by Martial Libera, and Birte Wassenberg, 197–221. Brussels: P.I.E. Peter Lang.

Polanyi, Karl. 1944. *The Great Transformation*. Boston, MA: Beacon Press.

Rosanvallon, Pierre. 1987. "Histoire des idées keynésiennes en France." *Revue française d'économie* 2 (4): 22–56.

Ruggie, Gerald. 1982. "International Regimes, Transactions, and Change: Embedded Liberalism in the Postwar Economic Order." *International Organization* 36 (2): 379–415.

Schild, Joachim. 2011. "Quel leadership franco-allemand en matière de gouvernance économique éuropéenne?" *Annuaire Français des Relations Internationales* 12: 493–510.

Schild, Joachim. 2013. "Leadership in Hard Times: Germany, France, and the Management of the Eurozone Crisis." *German Politics & Society* 31 (1): 24–47.

Schmidt, Vivien A. 2002. *The Futures of European Capitalism*. Oxford: OUP.

Seidel, Katja. 2016. "Robert Marjolin: Securing the Common Market through Economic and Monetary Union." In *The Architects of the Euro*, edited by K. Dysonand I. Maes, 51–74. Oxford: OUP.

Sinn, Hans-Werner. 2014. *The Euro Trap. On Bursting Bubbles, Budgets, and Beliefs*. Oxford: Oxford University Press.

Skidelsky, Robert. 2000. *John Maynard Keynes, 1937–1946: Fighting for Britain*. London: Macmillan.

Spiegel online international. 2012. "Rescue Fund Controversy: France and Italy Seek Ultimate Firepower for ESM." 31 July 2012. Accessed March 14, 2016. URL: http://www.spiegel.de/international/europe/euro-zone-states-discuss-plan-to-give-esm-unlimited-funding-from-ecb-a-847415.html

Triffin, Robert. 1954. "Convertibilité ou intégration." *Economie appliquée, T VII* 1954 (4): 359–375.

Triffin, Robert. 1957. *Europe and the Money Muddle*. New Haven, CT: Yale University Press.

Ungerer, Horst. 1997. *A Concise History of European Monetary Integration: From EPU to EMU*. Westport, Conn.: Quorum Books.

Uterwedde, Henrik. 1988. *Die Wirtschaftspolitik der Linken in Frankreich. Programme und Praxis 1974 - 1986*. Frankfurt/Main: Campus.

Vail, Mark. 2010. *Recasting Welfare Capitalism*. Economic Adjustment in Contemporary France and Germany. Philadelphia PA: Temple University Press.

Vines, David. 2003 June. "John Maynard Keynes, 1937-1946: The Creation of International Macroeconomics." [Review of Skidelsky, 2000] *Economic Journal* 113: F3380–F361.

Drawing Algeria into Europe: shifting French policy and the Treaty of Rome (1951–1964)

Megan Brown

ABSTRACT

In France and Europe today, claims arise defining so-called Muslim and European 'worlds' and labelling them irreconcilable. These claims ignore the intertwined history of France and North Africa. When the six founding members of the European Economic Community (EEC) signed the Treaty of Rome, French administrators still considered Algeria to be a constituent part of France, despite the ongoing war. The Algerian question was central to negotiations for the Treaty of Rome and during them, French officials attempted to inscribe Algeria within the founding documents of the European project through a policy of 'Eurafrique'. Their partners, eager for France's signature on the Treaty, accepted a vision of integrated Europe with borders crossing the Mediterranean. This decision raised thorny issues in the months and years to come, first in debates of how or even if the Treaty could be implemented overseas, then when independent Algeria attempted to define its relationship with the EEC. These episodes of negotiation and interaction reveal the centrality of the question of empire to the foundations of integrated Europe.

RÉSUMÉ

En France et en Europe il est courant d'entendre aujourd'hui que les soi-disant « mondes » musulmans et européens ne sont pas conciliables. Ces déclarations sous-estiment l'histoire entremêlée de la France et de l'Afrique du Nord. Quand les six membres fondateurs de la Communauté économique européenne (CEE) ont signé le Traité de Rome, les administrateurs français considéraient l'Algérie une partie intégrante de la France, et ce malgré la guerre en cours. La question algérienne fut centrale dans les négociations pour le Traité de Rome. C'est au cours de celles-ci que les officiels français promeuvent leur politique de l'Eurafrique, et tentent donc d'inscrire l'Algérie dans les documents fondateurs du projet européen. Ses partenaires, dans leur souhait de voir la France signer le Traité, ont accepté une vision de l'Europe intégrée avec des frontières traversant la Méditerranée. Cette décision a soulevé des questions délicates dans les mois et les années à venir, d'abord concernant comment ou même si les conventions du Traité pourraient être mises en œuvre outre-mer, puis une fois que l'Algérie indépendante a cherché à préciser son lien avec la CEE. Ces épisodes de négociation et d'interaction révèlent la centralité de la question de l'empire dans les fondations de l'Europe intégrée.

When Belgium, France, Italy, Luxembourg, the Netherlands, and West Germany (the Six) signed the Treaties of Rome in 1957, establishing the European Economic Community (EEC) and Euratom, an Italian poster celebrated this moment of unity with an image of six pert women with pale skin, bedecked in skirts fashioned out of their respective national flags, a map of Europe looming behind them (Image 1).[1] With their small waists and wide smiles, these ladies reveal both how integration proponents represented the EEC to the wider European public and how many historians continue uncritically to understand it today: white, Christian, firmly on the continent.[2] But masked by the women's kitten heels and a ribbon labelling each respective state is a region crucial to the history of European integration: North Africa and, more specifically, Algeria.

Image 1. Poster celebrating the Treaty of Rome. Source: Europa Grafica—DG X—Représentation de la Commission européenne au Luxembourg.

Most histories of the EEC overlook that four of the six original members still possessed formal colonies or administered UN trust territories at the time of the institution's creation.[3] Indeed, the EEC's history is not only concurrent to, but also intertwined with, evolutions in empire and the post-war emergence of successful decolonising efforts.[4] French administrators in Brussels pushed their European partners to accept the inclusion of French overseas holdings within the EEC, seeing the supranational stage as a key site for asserting the legitimacy of their imperial project. Wielded as a political tool, French administrators attempted to use the policy of 'Eurafrique', or Eurafrica, to draw European support for colonial endeavours while maintaining control over existing African trade networks.[5]

This is perhaps best illustrated in French attempts to inscribe the crown jewel of its empire, Algeria, into emerging Europe. Unlike the rest of the French Union, Algeria's status marked it as a juridical part of France.[6] French officials' insistence on Algeria's exceptional position, which to them proved it belonged in the EEC, reveals that France's domestic crisis—the Algerian War—directly impacted France's formulation of European integration policy. An analysis of French administrators' elastic understandings of Europe's limits in the 1950s and early 1960s unsettles traditional discussions of European integration that too often unquestioningly follow the image of Europe presented in propaganda such as the poster of the six lithe women. It challenges histories of European integration that take the current shape of 'Europe' as a given, arguing that indeed, not only did empire influence decisions at the time of the EEC's formation, but the precise borders of Europe even after decolonisation hardly appeared evident to the administrators in these new institutions.[7] While historians have begun to examine the long ties between Europe and sub-Saharan Africa, this study asserts the significance of Algeria to Eurafrican policy.[8]

By the time French administrators entered negotiations for the EEC, maintaining strong ties with overseas holdings had become a top priority. Indeed, at the 'periphery' of hexagonal France (and at the heart of its empire), understandings of citizenship rights and the legal status of the land remained contested and confused.[9] Debates among French administrators and jurists and between French and European officials disputing the definition of Algeria's legal status within France reveal the messiness of seemingly firm juridical distinctions across France's empire.[10] In the 1950s, the lack of consensus even among French legal scholars about the juridical difference between Algeria and the metropolitan departments allowed French administrators to make claims in Brussels on behalf of French economic interests while evading decisions on how to extend metropolitan rights overseas. This would echo after the decolonisations of the 1950s and 1960s, as the French state continued to find military and economic uses for overseas French departments and pushed for the continuity of trade ties with sub-Saharan Africa that it no longer enjoyed with Algeria (Trépied 2013).

The first part of this article asks how and why France attempted to convince its European partners that the French Union must be included in an integrated Europe. Although the colonies of the other European states were discussed in some of these negotiations, French officials remained the most vocal proponents of Eurafrica. As the second part of this study will discuss, even after colonial states began to claim independence in the years following the Treaty of Rome's signing, it was unclear to French officials exactly how to square Eurafrican policy with the impending independence of most imperial holdings. The third section will demonstrate that after 1962, Algerian leaders began to assert their own version of Eurafrica. The archival record reveals the willingness of European officials to allocate a European status to Algeria and even to consider extending such a status to independent Algeria after

1962. While the Italian poster may have depicted the public image of the EEC as a bounded community, internally, the question of Europe's frontiers was far from settled. In France, French officials' lingering aspirations for continuing Franco-Algerian ties suggest a longer life for imperial relations, extending into the early independence period and even beyond.

L'Algérie française and the case for integrating the French Union (1951–1957)

The term 'Eurafrica' first came to prominence in interwar publications and political tracts. Proponents portrayed Africa as the key to European prosperity, promising easy access to abundant raw materials and warning that European states must share in Africa's bounty in order to promote peace. Such ideals celebrated imperialism and some flirted with fascist principles that aligned with a German vision of *Mittelafrika* (Smith 1986, 133–140). Although rarely acknowledged in laudatory histories of European integration, early advocates of a united Europe, such as the Austrian Richard Coudenhove-Kalergi, included a shared African empire within their programme. Like the post-war proponents of Eurafrica, interwar advocates, including the political scientist Eugène Guernier, pinpointed it as the only way for Europe to remain relevant in light of the increasingly powerful United States and USSR.[11] Others, notably the writer Louis Bertrand, emphasised the roots of a 'Latin Africa' in North Africa (Dridi and Mezzolani Andreose). This bolstered claims that the Mediterranean was an 'internal lake' in a Eurafrican continent, which fit with the fascist ideology of a Mediterranean civilisation promoted by Mussolini, among others (Antonsich 2009). Some Vichy collaborators embraced Eurafrica as part of a new world order (Nordblad 2014, 726). After World War II, the newly installed Fourth Republic renamed France's empire the French Union in a shift that in part marked distaste for overt expressions of European superiority. Despite its origins, the term 'Eurafrica' remained elemental to European integration discussions, even as the rhetoric surrounding the term came to emphasise partnership between Europe and Africa, rather than domination.

To understand the insertion of Algeria in the EEC, we must first note an earlier iteration of post-war European integration, the European Coal and Steel Community (ECSC, Treaty of Paris, 1951), from which the colonies were excluded. The omission of overseas holdings cannot be viewed solely as the result of the absence of coal and steel in Africa. Much of the continental territory of the Six also lacked such natural resources. The evolution of an integrated Europe from the ECSC to the EEC reveals the swift change in policy in the early to mid 1950s as French administrators came to understand that the challenge to empire in Algeria and elsewhere was real and imminent. Eurafrica would become a tool for maintaining the imperial status quo, but in the early 1950s, French officials did not yet see it as necessary to keep order.

Yet the exclusion from the ECSC would not go unnoticed. How could Algeria's special French departmental status, dating from 1848, be understood in light of these exclusions? During an April 1952 meeting of the Council of the Republic, Abdennour Tamzali, an Algerian senator from the Rassemblement des gauches républicaines, decried the absence of a guarantee that Algeria would be considered part of the ECSC. While French officials emphasised 'the juridical and economic credo of the intangibility and indivisibility of our economic union with the metropole', the Treaty of Paris made the three departments of Algeria the 'subject of an arbitrary discrimination'. Tamzali warned: 'Our constituents will not easily understand why their territory is placed outside of the [Coal and Steel] pool, like a poor, second-rate relation!'[12] Tamzali need only have waited four years for a sharp change in French policy, although by then the Algerian War's escalation would have become a greater concern to his constituents than a supranational accord.

By the mid 1950s, French officials began to assert the place of empire within European institutions, a policy shift that would intensify following the discovery of oil in the Algerian Sahara in 1956. As colonial crises became more pronounced, these administrators saw a way to funnel aid money into their colonies and to persuade their European partners to agree in writing to the French character of their overseas holdings. Thus, at the same moment Algerian nationalists began to gain international support, notably at the United Nations, the French were shaping supranational accords to name and include explicitly the totality of the French Union and, most importantly, Algeria.[13] Eurafrican policy, in effect, became one more tool for attempting to maintain control of increasingly uncontrollable circumstances. The French insisted that Algeria be included in Europe, and France's European partners, eager for France's signature on the Treaty of Rome, agreed.[14] Thus, into the early post-war era, the international community continued to uphold empire as an acceptable part of the political landscape. During French debates on European integration, officials fretted that Eurafrican policy would demand extended voting rights to all Africans, as some suggested during discussions of the European Defence Community.[15] However, as French Union *conseiller* Georges Monnet warned, exclusion of the French Union from the EEC would lead to a 'centre of gravity … on the Rhine'.[16] United in their demands in Brussels, French officials' internal discussions suggest a more ambivalent attitude toward Eurafrican goals.

Yet looking toward Brussels, French officials sought not just the signatures of the Six marking Algeria as part of France, but also partners with whom to share the burden of development aid. Such funds would allow for the construction of hospitals and the expansion of industrial facilities in North and sub-Saharan Africa.[17] When the empire began to erode, and only then, did French officials see the value of demanding territorial association within a unified Europe. In order to maintain France's sovereignty in Africa, French officials understood they would have to cede some sovereignty to Europe.

French pressure for the inclusion of the empire in the EEC came from administrators whose ministerial or departmental position demanded an interest in overseas affairs. Notable among them was Gaston Defferre, Minister of Overseas France (Ollivier 2005). In 1956, one month before his eponymous *loi-cadre* introduced major administrative changes to the French Union's governance and during the preparatory work for the Conference of Venice, he informed the Ministry of Foreign Affairs that the overseas territories must be integrated into the economic community now being crafted by the Six. Under the Fourth Republic, France's overseas territories were administered separately from Algeria and the overseas departments, yet it is clear from ministerial communications that borders were sometimes ignored during discussions about aid distribution and the applicability of trade and labour regulations. Defferre argued that the exclusion of Africa from the European Common Market jeopardised the *zone franc* and risked grave outcomes, including 'political secession'.[18] Two years after the loss of Indochina (1954) and the start of the Algerian War, and mere weeks after the declarations of Morocco's and Tunisia's independence (1956), this was no empty threat. Defferre insisted that France enter into the European Common Market only on the condition that the overseas territories closely integrate, as well. Minister of Foreign Affairs Christian Pineau took Defferre's suggestions seriously, telling his European counterparts that France 'could not participate in a common market from which the overseas territories would be excluded'.[19]

Despite potential conflicts between the goals of the Ministry of Overseas France, concerned with maintaining order in the French Union, and the Ministry of Foreign Affairs, eager to build new European institutions, imperial exigencies took precedence, helping to explain Pineau's embrace of Eurafrican policy. Many of the documents pertaining to such a policy were penned by unnamed officials within these ministries, often in conversation with the Ministry of Finances and Economic Affairs (and the Plan, under some administrations) and economic offices in other ministries, as well. As these administrators observed overseas upheaval, they maintained pressure for Eurafrican policy, even, as we will see, after 1960.[20]

French administrators negotiating the Treaty of Rome did not shy away from noting the strong commercial ties between the metropole and the French Union, which they cast as a lucrative incentive to entice the other members of the Six.[21] Africa was a fertile ground for acquiring raw materials and access to new consumers, which France could offer to the Six. Pineau promised France's partners that they would benefit from Eurafrica, as it would invite preferential trade agreements and protect Europe from the risk of an unstable (or even Communist) Africa.[22] This 'progressive and non-discriminatory opening' of the overseas markets would allow for a marked increase in European exports to Africa.[23] In return, the French would expect the Six to contribute to overseas development aid, an answer to critics such as the journalist Raymond Cartier.[24]

Forging this new Eurafrican partnership between metropolitan France, the French Union, and integrated Europe gained urgency for French officials by the mid 1950s, as calls for decolonisation grew louder across Africa. The Treaty of Rome would offer French officials the chance not just to reaffirm trade partnerships in Algeria and secure assistance in development and industrial projects in the warring territory, but it also would allow France to garner five signatures affirming Algeria's status as a part of France at the exact moment that the Algerian War intensified and expanded.[25] This was no territory or far-off colonial land, according to the France's Ministry of Foreign Affairs, this was 'the most underdeveloped' region of the European community. For those European states most interested in 'the construction of a Eurafrica ...', Algeria must necessarily comprise the most important African element'.[26] Such statements served two purposes. First, labelling Algeria an undeveloped region of Europe normalised it, as member states, notably Italy, also confronted extreme poverty and unemployment in some regions.[27] Second, depicting Algeria as the key to Africa added Cold War urgency to maintaining French Algeria, reinforcing the geographic and political imaginary of a Eurafrican bloc as a third force in an increasingly bipolar world.[28]

The Six agreed to stipulations that would explicitly name the French Union, along with other colonial holdings. Article 227 delineated where the Treaty of Rome would be applicable. Section 1 named the Six, while Section 2 declared that 'general and particular provisions', including some agricultural regulations, the liberalisation of services and the movement of goods, would apply 'to Algeria and the French overseas departments' once 'this Treaty enters into force'. Section 3 guaranteed 'special arrangements for association' that would apply to overseas countries and territories. This would include French, Belgian, Italian and Dutch holdings. A fourth section addressed the Saar.[29]

This wording guaranteed that the Treaty of Rome would apply unevenly to Algeria. The application of regulations related to work, agriculture and the movement of capital was delayed in the northern departments and its timeline for implementation even less clear in the newly demarcated departments of the Sahara and Oasis.[30] A notable sticking point was the European stipulation for the free movement of labour. Among the Six, Italy was particularly concerned by the possibility of the unchecked entry into Europe of Algerians and other French Union subject-citizens.[31] This risked competition for the labour force of unskilled Italians, who could benefit from free circulation clauses.[32] Italian reticence concerned administrators in France's Ministry of Foreign Affairs, but the threat of Italian anger was not enough to dissuade the French from pursuing Eurafrican policy.

Although the Six agreed to the wording of Article 227, they did not plan for its immediate application. This was typical of Treaty of Rome implementation. Thus, it is hard to determine if European negotiators expected Article 227 to be fully implemented within a few years, or if they expected that independence movements would render moot at least some of the issues at hand. However, the signatures were significant, as they reveal the importance of France to the integration equation. The colonies could be a bargaining chip, used to appease France with pledges of financial assistance or to tempt the other members of the Six with promises of new markets for exports. Regardless of concerns within and outside of France, on 25 March 1957, representatives of the Six signed the Treaty of Rome, laying the groundwork for an extension of Europe beyond the continent.

Enforcing the long reach of the Treaty of Rome (1958–1962)

From the EEC's start until the independence of Algeria in 1962, a brief period that witnessed the independence of nearly all of the African continent, French concerns about extra-metropolitan territory continued to influence how administrators approached European decision-making. This section investigates the ambiguity surrounding Algeria's legal status within France and within Europe, demonstrating that France's push for overseas inclusion in the EEC opened new avenues for understanding the reach of integrated European institutions. The Treaty of Rome went into effect on 1 January 1958, but administrators in Brussels tasked with implementing it did little to clarify Algeria's position.[33] This suggests domestic disorder in France, as administrators attempted to catch up with rapidly evolving realities overseas and struggled to define how Algeria fitted into France's territorial organisation. For example, in late May 1958, Jacques Pélissier, the Director of Agriculture and Forests in Algeria, complained about terminology to the Minister of Agriculture in Paris. The working group examining the integration of French agricultural policy within the European Common Market had inadvertently stumbled because of the litany of juridical definitions. Pélissier lamented:

> In certain already completed reports, Algeria is considered an overseas territory, which causes confusion, as the overseas territories are associated with the Common Market, while Algeria is integrated into it (Article 227 of the Treaty of Rome). Algeria is even sometimes treated [*assimilée*] as a foreign country, meaning a third-party state, in [relation] to the Common Market.[34]

Pélissier argued that standardised terminology would 'definitively clarif[y] a situation that will be susceptible to creating unfortunate confusion'.[35] Even within French ministries, it proved increasingly difficult to establish how Algeria's legal relation to France—and, by extension, to Europe—might be understood.

Yet a lack of clarity also had uses, allowing French administrators to sidestep complicated and potentially polarising questions about the Treaty's applicability in Algeria, which concerned French and other European ministers. For the French, the stakes were multiple, and ambiguity was perhaps as useful as it was perplexing. Indeed, internally and in the halls of Brussels, French administrators avoided labelling Algeria as an Overseas Department (DOM) or an Overseas Territory (TOM), even as it was clear that they did not view it as a North African Alpes-Maritimes, either. Were they to acknowledge that Algeria was not the same as a metropolitan department, they would promote a reading of its juridical status that undermined the very reasoning for France's deep embroilment in Algeria's war for independence. Were they to insist fully on Algeria's French quality, domestic policies would need to shift to incorporate the millions of new citizens and the administrators risked alienating their European counterparts.

Eric de Carbonnel, Permanent Representative of France before the European Communities, offered a particularly novel solution. He suggested that '[t]he problem of the domain of the application of this regulation as it concerns Algeria can be treated by preterition'.[36] Preterition is the rhetorical device of omission, or of feigning omission. Carbonnel thus implied that by *not* addressing Algeria outright—or by insisting that there was no reason for Algeria to be discussed explicitly—the French could tacitly create a legal environment in which its partners would accept the by now less-than-tenable claim of the territory's Frenchness.

The 1958 emergence of the Fifth Republic, with a new constitution and a new government led by Charles de Gaulle, added little clarity to the place of Algeria within the EEC and did little to alter France's approach to Eurafrican policy. Nor did the new constitution calm debates surrounding French administrators' ambivalent understanding of Algeria's juridical status (Viard 1960). Indeed, even as French officials implemented the Constantine Plan and as French and Algerian negotiators were meeting in Evian in 1961, some administrators of the Fifth Republic continued to push the application of the Treaty of Rome to Algeria.[37]

These seemingly opposing endeavours—independence or integration—suggest that French officials and Algerian nationalists alike did not foresee that Algeria would lose nearly its entire 'European' population to *l'exode* in 1962 (Cohen 2003). This cautious approach to reshaping (or maintaining) ties extended to sub-Saharan Africa, as well. The accession to independence of nearly all of France's sub-Saharan territories in 1960 renewed debates in Brussels about the French Community's (as the Union was renamed under the Fifth Republic) relations with the EEC. Prior to independence, French administrators leveraged Eurafrican policy to remain instrumental in African economic and political affairs. After independence, it appeared the only way for France to maintain its status in Africa.

The continuity of Eurafrican pressure reveals that de Gaulle's evolution from seeking reform to releasing colonial holdings was more gradual and tentative than historians often contend. De Gaulle's Eurosceptic prime minister Michel Debré argued that the French must make clear in this moment of African independence that France was still the principal power interested in, and working with, these states. In a lengthy discussion with EEC Commission President and West German statesman Walter Hallstein in July 1960, Debré emphasised that France was the leader (*chef de file*) regarding questions about the African states:

> Regarding Africa, there must not be two capitals—Brussels must not compete with Paris. There should not be outbidding; there must not even be a feeling that Brussels may be a recourse against Paris.[38]

The meeting, which Debré deemed 'very cordial', mirrored the deepening ties between de Gaulle and Konrad Adenauer, evidenced well beyond Eurafrican policy.[39] In contrast, the Dutch came to view France's attachment to Algeria and to its former empire as a weak point through which it could attack France, whose blocking of United Kingdom entry into the EEC angered Dutch administrators.[40] Georges Gorse, Carbonnel's replacement as

France's Permanent Representative in Brussels, worried that a negative message from the Netherlands and the EEC as a whole would imbue a sense of ill-will toward Europe in newly independent African states.[41] Ultimately, Dutch obstructionism did little to diminish France's greater power of persuasion within the EEC.[42] Thus, it is clear that in the period of the Treaty's implementation, nearly concurrent with the emergence of the Fifth Republic and only two years before the majority of France's overseas holdings acceded to independence, French administrators continued to pursue Eurafrican goals.

A Eurafrica for independent Algeria? (1962–1964)

Algeria's independence became official on 3 July 1962, but France's empire continued to haunt the halls of Brussels. In this moment, Algerians ceased to be silent on the issue of Eurafrica, revealing yet another use of the term. Without ignoring very serious and credible contentions by some Africans, sympathetic Europeans, and historians alike suggesting that Eurafrican policy smacks of neo-colonialism, it could also be instrumentalised as a tool for leaders in independent Algeria to guarantee protections at the very moment the fledgling economy needed assurances of support and aid.[43] On 24 December 1962, Ahmed Ben Bella, who would become the first elected president of independent Algeria, wrote to the president of the EEC Council. Ben Bella announced that the Algerian government intended to 'inquire through negotiations … what will be the possible future relations between Algeria and the Community', pointing out that Article 227 named Algeria as a beneficiary of some EEC provisions. Ben Bella hoped that until the situation was clarified, Algeria could 'see the maintenance for Algeria of the benefit of the regulations that are currently established', affirming the usefulness of a Eurafrican policy for a former colony.[44] This demonstrates one method in which Algerian officials attempted to 'escape [Algeria's] geographical fate', as Jeffrey James Byrne describes. This existed in tandem with efforts by the young government to strengthen its diplomatic ties across the 'Third World'.[45]

The Six struggled to agree on what sort of response they should send Ben Bella. The Dutch wanted the Community to re-examine Algeria's right to be included in the Treaty's programmes. The French delegation emphasised that Algeria was unique among overseas states—a holdover from over a hundred years of claiming the soil as France, perhaps, or a recognition of the continued presence of French business interests there—and thus not to be considered a third-party state.[46] Commission representatives feared a delay in replying to Ben Bella, owing to 'the political and psychological importance of' the question.[47] By way of reply, the acting president of the EEC Council sent an acknowledgment of receipt to Algiers on 24 January.[48] Ben Bella would have learned little from such a reply, and the issue of Algeria's relationship to the EEC was not laid to rest.

In the earliest years of Algerian independence, French and Algerian officials alike investigated how the turn to autonomy would impact EEC policy, and how Eurafrica could, or could not, incorporate the new state. Having worked so hard to include Algeria within the EEC, French administrators were now faced with the unenviable task of uncoupling the French and Algerian economies. As these French administrators attempted to make sense of the new reality, there existed no plan for extracting Algeria from France and Europe, despite the Treaty of Rome's regulations not yet extending across the Mediterranean (they never would).[49] One month after Algeria's independence, Jean-Marc Boegner, Gorse's replacement in Brussels, deemed it 'wise' to continue treating Algeria under Article 227 of the Treaty, as 'it was juridically possible not to consider Algerian a third-party state'.[50] Even after Algeria's hard-won war of independence, French officials were not entirely convinced that Algeria had lost its unique status. Algeria was now definitively *not* France, but French administrators could not yet imagine labelling Algeria a third-party state, akin to Brazil, Japan, or the United States.

The question thus became, how would an independent state located on the continent of Africa be connected to the European Economic Community, and what legal and economic rights might this entail? The other members of the Six expected France to find the answer, in part by clarifying Franco-Algerian relations through bilateral discussions. The French, unsure of exactly how Algeria would fit into the EEC, deemed themselves to be in 'an important and delicate role'.[51] Yet, as one official within the Ministry of Foreign Affairs noted, it was 'obviously absurd' to suggest that Algeria might 'become the seventh member of the European Community'.[52]

The situation's complicated nature only became more confused as Algerian officials explored their country's place in the global economic and political landscape, and as France forged ahead with its own diplomatic agenda. Boegner expressed increased frustration with the Algerians, whose inaction and vagueness on the subject of EEC–Algerian relations were beginning to appear obstructionist. In their talks with the Commission, Algerian delegates inquired on diverse policies, notably the statute covering Algerian workers in the Community, which included professional training in both Algeria and Europe; guarantees of technical assistance; and the continuation of financial aid, extended to the completion of projects that had begun under the former development fund. But the potential benefits of a close relationship to the Six appeared to be increasingly off-limits to Algeria. A final decision was delayed as the Algerian delegation declared itself unable to respond to EEC questions until its relation with France was 'resolved', a position with which the Commission concurred.[53]

By mid 1964, it was clear to French officials that upholding a relationship with Algeria no longer held the benefits they once thought. The Secretary of State under the Prime Minister charged with Algerian affairs declared, 'the maintenance of this status will present more inconveniences than advantages'.[54] We are a long way from French assertions of the 1950s, or even from the more cautious declarations of 1962–1963. This rapid shift reveals changes in France's calculus of diplomacy. Now that Algeria was indisputably not l'Algérie française, a reality cemented by the exit of nearly the entire population of European origin by the summer of 1962, France turned increasingly to the same European neighbours that it risked alienating in pushing for Eurafrican policy in the first place. At the same time, independent Algeria's negotiating methods with Europe reflected their own domestic and international concerns. Algeria now saw opening before it a choice between the *grands ensembles* offered by closer ties to a so-called Muslim or pan-Arab world, whose leaders antagonised former colonial powers, and the economic and political benefits that Europe might offer (Shepard 2012).

Conclusion

In under a decade, leaders claiming to speak for Algeria had presented it in turns as undeniably French, worthy of approaching the EEC on its own and as a partner in a burgeoning North African ensemble. Such shifts are revealed in the planning for a variety of futures, none of which were realised.[55] Two years after the war's end, France appeared ready—even eager— to reduce significantly its connection to Algeria. French officials would by the mid 1960s attempt to wipe their hands clean of claims to Algeria's Frenchness, after over thirteen

Image 2. Cartoon suggesting expansion of the EEC. Source: Archives nationales d'outre-mer 81 F 1811: *Communauté européenne* (January 1960): 5.

decades of colonial rule and eight years of bitter conflict. However, even this brief interlude demonstrates that historians must push beyond 1962 when considering the timeline of Algerian independence. Yet, in turning towards a new European market, the French would see political and economic benefits much greater than what had existed in Algeria (Marseille 2005, 499–505; for Franco-Algerian relations, see Lefeuvre 2005; Saul 2016). Algerians would never enjoy the labour privileges in Bonn or Rome that their metropolitan counterparts could expect; the development aid promised under Article 227 would never fully materialise; and the unity of a Maghrebi or pan-Arabic community was marred by the cults of personality surrounding former heroes of decolonisation. At the same time, the path of development aid toward the former French Union (rather than, say, Brazil) attests to the long-term impact of Eurafrican policy on the economies of non-Western states (Grilli 1993).

The consternation Ben Bella stirred by sending his letter to Brussels speaks to the possibilities of the moment of decolonisation, when it was not entirely clear why Algeria could not be a part of Europe, although the crown jewel of the French empire shone less bright as the possibilities of close European partnerships expanded in the boom years of the *trentes glorieuses*. But if France was now willing to draw its own southern border along the Mediterranean's northern coast, the shape of Europe was anything but fixed. The historian Yves Montarsolo argues that the Six answered the question 'Europe until where?' by recognising Africa only as 'a "market", a "periphery"' (Montarsolo 2010, 261). However, as this article has demonstrated, French officials viewed the limits of Europe as malleable, and the case of Algeria reveals the other possible shapes that Europe could have taken. These episodes of administrative wheeling and dealing, at turns dominated by political one-upmanship or handwringing, challenge the image of the EEC as six slim, grinning women dancing across the continent. This image obscures the much messier reality of negotiations for the Treaty of Rome and the implementation of its regulations in extra-metropolitan territory after its signing.

Indeed, we can locate other visions of Europe that appear decidedly less 'Western', markedly less 'European'. In the earliest discussions in Brussels regarding which states would join the Community upon its first expansion, European delegates frequently suggested that the obvious *champs d'expansion* would be Greece and Turkey.[56] A 1960 illustration shows the Six as cartoonish men, hands held as they stretch eastward across the Continent (Image 2).[57] Reaching out to join them are Greece and Turkey, donning traditional-looking clothing (including a turban of sorts on the Turk—far from Ataturk's fedora). Idealistic and stylised as the illustration is, it nonetheless portrays a different vision of where Europe might stretch its arms and who could enjoy inclusion.[58] Meanwhile, through the Yaoundé (1963, 1969) and Lomé I (1975) conventions, former colonial holdings secured Eurafrican trade privileges similar to those France had sought during early stages of European integration.[59] Thus, we see the Algerian question as one piece of a larger puzzle as France and its European partners attempted to understand the shifting geopolitical landscape of the post-war, Cold War era. Such ambiguous notions of political borders and geographical limitations (or openings) upend claims made today of strict lines between 'civilisations' and should give us pause as we attempt to make sense of contemporary interrogations of Europe's borders and citizenship regimes. In economic, political and geographic terms, Europe was never only on the continent. Indeed, its greatest advocates could not even agree on where Europe ended and an African, Muslim or Arab world began.

Notes

1. Their joyous femininity contrasts to the masculine images of the wartime era. "Poster Publicising the Signing of the Rome Treaties (1957)." Centre virtuel de la connaissance sur l'Europe. Accessed March 4, 2016. http://www.cvce.eu/en/obj/poster_publicising_the_signing_of_the_rome_treaties_1957-en-77920b2d-2b40-4849-9f06-f7336bc355f5.html. For a concise history of post-war European integration, see Bossuat (1996) and Dedman (2010).
2. Todd Shepard (2006, 2–3) employs quotation marks around terms such as 'Muslim' and 'European'. While acknowledging the complex web of identities at play in French Algeria, I will not use quotation marks, but readers should be critical of religious or national labels.
3. Aside from France, the others were Belgium (Belgian Congo and trusteeship of Ruanda-Urundi), Italy (trusteeship of Somaliland) and the Netherlands (Suriname and Guyana). Recent studies that examine the impact of decolonisation on metropolitan states include Bailkin (2012), Bandeira Jerónimo and Costa Pinto (2015), and Mazower (2009).
4. Though the EEC is but one example of post-war experiments in supranational organisation, its evolution offers a unique vantage from which to understand the place of empire within European integration. For a survey of post-war European integration, including the formation of the EEC, see Urwin (2014).
5. This article focuses on Eurafrique as French administrators and continental Europeans (as well as citizens and subjects of their empires) employed the term. For the British Commonwealth and Eurafrica, see Kottos (2012) and Schenk (1996).
6. The organisation of extra-metropolitan territory under the Fourth Republic was: Overseas Departments (DOM): French Guiana, Guadeloupe, Martinique, La Réunion; Overseas Territories (TOM): Western French Africa (AOF—Senegal, Sudan, Guinea, Ivory Coast, Dahomey, Mauritania, Niger, Upper Volta), Equatorial French Africa (AEF—Moyen-Congo, Ubangi-Shari, Chad, Gabon), Saint-Pierre and Miquelon, the Comoros, Madagascar, French Somaliland, New Caledonia, French Establishments in Oceania (today's French Polynesia), the French Southern and Antarctic lands; and trustee territories: the Republic of Togo and Cameroon.
7. The term *l'hexagone*, now synonymous with France, was not employed until Algerian independence effectively shrunk the map of France. Shepard (2006, 269).
8. Key works on Eurafrica include: Adebajo and Whiteman (2012), Ageron (1975, 449–450), Bitsch and Bossuat (2005), Garavini (2012), Girault (1989), Hansen and Jonsson (2014), Montarsolo (2010), Rempe (2011), and Sicking (2005).

60 YEARS OF FRANCE AND EUROPE

9. Karis Muller interrogates these 'elastic' boundaries. See, for example, Muller (2001, 2000, 2012).
10. Jurists published extensively on questions of Algeria's legal status. See Gonidec (1958) and Lambert (1952). For a contemporary analysis, see Renucci (2011).
11. For an introduction to Guernier's work, Coudenhove-Kalergi's Pan-Europa, and the Eurafrican ideals of Italian nationalist Paolo Orsini di Camerota, see Hansen and Jonsson (2014, 25–40).
12. All translations are my own. Archives nationales d'outre-mer (CAOM) 81 F 2136: "'L'Algérie ne doit souffrir – ni économiquement, ni socialement – de sa non-intégration dans le pool charbon-acier' a souligné M. le sénateur Tamzali au Conseil de la République." *Dépêche quotidienne d'Algérie*, April 3, 1952.
13. Archives nationales (AN) 20000293/4 (dérogation): Le secrétaire d'État aux Affaires étrangères to Monsieur le secrétaire d'État à l'Algérie, Bureau économique et financier, "Application à l'Algérie des dispositions du Traité de Rome relatives à l'agriculture," October 19, 1957, recirculated July 8, 1959 by Morin to the ministère des Affaires économiques et financières. Johnson (2016, 157–183).
14. Algeria was only one point of contention. Boerger-De Smedt (2012, 348–351).
15. CAOM FR ANOM 61 COL 2314: Commission pour la Communauté politique européenne, "La Communauté Européenne de Défense et la Communauté Politique Européenne," likely May 1954.
16. CAOM FR ANOM 61 COL 2316: Analytic Summary, Assembly of the French Union, January 24, 1957.
17. Centre des Archives économiques et financières (CAEF) B 0062126 (formerly B 25343): Ministère de l'Économie et des Finances, Direction des Finances extérieures, Comptes-rendus de réunions des conseillers financiers français à Paris, October 9, 1959. Such promises comprised part of colonial France's last-ditch effort to maintain stability in the French Union. Frederick Cooper argues that mid-1950s 'developmentalism' backfired on French officials (1996, 406).
18. Centre des Archives diplomatiques du ministère des Affaires étrangères (MAEF) 20QO/792: Gaston Defferre, Ministre de la France d'Outre-Mer to Monsieur le Secrétaire d'État aux Affaires Étrangères, "Problèmes posés pour la France d'outre-mer par le projet de Marché Commun Européen," May 17, 1956, 8 pages. Because France already engaged in a common market with Africa, some administrators warned that committing to a second common market without the French Union would amount to 'bigamy'. Centre d'Histoire, Sciences Po PM 24, Fonds Pierre Moussa: Pierre Moussa, "L'Intégration des Territoires d'Outre-Mer et le Marché Commun." *Politique étrangère* 22 (1) (December 4, 1957): 39–50.
19. MAEF 20QO/719: "Note d'Information sur les Territoires d'Outre-Mer et le Marché Commun," n.d. but likely August 1956.
20. Some French officials in Brussels first worked in colonial administration. See Dimier (2011, 251–274).
21. Such ties were less beneficial than French officials asserted. See Marseille (2005).
22. French administrators were explicit in their Cold War tack: "If Europe became disinterested in [the territories], would it be possible to keep these countries in the Western orbit for much longer?" MAEF 20QO/719: "Note d'Information sur les Territoires d'Outre-Mer et le Marché Commun," n.d. but likely August 1956.
23. Bibliothèque de documentation international contemporaine O 42174 (83): Pierre Moussa, *Les Chances économiques de la Communauté Franco-Africaine*, Cahiers de la Fondation Nationale des Sciences Politiques Nº 83 (Paris: Librairie Armand Colin, 1957), 19. On Directeur des Affaires économiques et du Plan au ministère de la France d'Outre Mer Pierre Moussa, see Marseille (2005, 42–43, 373–375).
24. In 1956, Cartier argued in *Paris Match* that the French Union's costs outweighed its benefits. Moussa dubbed such thinking 'le complexe hollandaise'.
25. The 'internationalisation' of supposedly domestic colonial crises is a theme in post-war French history. See Atwood Lawrence (2008), Connelly (2002), and Wall (2001).
26. MAEF 20QO/726: Ministère des Affaires étrangères, direction des Affaires économiques et financières, service de coopération économique, Marché commun, "Note sur les observations et conditions principales à prendre en considération pour l'entrée de l'Algérie dans la Communauté du marché européen," August 21, 1956.

27. Multiple French officials drew comparisons between Algeria and the Mezzogiorno. For example, CAOM BIB AOM 20773/1959: Jean Pouderoux, "La Communauté économique européenne et l'Algérie." *Communautés et Continents* 51 (3) (July–September 1959): 5–13.
28. This in turn harkened back to interwar depictions of spheres of influence. See Hansen and Jonsson (2014, 36–39). See also Ludlow (2007).
29. Murray (2012, 15–18). AN 20000293/4 (dérogation): "Note sur les dispositions du Traité de Rome relatives à l'Algérie," February 10, 1959.
30. Maison méditerranéenne de la science de l'homme, Médiathèque (MMSH) GL-20686: Banque nationale pour le commerce et l'industrie (Afrique), "L'Algérie et le Marché commun," n.d. but likely 1959: 13.
31. The term 'nationals' implied a 'quality of citizenship', but with fewer rights. Cooper (2014, 75). For a longer discussion of national identity and Algerians during the negotiations, see Hansen and Jonsson (2014, 226–234). See also Dozon (2003) and Finch-Boyer (2013, 109–140).
32. CAOM 81 F 1133: Y.R.B. to the ministre d'État chargé des Affaires algériennes, "Application à l'Algérie des dispositions sociales du Traité de Rome," March 22, 1961.
33. MAEF 20QO/712: Mille, telegram to Donnedieu de Vabres, secrétaire d'État et direction économique, April 12, 1958.
34. CAOM 81 F 2255: Directeur de l'Agriculture et des Forêts du ministère de l'Algérie to le ministre de l'Agriculture, "Production Agricole de l'Algérie – Intégration dans le cadre du Marché Commun Européen," May 30, 1958.
35. CAOM 81 F 2255: Directeur de l'Agriculture et des Forêts du Ministère de l'Algérie to le Ministre de l'Agriculture, "Production Agricole de l'Algérie – Intégration dans le cadre du Marché Commun Européen," May 30, 1958.
36. MAEF 20QO/721: Carbonnel telegram to Ministry of Foreign Affairs, August 5, 1958.
37. Muriam Haleh Davis contends that '[t]he goal of the Constantine Plan … was not merely to perpetuate a French Algeria, but to make Muslim Algerians compatible with the dictates of European integration' (Davis 2016, 3).
38. Centre d'Histoire, Sciences Po CM 7, Fonds Couve de Murville: Michel Debré to Maurice Couve de Murville, July 23, 1960.
39. Centre d'Histoire, Sciences Po CM 7, Fonds Couve de Murville: Michel Debré to Maurice Couve de Murville, July 23, 1960.
40. Great Britain's Commonwealth connection was cited (guilelessly) by French administrators as a reason why the British could not join the EEC. British requests to join were formally vetoed in 1963 and 1967. It joined the EEC in 1973.
41. MAEF 20QO/723: Gorse, telegram to ministère des Affaires étrangères, July 12, 1960.
42. Later, Dutch administrators used France's increasingly sore spot of colonial management as a way of expressing their frustration at de Gaulle's veto over the entry of Great Britain into the EEC. MAEF 21QO/1462: Telegram signed Crouy, in The Hague, to ministère des Affaires étrangères, June 20, 1963.
43. Although Hansen and Jonsson (2014) offer an important analysis of Eurafrican ideology, their emphasis on its neo-colonialist elements does not give voice to African uses of the term.
44. AN 20000293/4 (dérogation): F. de Schacht, telex to Premier ministre, Comité interministériel pour les questions de coopération économique européenne, Secrétariat général (SGCI) (copy), January 4, 1963; Historical Archives of the European Union (HAEU) CM2/1963-885: Herbst, Communauté économique européenne, Commission, Secrétariat, to Calmes, Conseil de la Communauté économique européenne, January 3, 1963.
45. Byrne (2016, 5–6). Former colonies also attempted to employ different geographic labels in the supranational context. See Pearson-Patel (2015).
46. This was compounded by the fact that the question of Algerian–EEC relations was discussed a few days before the suspension of negotiations with Great Britain, which the French felt limited their ability to insist upon a more 'attractive' (*engageante*) reply from their partners. MAEF 21QO/1462: Ministère des Affaires étrangères, direction des Affaires économiques et financières, service de coopération économique, "L'Algérie et la Communauté Économique Européenne," February 7, 1963.

47. HAEU CM2/1963-885: Conseils de la Communauté économique européenne et de la Communauté européenne de l'énergie atomique, "Addendum au Projet de Compte Rendu Sommaire de la réunion restreinte tenue à l'occasion de la 243ème réunion du Comité des Représentants Permanents (Bruxelles, les mardi 15, jeudi 17, vendredi 18, mardi 22 et mercredi 23 janvier 1963)," January 28, 1963.
48. MAEF 21QO/1462: Ministère des Affaires étrangères, Note, "Démarches algériennes auprès de la CEE," January 3, 1964.
49. This is not the only moment of contraction in European institutions: Greenland opted out of the European Union after it gained independence from Denmark in 1985. Dedman (2010, 7–8).
50. MAEF 21QO/1462: Boegner telegram to ministère des Affaires étrangères, "L'Algérie et la CEE," August 22, 1962.
51. MAEF 21QO/1462: Ministère des Affaires étrangères, direction des Affaires économiques et financières, service de coopération économique. "Note a/s Le Maghreb et la Communauté Économique Européenne," October 11, 1962: 1.
52. MAEF 21QO/1462: Ministère des Affaires étrangères, direction des Affaires économiques et financières, service de coopération économique. Note a/s Le Maghreb et la Communauté Économique Européenne," October, 11 1962: 2, 4, 8.
53. MAEF 21QO/1462: Boegner telegram to ministère des Affaires étrangères, May 19, 1964.
54. MAEF 21QO/1462: Morin, SGCI, to secrétaire d'État chargé des Affaires algériennes, ministre des Affaires étrangères, and ministre du Travail, "Application à l'Algérie des règlements no 3 et 4 sur la sécurité sociale des travailleurs migrants," June 3, 1964.
55. Indeed, Gary Wilder challenges historians to take seriously the importance of the political thinking behind such plans in the context of the French Union, arguing that '[t]he conflict over whether postwar France would be a national-imperial federation or a postimperial federal democracy underscores how fine the line was between the actual order and a possible alternative to it' Wilder (2015, 146–147).
56. See, for example, CAOM 81 F 2256: Délégation générale du Gouvernement en Algérie, commerce intérieur et extérieur, Premier ministre secrétariat général pour les Affaires algériennes, "Association de la Turquie à la Communauté Économique Européenne," April 9, 1960; CAEF B 0062126 (formerly B 25343): Ministère de l'Économie et des Finances, Direction des Finances extérieures, Comptes-rendus de réunions des conseillers financiers français à Paris, May 18, 1960.
57. CAOM 81 F 1811: *Communauté européenne*, January 1960: 5.
58. Greece acceded in 1981. Morocco's request to accede to the EEC was flatly rejected in 1987 on the grounds that Morocco is not in Europe. Turkey's application has been engaged in accession negotiations since 2005.
59. Adebajo and Whiteman (2012) and Bitsch and Bossuat (2005) both include several useful chapters on the Yaoundé and Lomé conventions.

Acknowledgments

I am grateful for the input of the editors, Helen Drake and Chris Reynolds and for the thoughtful feedback of the two anonymous reviewers. David Troyansky, Clifford Rosenberg, and Gary Wilder read drafts and offered invaluable advice. I received helpful critiques from the seminar *Pour une histoire sociale de l'Algérie colonisée* and thank Emmanuel Blanchard, Jim House, and Sylvie Thénault for their kind invitation to present a draft of this work. Karis Muller offered important comments. Kelsey Suggitt included me in the Re-imagining ends of empire Study Day at the University of Portsmouth, where I first presented this article's main ideas. I also thank Kyle Francis, Timothy Scott Johnson, Miranda Sachs, and Thea Goldring.

Disclosure statement

No potential conflict of interest was reported by the author.

Funding

The Fulbright Commission, the Council for European Studies at Columbia University, and the Camargo Foundation generously supported the research for this article.

References

Adebajo, Adekeye, and Kaye Whiteman, eds. 2012. *The EU and Africa: From Eurafrique to Afro-Europa.* New York: Columbia University Press.

Ageron, Charles-Robert. 1975. "Idée d'Eurafrique et le débat colonial franco-allemand de l'entre-deux-guerres." *Revue d'histoire moderne et contemporaine* 22 (3) (July–Sept.): 446–475.

Antonsich, Marco. 2009. "*Geopolitica*: The 'Geographical and Imperial Consciousness' of Fascist Italy." *Geopolitics* 14 (2): 256–277.

Atwood Lawrence, Mark. 2008. "Explaining the Early Decisions: The United States and the French War, 1945–1954." In *Making Sense of the Vietnam Wars: Local, National, and Transnational Perspectives*, edited by Mark Philip Bradley and Marilyn B. Young, 23–44. Oxford: Oxford University Press.

Bailkin, Jordanna. 2012. *The Afterlife of Empire.* Berkeley: University of California Press.

Bandeira Jerónimo, Miguel, and António Costa Pinto, eds. 2015. *The Ends of European Colonial Empires.* Basingstoke: Palgrave Macmillan.

Bitsch, Marie-Thérèse, and Gérard Bossuat, eds. 2005. *L'Europe unie et l'Afrique: de l'idée d'Eurafrique à la convention de Lomé I: Actes du Colloque international de Paris, 1er et 2 Avril 2004.* Brussels: Bruylant.

Boerger-De Smedt, Anne. 2012. "Negotiating the Foundations of European Law, 1950–1957: The Legal History of the Treaties of Paris and Rome." *Contemporary European History* 21 (3): 339–356.

Bossuat, Gérard. 1996. *L'Europe des Français, 1943–1959: la IVe République aux sources de l'Europe communautaire.* Paris: Publications de la Sorbonne.

Byrne, Jeffrey James. 2016. *Mecca of Revolution: Algeria, Decolonization, and the Third World Order.* Oxford: Oxford University Press.

Cohen, William B. 2003. "Pied-Noir Memory, History, and the Algerian War." In *Europe's Invisible Migrants*, edited by Andrea L. Smith, 129–145. Amsterdam: Amsterdam University Press.

Connelly, Matthew. 2002. *A Diplomatic Revolution: Algeria's Fight for Independence and the Origins of the Post-Cold War Era.* New York: Oxford University Press.

Cooper, Frederick. 1996. *Decolonization and African Society: The Labor Question in French and British Africa.* New York: Cambridge University Press.

Cooper, Frederick. 2014. *Citizenship between Empire and Nation: Remaking France and French Africa, 1945–1960.* Princeton: Princeton University Press.

Davis, Muriam Haleh. 2016. "'The Transformation of Man' in French Algeria: Economic Planning and the Postwar Social Sciences, 1958–62." *Journal of Contemporary History* 2016: 3. doi:10.1177/0022009416647117.

Dedman, Martin J. 2010. *The Origins and Development of the European Union 1945–2008: A History of European Integration.* 2nd ed. London: Routledge.

Dimier, Véronique. 2011. "Recycling Empire: French Colonial Administrators at the Heart of European Development Policy." In *The French Colonial Mind Volume I: Mental Maps of Empire and Colonial Encounters*, edited by Martin Thomas, 251–275. Lincoln, NE: University of Nebraska Press.

Dozon, Jean-Pierre. 2003. *Frères et sujets: la France et l'Afrique en perspective.* Paris: Flammarion.

Dramé, Papa, and Samir Saul. 2004. "Le projet d'Eurafrique en France (1946–1960): quête de puissance ou atavisme colonial?" *Guerres mondiales et conflits contemporains* 216: 95–114.

Dridi, Hédi, and Antonella Mezzolani Andreose. 2012. "'Ranimer les ruines': l'archéologie dans l'Afrique latine de Louis Bertrand." *Les Nouvelles de l'archéologie* 128: 10–16. doi:10.4000/nda.1613.

Finch-Boyer, Héloïse. 2013. "'The Idea of the Nation Was Superior to Race': Transforming Racial Contours and Social Attitudes and Decolonizing the French Empire from La Réunion, 1946–1973." *French Historical Studies* 36 (1): 109–140.

Garavini, Giuliano. 2012. *After Empires: European Integration, Decolonization, and the Challenge from the Global South.* Translated by Richard R. Nybakken. Oxford: Oxford University Press.

Girault, René. 1989. "La France entre l'Europe et l'Afrique." In *The Relaunching of Europe and the Treaties of Rome: Actes du Colloque de Rome 25–28 mars 1987*, edited by Enrico Serra, 351–378. Brussels: Bruylant.

Gonidec, P. F. 1958. "L'Association des pays d'outre-mer au Marché commun." *Annuaire français de droit international* 4: 593–621.

Grilli, and R. Enzo. 1993. *The European Community and Developing Countries*. Cambridge: Cambridge University Press.

Hansen, Peo, and Stefan Jonsson. 2014. *Eurafrica: The Untold History of European Integration and Colonialism*. London: Bloomsbury.

Johnson, Jennifer. 2016. *The Battle for Algeria: Sovereignty, Health Care, and Humanitarianism*. Philadelphia, PA: University of Pennsylvania Press.

Kottos, Laura. 2012. "A 'European Commonwealth': Britain, the European League for Economic Co-operation, and European Debates on Empire, 1947–1957." *Journal of Contemporary European Studies* 20 (4): 497–515.

Lambert, Jacques. 1952. *Manuel de législation algérienne*. Algiers: Librairie des Facultés.

Lefeuvre, Daniel. 2005. *Chère Algérie. La France et sa colonie, 1930–1962*. 2nd ed. Paris: Flammarion.

Ludlow, N. Piers, ed. 2007. *European Integration and the Cold War: Ostpolitik-Westpolitik, 1965–1973*. London: Routledge.

Marseille, Jacques. 2005. *Empire colonial et capitalisme français: histoire d'un divorce*. 2nd ed. Paris: Albin Michel.

Mazower, Mark. 2009. *No Enchanted Palace: The End of Empire and the Ideological Origins of the United Nations*. Princeton: Princeton University Press.

Montarsolo, Yves. 2010. *L'Eurafrique: contrepoint de l'idée d'Europe: le cas français de la fin de la Deuxième Guerre mondiale aux négociations des Traités de Rome*. Aix-en-Provence: Publications de l'Université de Provence.

Muller, Karis. 2000. "'Concentric Circles' at the Periphery of the European Union." *Australian Journal of Politics and History* 46 (3): 322–335.

Muller, Karis. 2001. "Shadows of Empire in the European Union." *The European Legacy* 6 (4): 439–451.

Muller, Karis. 2012. "Between Europe and Africa: Mayotte." In *European Integration and Post-Colonial Sovereignty Games*, edited by R. Adler-Nissen and Ulrik Gad, 187–203. London: Routledge.

Murray, Fiona. 2012. *The European Union and Member State Territories: A New Legal Framework under the EU Treaties*. The Hague: Asser Press.

Nordblad, Julia. 2014. "The Un-European Idea: Vichy and Eurafrica in the Historiography of Europeanism." *The European Legacy* 19 (6): 711–729.

Ollivier, Anne-Laure. 2005. "Entre Europe et Afrique: Gaston Defferre et les débuts de la construction européenne." *Terrains et Travaux*, no. 8: 14–33.

Pearson-Patel, Jessica. 2015. "Remapeando as fronteiras da saúde imperial: a Organização Mundial de Saúde e os debates internacionais sobre a regionalização do Norte de África francês, 1945–1956", translated by Luís Domingos, in *Os passados do presente: internacionalismo, imperialismo e a construção do mundo contemporâneo*, edited by Miguel Bandeira Jerónimo and José Pedro Monteiro, 295–322. Lisbon: Almedina.

Rempe, Martin. 2011. "Decolonization by Europeanization? The Early EEC and the Transformation of French–African Relations." KFG Working Papers. Free University Berlin. Accessed August 24, 2016. http://userpage.fu-berlin.de/kfgeu/kfgwp/wpseries/WorkingPaperKFG_27.pdf

Renucci, Florence. 2011. "La 'décolonisation doctrinale' ou la naissance du droit d'outre-mer (1946-début des années 1960)." *Revue d'histoire des sciences humaines* 24 (1): 61–76.

Saul, Samir. 2016. *Intérêts économiques français et décolonisation de l'Afrique du Nord (1945–1962)*. Geneva: Droz.

Schenk, Catherine R. 1996. "Decolonization and European Economic Integration: The Free Trade Area Negotiations, 1956–58." *The Journal of Imperial and Commonwealth History* 24 (3): 444–463.

Shepard, Todd. 2006. *The Invention of Decolonization: The Algerian War and the Remaking of France*. Ithaca: Cornell University Press.

Shepard, Todd. 2012. "À l'heure des 'grands ensembles' et de la guerre d'Algérie: l'"État-nation' en question." "Translated by Jennifer Dybmann. *Monde(s): Histoire, Espaces, Relations* 1: 113–134.

Sicking, Louis. 2004. "A Colonial Echo: France and the Colonial Dimension of the European Economic Community." *French Colonial History* 5: 207–228.

Smith, Woodruff D. 1986. *The Ideological Origins of Nazi Imperialism*. New York: Oxford University Press.

Trépied, Benoît. 2010. "'Two Colours, One People'? The Paradoxes of the Multiracial *Union Calédonienne* in the Commune of Koné (New Caledonia, 1951–1977)." *The Journal of Pacific History* 45 (2): 247–264.

Trépied, Benoît. 2013. "La décolonisation sans l'indépendance? Sortir du colonial en Nouvelle-Calédonie (1946–1975)." *Genèses* 91: 7–27.

Urwin, Derek W. 2014. *The Community of Europe: A History of European Integration since 1945*. 2nd ed. London: Routledge.

Viard, Paul-Émile. 1960. *Traité élémentaire de droit public et de droit privé en Algérie. 1re partie – Les Caractères politiques de l'Algérie*. Algiers: Bibliothèque Faculté de Droit et des Sciences Économiques d'Alger.

Wall, Irwin M. 2001. *France, the United States, and the Algerian War*. Berkeley: University of California Press.

Wilder, Gary. 2015. *Freedom Time: Negritude, Decolonization, and the Future of the World*. Durham, NC: Duke University Press.

European democracy deferred: de Gaulle and the Dehousse Plan, 1960

Eric O'Connor

ABSTRACT

This article examines the first debate within the European Economic Community (EEC) over democracy following the Treaty of Rome. The treaty called for the newly created European Parliament to draw up a proposal for direct, transnational parliamentary elections. A plan in 1960 led by Fernand Dehousse emerged as the consensus choice. Charles de Gaulle, however, opposed the plan and succeeded in defeating it. We see during the 1960 debate over the Dehousse Plan competing interpretations of democracy in European unity that still frame the issue today. At stake was the democratic character of the new EEC as well as the proper role of the public in the uniting of Europe. Should the public vote on matters of European integration via transnational parliamentary elections, national referendums or neither? By analytically reconstructing the key participants' democratic worldviews, the article contributes to developing a deeper understanding of the debate over direct elections to the European Parliament, a fuller comprehension of the early life of the Treaty of Rome and a sharper realisation of the essential interconnectedness of the development of the EEC and the resumption of national democracy in post-WWII Western Europe.

On the 60th anniversary of the 1957 Treaty of Rome, as national referendums increasingly decide national policy toward the European Union, now is a good time to reconsider how one of the first consequential debates after the treaty went into effect was about how to incorporate voters into the European Economic Community (today's European Union). This paper examines a largely forgotten debate in 1960 over direct elections to the newly created European Parliament (EP). Article 138, paragraph three of the Treaty of Rome read: 'The assembly[1] shall draw up proposals for elections by direct universal suffrage in accordance to a uniform procedure in all member states.' By 1960, the parliament had completed its task of drawing up a plan, but direct elections did not take place until 1979. The 1960 proposal, known as the Dehousse Plan, never received full consideration. Why, especially during the treaty's initial 'honeymoon' (Marjolin 1998, 308) phase as other issues garnered easier agreement, was the treaty's section on direct elections seemingly neglected? This article demonstrates that debate on democracy in the European Economic Community (EEC) during the early implementation of the Treaty of Rome was not absent, but rather burned momentarily bright in 1960 before being extinguished for much of the rest of the decade. In doing so, the article contributes to developing a deeper understanding of the debate over direct EP elections, a fuller comprehension of the early life of the Treaty of Rome and a sharper realisation of the essential interconnectedness of the development of the EEC and the resumption of national democracy in post-WWII Western Europe.

Two democratic worldviews collided in 1960 that crystallised competing notions of democracy in Europe, and hardened the battle lines that still inform the debate today over democracy in the European Union. Intra-EEC balance of power and representation considerations help explain the Dehousse Plan's defeat, but unbridgeable notions of how democracy should operate in the post-war world conditioned such considerations. Should member-state voters be involved in European integration at all, and if so, were transnational elections or national referendums most appropriate? Fernand Dehousse, a Belgian socialist who spent much of his career in various transnational assemblies, best represented the view that popular voting should enter into the EEC via transnational parliamentary elections. Dehousse led the working group from 1958–1960 within the EP that created the plan that bore his name. On the other side of the democratic divide was French president Charles de Gaulle, who endorsed national referendums. Both Dehousse and de Gaulle advocated for greater popular participation within the EEC, but they viewed each other's methods as incompatible. The debate in 1960 over how to address citizen voting within the EEC was not a battle of two individuals, but rather two ideas, best represented by these two men. They were both the purest manifestations of their respective democratic worldviews. They represented the cleanest fault line of disagreement. Juxtaposing these two figures makes concrete the broader intellectual debates on popular political participation in European unity that characterise this episode. While direct elections to the EP always faced a tough road, it was made tougher by each side staying unyieldingly attached to its dearly held democratic worldviews, contributing to stalemate and inaction on the issue of greater democracy in the EEC.

Historiographically, this article contributes to our knowledge on the history of democracy in European integration. The standard account in the scholarly literature is quite simple: there is no meaningful history of democracy in the process of European integration, at least not until national referendums in the 1970s and the inaugural EP elections of 1979 (Dinan 2004; Gilbert 2012). This article challenges that prevailing wisdom by demonstrating that popular political participation was a central question posed by the Treaty of Rome, and that one of the very first debates that occurred during its implementation was over how to introduce elements of democracy into the process of European integration. Furthermore, diving deep into the 1960 debate over direct EP elections allows us to better comprehend the history of the European Parliament. Established historiography is minimal on the early years of the European Parliament. In the last few years, scholars have begun to take a stronger interest in the EP's history (Gfeller, Loth, and Schulz 2011), but it is still the most under-studied institution from a historical perspective. In two notable histories of the European Parliament by Julie Smith (1999) and Berthold Rittberger (2007), the authors virtually ignore the critical period of the early 1960s. Scholars generally regard direct EP elections and greater democracy in European unity in the 1950s and 1960s as unrealistic federalist fantasies (Schulz-Forberg and Stråth 2010). We see instead in this article that debate over greater democracy in European unity was a viable issue that went unrealised in the 1960s not because it was unrealistic—it was after all stipulated in the Treaty of Rome—but in part because of oppositional, hardened conceptions of how democracy should operate at the European level that could not be reconciled. The debate sparked by the Treaty of Rome was not *whether* voters should be included in the dynamics of European integration, but rather *how* to do so.

This article also expands our understanding of the idea of democracy more broadly in post-WWII Western Europe. Democracy is of course far more complicated than the act of holding free elections, but they are a necessary condition of democracy. Therefore this article examines basic notions of how to democratically incorporate popular voting into the process of European integration. I emphasise that important conceptions of democracy that competed at the national level also competed at the EEC level. Martin Conway (2002, 2004; Conway and Depkat 2010) and others have shown that political leaders re-founded democracy after WWII throughout much of Western Europe on national parliaments. Parliaments were considered the safest, most cautious vessel through which to channel the will of the people. This article shows how the Dehousse Plan attempted to transpose a parliamentary-centred notion of democracy, dominant at the national level, to the EEC level. The same dynamic is true in de Gaulle's case. Copious literature exists that details de Gaulle's plebiscitary conception of national democracy (Jackson 2003; Lacouture 1970; Roussel 2002). A nearly equal quantity examines his relationship to European integration. Some cast him as a villain (Pinder 1963), an unheralded protector and architect (Sutton 2007; Warlouzet 2011), an obstacle (Ludlow 2005) or a realist (Moravcsik 2000), among others. Yet few connect his national democratic strategy to his EEC or EP strategy. This paper synthesises what we already know about de Gaulle's European and democratic worldviews and analytically interprets these rarely combined ideological strands in regard to the understudied Dehousse Plan. Doing so allows us to better understand why de Gaulle, one of supranationalism's most vocal critics of the 1960s, was willing to compromise in a supranational direction on some issues, most notably in agriculture, but not on others. In his opposition to the Dehousse Plan, we see de Gaulle beginning to implement a strategy he later abandoned to transpose his referendum-based, plebiscitary conception of democracy to the EEC level. Thus the EEC became a new canvas for competing notions of democracy—parliamentary centred or plebiscitary—in post-WWII Western Europe.

The Dehousse Plan

The Dehousse Plan was the culmination of a decade of democratic activism on European integration, just as the European Parliament was the culmination of decade of transnational parliamentary experimentation. At least six transnational parliaments had preceded the European Parliament in the previous decade, including parliaments attached to the North Atlantic Treaty Organization, the Nordic Council, the Western European Union, the Benelux Union, the Council of Europe, and the European Coal and Steel Community (Hovey 1966). Each was the least powerful branch of a novel international institution. Member-state national parliaments or governments chose the representatives of each assembly. Though none were directly populated by voters, each assembly existed to provide democratic accountability to an international organisation, and to include national parliamentarians in international relations. It began a quest to 'democratize diplomacy' in the wake of war (Haas 1960, 12). Transnational parliaments existed in part because they symbolised the parliamentary democratic renaissance taking place at the national level in Western Europe. Presidential, judicial, plebiscitary and corporatist conceptions of democracy did not disappear, but none rivalled liberal parliamentary democracy as the dominant organising principle, especially in the original EEC countries. 'Never perhaps since the *ancien régime* monarchies of Europe in the eighteenth century had a single political model acquired, and more importantly maintained, such a dominance,' historian Martin Conway wrote regarding parliamentary democracy in post-war Western Europe (Conway 2002, 59). Transnational parliaments, though unelected and powerless at first, represented an incomplete transposition from the national to the European level of the notion that parliaments represented the paragon of democracy. Federalists across Western Europe in the 1950s were powerful enough to parlay mainstream politicians' fidelity for parliaments into a newfound general acceptance that any new international institution must contain a parliament, but were not powerful enough to convince a sufficient number of their colleagues to bestow significant power or popular legitimacy upon the parliaments.

Yet federalists, including Dehousse, tried unsuccessfully throughout the 1950s to institute direct elections to the new transnational assemblies. Examples include proposals to directly elect the Council of Europe Consultative Assembly in 1949–1951 (Reynaud 1951, 192–193; Union of European Federalists Extraordinary General Assembly 1991), the unrealised 1952–1954 European Political Community's bicameral legislature (Griffiths 1994) and radical federalist Altiero Spinelli's Congress of the European People from 1957 until the early 1960s (Pistone 2008, 87–122). Additionally, the treaty that created the 1952 European Coal and Steel Community Common Assembly explicitly allowed member states to hold direct elections for their own assembly representatives, but no state chose to do so. Therefore by the end of the 1950s, the European Parliament was the newest, most promising creation in an explosion of transnational assemblies, yet it also inherited a decade of failed activism toward electing transnational assembly members by direct suffrage (Scalingi 1980, 13–48).

When the European Parliament met for the first time in March 1958, its members had direct elections on their minds. The European Coal and Steel Community Common Assembly had closed down less than a month before, and more than 50 of its 78 members joined the new 142-member European Parliament. Among those who migrated to the new parliament was Fernand Dehousse, who became the logical choice to continue the charge toward direct election of a transnational parliament. Dehousse was a veteran of the previous decade of transnational parliamentary experimentation, having served after WWII within the European Parliament, Council of Europe Consultative Assembly, the European Coal and Steel Community Common Assembly, and the Ad Hoc Assembly charged with creating a European Political Community within the failed European Defence Community. After the war he became a committed federalist, advocating the virtues of federalism for both Belgium and Europe as a lawyer and during a 19-year career in transnational assemblies from 1952–1971. He was a prototypical activist for direct EP elections in that he served in many transnational assemblies, he subscribed to the post-war consensus that democracy must centre on parliaments, and he had emerged after 1945 determined to eradicate war through federalism (Carlier 1986, 1989). Dehousse does not stand out in the historical literature in the same manner as other so-called founding fathers of European integration. He was simply representative of a particular belief, widespread in the new European Parliament, that a united Europe must include the direct participation of its people. But, given his background and commitment to the cause, other EP members looked to him in 1958 to coordinate the creation of a plan for direct EP elections in accordance with the Treaty of Rome.

As public attention centred on the EEC's negotiations toward the Common Market from 1958–1960, the committee led by Dehousse quietly finished its work in early 1960. It became immediately clear that the Dehousse Plan was designed to achieve the broadest base of support. It was deferential to the member states and rejected the most radical federalist proposals. Rather than directly electing the entire parliament all at once, the public would initially elect only two-thirds of the assembly (European Parliament 1960). Member states would still appoint one-third of the members in the previous manner during an unspecified transition period. Any member-state citizen at least 21 years old could vote in the elections, and potential representatives could stand for election at age 25. Dehousse decided that EP direct elections should take place separately from national elections to demonstrate to voters the distinctness of the European Parliament from national parliaments. In order to begin to live up to its name, the parliament decided to broaden representation by increasing the number of parliamentarians from 142 to 426 to represent the 170 million citizens in the six member states.

The reimagined EP would not, however, possess additional competencies or powers under the Dehousse Plan. As had been the case with all previous post-war transnational assemblies, the European Parliament was the EEC's weakest branch. It was a pale comparison to a national parliament, as it possessed very little power or responsibility. EP members were usually some of the most pro-integration elected officials, thus the parliament lacked the self-conscious opposition found in national parliaments. Furthermore, it possessed no formal connection to the EEC's most powerful branch, the Council of Ministers, nor did it have the power to initiate legislation like the Commission. The EP could offer its opinion on European matters, and it could censure and dissolve the Commission by a two-thirds vote, but it had no legislative or meaningful budgetary powers.

Although divided on this matter, a majority of Dehousse's committee considered direct elections more urgent than a more powerful EP. The powers of the EP eventually should increase, Dehousse insisted, but direct elections could not wait. The very reputation and reason for being of the entire European project was at stake: 'The election is justified because the Europe that's necessary to build has always been known as a democratic Europe, and by definition democracy implies the direct participation of the people. For this reason the argument of legitimacy occupies a place of equal importance to the argument of effectiveness,' Dehousse wrote (1960a, 11). Dehousse understood that voters might view elections to a powerless parliament as a useless gesture. But he supported direct elections immediately—even at the expense of keeping the parliament nearly impotent. In time he was certain that the European Parliament's newfound prestige as a directly elected body would lead to increased powers.

Dehousse (1960b) and his committee argued that directly electing the parliament, even an extremely weak parliament, would 'administer a salutary shock' to the people of Europe to stand up and dedicate their full attention to the process of European unity taking place over their heads. The 'shock' to which Dehousse referred was intended to alter the technocratic orbit Jean Monnet had initiated, and, crucially, to accustom voters to participating at the level beyond the nation state. Directly electing the European Parliament 'protects the community from technocracy,' Dehousse wrote (1969a, 19). In addition, studying the problem of direct elections had revealed a clear 'fault' in the process of European integration: 'What is largely lacking in the European Communities … is popular support, the realisation by the European people of their solidarity, the shared sentiment that national settings are too constricting and that the future of Europe will come, if at all, through the European Communities' (Dehousse 1960b). Direct elections would begin to address this perceived defect by beginning to foster a European political consciousness. European elections on the same day in all six nations could electrify the people, and give birth to a genuine transnational political community in Western Europe. In his view, campaigners and media companies would be forced to view the EEC as a single political space.

The Dehousse Plan distilled a decade of federal activism down to a single document set. Direct elections would add the missing ingredient—namely popular political participation—to European unity that federalists so ardently identified in the 1940s and 1950s. Capturing the voters' attention and habituating them to political participation with implications outside of the nation state would not be quick or easy, Dehousse accepted. National political communities had thoroughly conditioned citizens to conceive of themselves as local and national political actors only. In addition, few citizens held informed or sophisticated opinions about European integration: 'The Communities have until now been the domain of a few hundred specialists, politicians, and officials,' Dehousse wrote (1960b). 'The public only knows a fraction of its activity. Some have held this to be a perfectly normal state of affairs, given the general public's inability to grasp the subject matter. This is an incorrect assertion.' He continued: 'It is therefore time that the people be drawn into this venture, that they grasp what is at stake, and make known their will.' Dehousse conceded in 1960 that the EEC existed in the dark. But he posited that one hundred years previously, newly franchised voters had hardly understood their own national political environment at first. Potential European voters probably comprehended just as little as all new voters. History instructed Dehousse that the political education elections engendered took time.

In addition to redefining the EEC as a democracy-in-progress and accustoming voters to casting a ballot at the European level, direct elections would cement the parliamentary renaissance in Western Europe. 'The first [reason for direct elections] is undoubtedly that it reflects our faith in parliamentary democracy,' Dehousse wrote (1969a, 20). 'What could be more natural, if it is wanted to build a united Europe, than to elect a European Parliament?' The Dehousse Plan fit perfectly into the post-WWII Western European democratic milieu which historian Martin Conway (2002, 2004, 2010) describes in which parliaments were the paragon of democratic organisation. Dehousse simply transposed to the European level the values and techniques that guided founders of the new post-WWII national political systems in France, Italy and West Germany. These new systems championed parliamentary elections that delicately incorporated voters into a stable and orderly democratic framework, yet that were far freer than the so-called people's democracies to the east. 'The case that is being tried in this house is that of democracy, of the virtue of association. The question is whether this democratic idea can overcome the obstacles and the difficulties of our time,' Dehousse said on the EP floor in May 1960 (1969b, 78). The plan would begin to fulfil the democratic destiny many federalists believed a united Europe possessed, and would further the renewed cause of parliamentary democracy in Western Europe. Therefore, the Dehousse Plan did not simply provide a blueprint for conducting direct elections to the European Parliament, it also represented a manifesto for how democracy should operate in Western Europe. It reflected the previous ten-plus years of democratic development since the end of the war and the resurrection of parliamentary democracy in Europe. The Dehousse Plan appeared promising: the Treaty of Rome called for it, the necessary institutional infrastructure already existed and it conformed to most officials' democratic instincts.

Despite some members' concerns, the full European Parliament approved a slightly amended version of the Dehousse Plan on 17 May 1960. The broad strokes of the plan stayed intact, and the parliament recommended that elections proceed first without an increase in its powers. The historical context of the Dehousse Plan was clear: like the European Parliament itself, it emerged from the federalist desire to accompany the uniting of Europe with popular representation. It reinforced the dominant democratic thinking at the time that democracy emanates most powerfully from parliaments. The implications of direct elections, had they been enacted, were less clear. Would they have energised the public into taking greater interest and ownership in European integration? Or would they have embarrassingly exposed the powerlessness of the European Parliament, as well as the powerlessness of the European electorate, on matters of European unity? As these questions lingered, the EP awaited a response from the Council of Ministers, the forum of national government ministers within the EEC empowered to grant the proposal final approval. And it waited. The EP never received an answer.

De Gaulle and democracy

In Charles de Gaulle, federalists confronted not only a fearsome opponent to their designs for European unity, but also an unwavering critic of their most basic understanding of democracy. He endorsed national referendums on European integration rather than direct EP elections. De Gaulle possessed a dim view of supranationalism, European federalism and parliamentary democracy; the European Parliament brought all of these powerful post-war ideas together in a single institution. De Gaulle's relationship to the European Parliament and its founding ideals cast in relief the supreme difficulty of advancing the Dehousse Plan or expanding parliamentary democracy outside the bounds of the nation state.

We must remember that the Treaty of Rome was created in one era, and implemented in another. A severe political and military crisis over France's role in Algeria in May 1958 occasioned the return of General Charles de Gaulle to power in France just two months after the opening of the European Parliament. On the one hand, European activists took heart that de Gaulle preliminarily bestowed his cautious approval upon the EEC he inherited. Signed on 25 March 1957, the Treaty of Rome had predated de Gaulle's return and had been negotiated by the people de Gaulle and his administration replaced. De Gaulle's initial support for the Treaty of Rome was a bit surprising considering that Gaullists during de Gaulle's self-imposed political exile from 1946–1958 had been reliable opponents of the various blueprints for European integration. While Gaullists did not always present a unified front on European integration (Manigand 2012) and were not a priori opposed to European unity (Loth 1991), they wholeheartedly rejected democratic European federalism.

De Gaulle's return so soon after Treaty of Rome took effect set the stage for a battle of democratic conceptions that irrevocably marked the European project. In nearly all the free democracies of Western Europe, the post-war consensus in favour of parliamentary-centred democracy endured through the mid 1970s (Conway 2010, 141). France after de Gaulle's return in 1958 was the major exception to the parliamentary trend. De Gaulle's theory of politics centred on a more personal manner of governing, preferring to personally embody the spirit of the French people rather than endure drawn-out debates among special interests and political parties. Historian Julian Jackson (2003) notes that de Gaulle's notion of democracy was 'plebiscitary': 'He saw democracy less as a means for the expression of legitimate opposition [as in a parliament] than as a way of affirming national unity, less as an articulation of the tensions of a pluralistic society than as a ratification of policy' (63).

For de Gaulle, democracy was best reflected in the mandate the French people bestowed directly upon him to be a powerful head of state, rather than in elections to a 'mediocre' parliament. 'For myself, the separation of powers, the authority of a genuine chief of state, the recourse to the people by means of a referendum whenever its destiny or its institutions were in question—these were the necessary bases of democracy in a country like ours,' de Gaulle wrote (1998, 785). Rather than share his colleagues' conviction that parliaments were the epitome of democracy, de Gaulle viewed parliaments as the space for self-interested parties to divide and weaken the state. Echoing the anti-liberal opponents of the inter-war period, de Gaulle viewed parliaments as sites that specialised in prolonged discussions and subsequent inaction.

For this reason, de Gaulle was pleased to dispose of the Fourth Republic's constitution, in which governments were indirectly chosen by parliament and referendums were taboo, and wrote a new constitution. Soon de Gaulle would have himself directly elected and freely utilise the controversial practice of national referendums. In what much of Western Europe's political class at the time considered an affront to Europe's democratic traditions, de Gaulle would become the first directly elected leader of France since Louis-Napoleon in 1848, and the only directly elected head of state or government within the EEC. Although de Gaulle's grip on power to a significant degree rested on strong Gaullist performance in parliamentary elections, his constitutional reforms allowed him to often bypass a national parliament's two most important tasks: choosing a government and passing legislation. The Third and Fourth Republics, those decadent, effete parliamentary regimes in de Gaulle's view, had inevitably failed the French people at critical moments because of their inability to handle crises which, he argued, required a powerful leader and a muscular unified state. 'The mass of French people confuse the word democracy with the parliamentary regime as it operated in France before the war,' he wrote in summing up the Third Republic in 1941. 'That regime has been condemned by events and public opinion' (cited in Mazower 1998, 184). Now given the chance to institute his ideal polity type amidst crisis in 1958, de Gaulle vowed to ensure his Fifth Republic was up to the challenge.

Just as de Gaulle's concept of democracy differed from his peers, so too did his overall conception of European unity. Rather than a federation, or a functional federation-under-construction, de Gaulle envisioned a confederation of sovereign nation states. 'It is only the states that are valid, legitimate and capable of achievement,' de Gaulle said during a 1962 speech (1964, 176). 'I have already said, and I repeat, that at the present time there cannot be any other Europe than a Europe of states, apart, of course, from myths, stories, and parades.' To him, supranationality was a disease that weakened the French state. He defined supranationality as 'France's submission to a law that was not her own' (de Gaulle 1971, 169). Yet de Gaulle was no isolationist, and he ardently believed that European cooperation was essential for France's national interests. He understood the agricultural benefits for France in the Common Market, and like most of Europe's political class at the time, he considered European collaboration a promising, natural and flexible political model. Yet he did so in the service of a strategy that differed from nearly all of his EEC partners.

Gaullists and federalist found common ground, however, on the necessity of popular political participation in European integration. Concurrent to federalist exhortations for direct elections to transnational parliaments throughout the 1950s, Gaullists repeatedly called for national referendums on topics of European unity. Gaullists, organised into the Rassemblement du peuple français, advocated for national referendums on the European

Coal and Steel Community in 1951–1952, and on the European Defence Community in 1953–1954. They did so primarily to block progress toward supranationalism, but also because, in the words of de Gaulle, European integration should be the result of 'deep, popular roots' via referendums (*Le Monde*, January 5, 1953). Gaullists issued a communiqué in 1952 that stated, '[Europe] should be established on a democratic base with the people, via universal suffrage, giving their approval to the governments' (*Le Monde*, November 13, 1952). Gaullists remained out of power for much of the 1950s, so national referendums on European integration never took place. Furthermore, federalists and functionalists recognised their call for referendums as a strategy to potentially wield public opinion against supranational proposals, and also found proposals for referendums reckless (as we will see below) in a post-war environment that was recovering from the perceived abuse of interwar national referendums.

Among the Gaullists of the era, French prime minister Michel Debré (1959–1962) is a revealing example of the Gaullist democratic worldview at work in the European assemblies. Unlike most Gaullists, Debré possessed first-hand experience within the era's new transnational assemblies, having served as a rare Gaullist representative within various transnational assemblies before he became prime minister, including in the European Coal and Steel Community Common Assembly and the Ad Hoc Assembly. For instance, Debré was one of only three Gaullists out of 18 total French representatives in the Common Assembly (Manigand 2012, 13). Although Debré understood transnational assemblies well and strongly endorsed greater European cooperation (Frank 2005), he firmly rejected supranationalism or expanding democracy beyond the nation state. Debré and Dehousse collided occasionally on the issue of transnational parliamentary elections, as in 1953 within the Ad Hoc Assembly when they publically engaged in a bit of chicken-and-egg wordplay: Dehousse endorsed European elections to bring a European nation into existence, while Debré rejected elections because no such thing as a European nation existed (Debré 1953, 50–51). Debré's participation in the Common Assembly and the Ad Hoc Assembly illustrated that even the most parliamentary-focused and European-minded Gaullist could not countenance direct elections to a transnational assembly.

Once in power after de Gaulle's return, Debré utilised his parliamentary expertise and experience to install de Gaulle's views on democracy into the Fifth Republic's constitution. Debré helped design the new French parliament, and then became its leader as prime minister. While the rest of the EEC member states were satisfied with their parliamentary-centred constitutions, France went in a different direction in 1958. Debré often declared his fidelity to the reorganised parliament while undermining its power. 'One cannot conceive of democracy in France without its parliament,' he wrote (1958, 21–22). 'But the experience of a half century and more teaches us that we should not go overboard with faux-parliamentarianism where the assemblies, above all elected by direct suffrage, absorb the government … because it is then … the end of democracy.' Debré's ideal parliament corrected these perceived flaws: 'A parliament that's small, meets less frequently, is less anarchic, has fewer competencies, and is less arbitrary in its decisions,' he wrote (27). Thus Debré, a parliamentary veteran of the 1950s, helped fundamentally change the nature of democracy in France away from a parliamentary-exclusive conception. Nevertheless, Debré would soon be sacrificed together with the newly diminished parliament that he created and led, as de Gaulle forced him to implement policies regarding Algeria with which he did not agree. In 1962 de Gaulle's marginalisation of the French parliament was complete. Against the wishes of all of France's other political parties, he successfully held a referendum that allowed direct election of the

Fifth Republic president, and he replaced the long-time parliamentarian Debré with the unelected banker Georges Pompidou as prime minister.

It is difficult to overstate the thunderclap that de Gaulle's return prompted within the emerging European community. De Gaulle opposed everything the Dehousse Plan stood for: employing parliamentary elections for the purposes of strengthening the public's connection to a supranational organisation with federalist ambitions. De Gaulle and the federalists did not simply possess different political opinions—a gaping chasm separated their democratic worldviews. As the European Parliament strove for greater legitimacy and power, it came up against a staunch opponent of its inherent justification for existence.

Stalemate, 1960

The battle of ideas that de Gaulle's philosophy and the Dehousse Plan represented would not amount to much of a battle. The European Parliament was a nearly powerless collection of parliamentarians in Strasbourg, while Charles de Gaulle was one of the most powerful men in Europe. But the brief intersection of two grand EEC programmes of the early 1960s—federalist and Gaullist—established a narrower and more desperate course for advocates of popular political participation in European unity. The EP sent the Dehousse Plan to the EEC's member-state representatives in the Council of Ministers for their consideration on 17 May 1960. All six member-state governments would have to agree to the plan for it to take effect. The EEC produced only unanimous decisions at this point in its young existence. All eyes were on France. The other member states had concerns about the specific details of the Dehousse Plan, but none of the governments or non-Communist political parties outside of France possessed the Gaullists' powerful doctrinaire aversion to the type of integration and democracy that direct parliamentary elections represented.

After a summer that produced no momentum for the Dehousse Plan, its prospects dimmed further on 5 September 1960 during a de Gaulle press conference. Building on comments he made on 19 May 1960, de Gaulle branded federalist designs for Europe as unrealistic. '[We must proceed] not following our dream, but according to realities,' he said. 'What are the realities of Europe? ... [The] states are the only entities that have the right to order and the authority to act. To imagine that something can be built ... outside and above the states, this is a dream' (1964, 92–93). He then offered one of the clearest explanations of how he believed the EEC should be reorganised: regular, high-level consultations between governments, a permanent secretariat subordinate to each government, an assembly of appointed national parliamentarians, and national referendums, 'so as to give this launching of Europe the character of popular support and initiative that is indispensable' (93). De Gaulle wanted to be more personally involved and to incorporate more heads of state summits into the mechanics of European integration. And rather than parliamentary elections, de Gaulle preferred simultaneous national referendums on aspects of European unity in each member state. In concluding his thoughts on Europe, de Gaulle left little room for negotiation: 'Let me repeat, this is what France is proposing. It is all this and nothing else' (93).

A Gaullist-led referendum regarding European unity was a prospect that made most federalists shudder. Their primary goal was voter participation in European unity, but a referendum, particularly national referendums in de Gaulle's new era of referendums, might completely undermine their cause. Direct European Parliament elections were supposed to open up new ways of conceiving of transnational democratic representation, not reinforce national political ecosystems. One must also remember France's exceptional support for the national referendum compared with its EEC partners at the time: national referendums were constitutionally banned in West Germany on nearly all issues, and in Italy, the Netherlands and Belgium the legality of a national referendum on European integration was constitutionally dubious. In May 1960, the Belgian federalist Georges Bohy responded to Gaullist referendum proposals on the floor of the European Parliament by saying that direct elections would better allow citizens to make their voices heard. 'The peoples will make known their views. They will do so, however, not through the exceptional medium of a referendum—for which I see no justification—but in the form customary in a democracy, namely through their freely chosen and freely elected representatives' (1960, 107). Bohy, a centre-left Belgian parliamentarian, embodied the political consensus in Western Europe after the war. He could not imagine a reputable conception of democracy not centred on parliamentary elections.

De Gaulle was a challenge that federalists could not overcome. They had previously been able to justify their defeats, or work around forces that on principle rejected democracy at a level beyond the nation state. When the British and Scandinavian countries had taken an anti-federalist position in the late 1940s and early 1950s and voted against direct elections to the parliament of the Council of Europe, European federalists were content to move on without them and work within the original six states willing to move forward with tighter integration. When Communists and Gaullists in France had rejected the European Defence Community in 1954, and with it the directly elected European assembly in the European Political Community, federalists could take heart that it was German rearmament and other geopolitical issues that elicited nearly all of the opposition to the plan, and not elections to a European assembly (Hitchcock 1998, 169–202). European suffragists understood that direct elections should be separated from controversial issues, including military integration or increasing the parliament's powers. In the Dehousse Plan, they had achieved what they considered the proper formula: a plan for direct elections in 'little Europe' that was not bundled to another controversial proposal, that was quite modest in scope and that was directly in accordance with the Treaty of Rome.

Nonetheless, de Gaulle instructed his representatives in the EEC Council of Ministers to reject the Dehousse Plan, effectively killing it. A French Foreign Ministry memo from a few years later sternly noted that in January 1961 France's representatives in the Council of Ministers 'clearly showed our intention to put an end to this premature discussion' (French Foreign Ministry Memo 1968). A popular mandate was sacred to de Gaulle, and such a precious thing could never legitimize the European Parliament. He detested the growing institutions of Brussels and Strasbourg that enjoyed the 'trappings of sovereignty' (de Gaulle 1971, 184). He could not write the words European Parliament without putting them in quotation marks to demonstrate its unworthiness of the name. 'The "European Parliament" … has no effective power,' de Gaulle wrote, and it provided Brussels with only 'a semblance of democratic responsibility' (184). In his view, the EEC was only role-playing democracy, while de Gaulle, the man who saved France from fascism, regarded it as a solemn national obligation.

De Gaulle was resolute in his opposition to European Parliament direct elections throughout the 1960s, which positioned him as an outlier in the EEC. Nearly all the other governments, political parties and publics increasingly supported direct EP elections. West Germany, Italy (Bill on the direct election of Italian representatives 1965) and France (Pistone 2008, 142) each garnered a majority of national parliament members to support direct EP elections at various points throughout the 1960s. Furthermore, all of the major non-Communist political parties in Luxembourg, the Netherlands and Belgium publically supported direct EP elections by the middle of the 1960s.

Even other Gaullists were willing to move forward on direct elections during the height of the Dehousse Plan discussions in 1960. Christian de la Malène and Alain Peyrefitte worked out a deal in November 1960 with the European Movement, an international pro-integration group, to rearrange the EEC to better match the Gaullist conception of European integration in exchange for direct EP elections. The two Gaullists were able to drum up enough support in the European Movement for the creation of a forum for high-level political negotiation among national leaders to discuss foreign policy, a permanent political secretariat in Paris and popular referendums. In return they agreed to direct EP elections (European Movement Resolution 1960). Many federalists in the European Movement hated the compromise, understanding that the deal would severely weaken the supranational aspects of the EEC. They viewed it as one step forward, but too many steps backward (Delmas 1960).

De Gaulle, however, was not willing to compromise at all on direct elections. They could never occur under his watch, even if it meant jettisoning his European blueprint. Laurent Warlouzet (2010) has cautioned against a de Gaulle-centred view of the EEC in the 1960s, but in the case of the development of the European Parliament, de Gaulle's singular influence is inescapable. The subsequent Fouchet Plans of the early 1960s, which outlined de Gaulle's personal vision of a reconstructed EEC, put forth all the suggestions that made his European colleagues uncomfortable—referendums, a political secretariat in Paris and meetings with heads of state/government—without any of the compromises de la Malène and Peyrefitte offered, most notably direct EP elections (Silj 1967). The EEC had no choice but to continually reject de Gaulle's proposed institutional rearrangement, prompting de Gaulle to view the EEC by the mid 1960s with alternating anger and indifference.

Thus compromise became impossible, and stalemate was the result. Federalists and functionalists within the EEC were unwilling to channel democracy in European unity into national referendums, and de Gaulle was steadfastly opposed to direct elections to the European Parliament. While functionalists continued to evaluate if the time was right for popular political participation in European unity, the oppositional positions of the federalists and Gaullists ensured that the status quo would remain; the EP would stay, for the moment, nearly powerless and unelected. Direct EP elections faced a difficult road even without de Gaulle's opposition: the Benelux countries had significant concerns about their voting powers in a changing EP, and some diplomats were relieved to use de Gaulle's intransigence to cover their own apprehensions. But there can be no doubt that without de Gaulle's outlier democratic worldview, the Dehousse Plan would have advanced into deeper stages of negotiation. Whether direct EP elections would have led to an increase in the powers or prestige of the EP, or whether such a development would have altered the EU's current undemocratic image, remain open questions. What is certain is that de Gaulle's obstinacy, resulting from his anti-parliamentary democratic conceptions that were unique within post-WWII Western Europe, helped produced a stalemate in which progress toward direct EP elections became impossible.

Conclusion

Today, both democratic conceptions—parliamentary and plebiscitary—have entered into the mainstream mechanics of European integration, and broader European politics. We see de Gaulle's reflection in the European Council, which was created after his death and in many ways adheres to his European strategy. But we especially witness it in the proliferation of national referendums on European integration. Even beyond the Brexit earthquake, national referendums have become the dominant method by volume of voter consultation on matters of European integration. Dehousse endorsed transnational elections to habituate voters to European elections, but since the 1970s there have been more than forty national referendums on European unity and eight European Parliament elections. This complements a broader de-emphasis on parliaments starting in the 1970s compared with the earlier post-WWII period. '[There was a] general mistrust of parliaments that became evident everywhere from the 1970s onward,' Mark Mazower recently wrote (2013, 410). Parliamentary democracy's grip on the imagination of Western Europe's political class dramatically loosened by the 1970s (Conway 2004, 87), and today appears to be receding further. After 1968, 'Direct democracy was to take the place of the highly cautious and restricted conception of democracy that European elites had endorsed after 1945,' wrote historian Jan-Werner Müller (2011, 178). Yet the federalist conception also persists. Inaugural direct EP elections took place in 1979 and reoccur every five years, matched by a steady increase since then of the EP's powers.

The brief existence of the Dehousse Plan in 1960 was a critical early moment in crystallising the parliamentary versus plebiscitary democratic notions that linger and influence today's EU in various ways. We have seen in this article that one of the very first major debates within the EEC after the Treaty of Rome centred on democracy. It was a topic embedded in the very foundation of the EEC. In the earliest years of the EEC, democracy was not absent, an afterthought or simply a rhetorical flourish by federalists in a hopeless attempt to redefine the EEC as a democratic entity. It was instead a pivotal issue worked out on the ground among participants with divergent conceptions of both democracy and European unity.

The crusade for direct elections was a fundamental dispute over how democracy would operate at the supranational level—it was in essence over what democratic conception, if any, would materialise at the European level. The stalemate beginning in 1960 ensured that neither the federalist conception, especially direct EP elections, nor the Gaullist conception, especially national referendums, would take hold in the EEC right away. A stalemate ensued that left the EP in its original condition: powerless and unelected, yet also an unmistakable democratic symbol in a period of renewed liberal parliamentary democracy. The stalemate perpetuated the original democratic design of European integration, in which democracy existed in shape and spirit, exemplified by a transnational parliament and its federalist representatives, but not in practice.

Notes

1. In March 1962, members voted to officially name the assembly described in the Treaty of Rome as the European Parliament.
2. See the internal Bundestag debates, especially Karl Mommer's proposal (Mommer-Antrag) in the European Parliament Bundeskanzleramt files, B136/8511, Bundesarchiv, Koblenz.

Disclosure statement

No potential conflict of interest was reported by the author.

References

"Bill on the Direct Election of Italian Representatives to the European Parliament Introduced in the Senate". February 8, 1965. In *The Case for Elections to the European Parliament by Direct Universal Suffrage, Selected Documents*, edited by the European Parliament Political Affairs Committee, 300–307. Luxembourg: Directorate-General for Parliamentary Documentation and Information.

Bohy, Georges. 1960. "Speech to the European Parliament, May 11, 1960." In *The Case for Elections to the European Parliament by Direct Universal Suffrage, Selected Documents*, edited by the European Parliament Political Affairs Committee, 107–111. Luxembourg: Directorate-General for Parliamentary Documentation and Information.

Carlier, Philippe. 1986. "Fernand Dehousse, fédéraliste wallon et européen." *Socialisme* 195–96: 221–226.

Carlier, Philippe. 1989. "Fernand Dehousse et le projet d'Union Politique." In *The European Integration from the Schuman-Plan to the Treaties of Rome: Projects and Initiatives, Disappointments and Failures*. Contributions to the Symposium in Luxembourg, May 17–19, 1989, edited by Gilbert Trausch, 365–377. Brussels: Bruylant.

Conway, Martin. 2002. "Democracy in Postwar Western Europe: The Triumph of a Political Model." *European History Quarterly* 32 (1): 59–84.

Conway, Martin. 2004. "The Rise and Fall of Western Europe's Democratic Age, 1945-1973." *Contemporary European History* 13 (1): 67–88.

Conway, Martin, and Volker Depkat. 2010. "Towards a European History of the Discourse of Democracy: Discussing Democracy in Western Europe, 1945-1960." In *Europeanization in the Twentieth Century: Historical Approaches*, edited by Martin Conway and Kiran Klaus Patel, 132–156. Basingstoke: Palgrave Macmillan.

De Gaulle, Charles. 1964. *Major Addresses, Statements and Press Conferences of General Charles de Gaulle, May 19, 1958 - January 31, 1964*. New York: French Embassy Press and Information Division.

De Gaulle, Charles. 1971. *Memoirs of Hope*. Translated by Terence Kilmartin. London: Weidenfeld and Nicolson.

De Gaulle, Charles. 1998. *The Complete War Memoirs of Charles de Gaulle*. Translated by Jonathan Griffin and Richard Howard. New York: Carroll & Graf.

Debré, Michel. 1953. "Speech in Ad Hoc Assembly, January 7, 1953." In *Debates of the Ad Hoc Assembly Instructed to Work Out a Draft Treaty Setting Up a European Political Community, Official Report September 1952–March 1953*, edited by Ad Hoc Assembly Instructed to Work Out a Draft Treaty Setting Up a European Political Community, 50–51. Paris: Ad Hoc Assembly.

Debré, Michel. 1958. *Refaire une démocratie, un état, un pouvoir*. Paris: Plon.

Dehousse, Fernand. 1960a. "Des Élections Européennes en 1962?" *Communes d'Europe*. Conseil des Communes d'Europe, March 1960.

Dehousse, Fernand. 1960b. "Rapport général de Fernand Dehousse, membre de l'Assemblée parlementaire européenne." Centre Virtuel de la Connaissance sur l'Europe. Accessed April 30, 1960. http://www.cvce.eu/obj/general_report_by_fernand_dehousse_member_of_the_european_parliamentary_assembly_30_april_1960-en-89c2a74e-fb16-4b7f-b796-d3759876ddfe.html

Dehousse, Fernand. 1969a. "Introduction." In *The Case for Elections to the European Parliament by Direct Universal Suffrage, Selected Documents*, edited by the European Parliament Political Affairs Committee, 13–20. Luxembourg: Directorate-General for Parliamentary Documentation and Information.

Dehousse, Fernand. 1969b. "Speech to the European Parliament, May 10, 1960." In *The Case for Elections to the European Parliament by Direct Universal Suffrage, Selected Documents*, edited by the European Parliament Political Affairs Committee, 70–78. Luxembourg: Directorate-General for Parliamentary Documentation and Information.

Delmas, André. 1960. "Note Relative a la conference tenue a luxembourg les 11 et 12 novembre 1960 par le Mouvement Européen." Archiv für christlich-demokratische Politik der Konrad-Adenauer-Stiftung e.V., Sankt Augustin, Nouvelles Équipes Internationales files, 09-002, 051/2.

Dinan, Desmond. 2004. *Europe Recast: A History of European Union*. Boulder: Lynne Rienner.

European Movement Resolution. 1960. "Conférence Internationales en faveur d'l'élection au suffrage universel direct de l'assemblée parlementaire Européenne, Luxembourg, 11-12 novembre 1960," November 12, 1960. Archives diplomatiques du ministère des Affaires étrangères, La Courneuve, Couve de Murville papers, box 346.

European Parliament. 1960. "Résolution portant adoption d'un projet de convention sur l'élection de l'Assemblée parlementaire européenne au suffrage universel direct." Textes relatifs à l'élection de l'Assemblée parlementaire européenne au suffrage universel direct, 17 May 1960. Centre Virtuel de la Connaissance sur l'Europe. http://www.cvce.eu/obj/texts_relating_to_the_election_of_the_members_of_the_european_parliamentary_assembly_by_direct_universal_suffrage_17_may_1960-en-1e0f998c-8649-42b9-a881-a33f906012b0.html.

Frank, Robert. 2005. "Michel Debré et l'Europe." In *Michel Debré: Premier Ministre (1959–1962)*, edited by Serge Bernstein, Pierre Milza and Jean-François Sirinelli, 297–316. Paris: Press Universitaires de France.

French Foreign Ministry Memo. 1968. "Election de l'Assemblée Parlementaire Européene au suffrage Universel," November 26, 1968. Archives des Affairs Étrangères, La Courneuve, Questions Internationales Européennes, box 2726.

Gfeller, Aurélie Élisa, Wilfried Loth, and Matthias Schulz. 2011. "Democratizing Europe, Reaching out to the Citizen? The Transforming Powers of the European Parliament." *Journal of European Integration History* 17 (1): 5–12.

Gilbert, Mark. 2012. *European Integration: A Concise History*. Lanham: Rowman & Littlefield.

Griffiths, Richard T. 1994. "Europe's First Constitution: The European Political Community, 1952-1954." In *The Construction of Europe: Essays in Honour of Emile Noël*, edited by Stephen Martin, 19–39. Boston, MA: Kluwer Academic Publishers.

Haas, Ernst B. 1960. *Consensus Formation in the Council of Europe*. London: Stevens and Sons.

Hitchcock, William. 1998. *France Restored: Cold War Diplomacy and the Quest for Leadership in Europe, 1944–1954*. Chapel Hill: University of North Carolina Press.

Hovey Jr, J. Allan. 1966. *The Superparliaments: Interparliamentary Consultation and Atlantic Cooperation*. New York: Frederick A. Praeger.

Jackson, Julian. 2003. *De Gaulle*. London: Haus.

Lacouture, Jean. 1970. *De Gaulle*. Translated by Francis K. Price. London: Hutchinson.

Loth, Wilfried. 1991. "De Gaulle und Europa, eine Revision." *Historische Zeitschrift* 253: 629–660.

Ludlow, N. Piers. 2005. *The European Community and the Crisis of the 1960s: Negotiating the Gaullist Challenge*. London: Routledge.

Manigand, Christine. 2012. "L'Europe des Gaullistes: Essai sur la place des gaullistes au sein des assemblées européennes (1948-1979)." *Vingtième Siècle. Revue d'histoire* 116 (4): 9–21.

Marjolin, Robert. 1998. *Memoirs 1911–1986: Architect of European Unity*. Translated by William Hall. London: Weidenfeld and Nicolson.

Mazower, Mark. 1998. *Dark Continent: Europe's Twentieth Century*. New York: Vintage Books.

Mazower, Mark. 2013. *Governing the World: The History of an Idea, 1815 to the Present*. New York: Penguin.

Moravcsik, Andrew. 2000. "De Gaulle Between Grain and Grandeur: The Political Economy of French EC Policy 1958-1970 (Part 1)." *Journal of Cold War Studies* 2 (2): 3–43.

Müller, Jan-Werner. 2011. *Contesting Democracy: Political Ideas in Twentieth-Century Europe*. New Haven, CT: Yale University Press.

Pinder, John. 1963. *Europe Against de Gaulle*. London: Pall Mall Press.

Pistone, Sergio. 2008. *The Union of European Federalists: From the Foundation to the Decision on Direct Elections of the European Parliament 1946–1974*. Milan: Guiffrè Editore.

Reynaud, Paul. 1951. *Unite or Perish: A Dynamic Program for a United Europe*. New York: Simon and Schuster.

Rittberger, Berthold. 2007. *Building Europe's Parliament: Democratic Representation Beyond the Nation-State*. New York: Oxford University Press.

Roussel, Eric. 2002. *Charles de Gaulle*. Paris: Gallimard.

Scalingi, Paula. 1980. *The European Parliament: The Three-Decade Search for a United Europe*. Westport: Greenwood Press.

Schulz-Forberg, Hagen, and Bo Stråth. 2010. *The Political History of European Integration: The Hypocrisy of Democracy-Through-Market*. New York: Routledge.

Silj, Alessandro. 1967. *Europe's Political Puzzle: A Study of the Fouchet Negotiations and the 1963 Veto*. Occasional Papers in International Affairs No. 17. Cambridge: Harvard University Center for International Affairs.

Smith, Julie. 1999. *Europe's Elected Parliament*. Sheffield: Sheffield Academic Press.

Sutton, Michael. 2007. *France and the Construction of Europe, 1944–2007: The Geopolitical Imperative*. New York and Oxford: Berghahn Books.

Union of European Federalists Extraordinary General Assembly. 1991. "Draft of a Federal Pact," Oct. 29–31, 1949." In *Documents on the History of European Integration*, volume 4, edited by Walter Lipgens and Wilfried Loth, 86. New York: Walter de Gruyter.

Warlouzet, Laurent. 2010. "Charles de Gaulle's Idea of Europe. The Lasting Legacy." *Kontur* 19: 21–31.

Warlouzet, Laurent. 2011. "De Gaulle as Father of Europe: The Unpredictability of the FTA's Failure and the EEC's Success (1956-58)." *Contemporary European History* 20 (4): 419–434.

Conclusion

Helen Drake and Chris Reynolds

Europe by proxy: France and Europe, 60 years on

Only time will reveal the significance of the year 2017 for France's relationship with the European Union (EU). Perhaps when viewed from the unforeseeable future, 2017 will appear as another decisive moment – a Macron moment – in France's history as an EU member state. Sixty years after the signing of the Treaty of Rome, did France in 2017 declare itself ready to take another leap towards closer relations with its fellow member states, much as it had at other times in its history? Was Parson's above diagnosis (1) of a 'distressing stalemate' and 'national inertia' in French politics towards the EU outdated? Was all the ailing patient needed an injection of self-confidence and renewed sense of the purpose of national life? To paraphrase Gaullist terminology, could Emmanuel Macron, France's eighth president since 1958, be poised to restore France to itself as a *primus inter 27 pares*, in an EU ripe for reform?

From the limited vantage point of 2018, a more sober perspective prevails. In what follows we develop this perspective with reference to the themes explored in the chapters that make up this volume; namely, presidents, parties, policy and ideas. 'Europe' was certainly significant in the 2017 elections as we shall see below; not because it was salient for voters as a distinct electoral issue but due to the extent to which it had become part of the 'organisational logic' of French political life (see above, 2) such that presidential candidates could not help but address it; and voters could not avoid engaging with it. Neither in 2012 nor in 2017 was 'Europe' *per se* at the forefront of a majority of voters' minds when casting their ballot in the presidential elections. On the contrary, the most significant issues for France's electorate in 2017 were security, migration and the economy (more precisely, spending power, immigration, unemployment and terrorism (IPSOS, 2017a)). The challenge for presidential candidates was to package Europe into their political offerings on these subjects. 'Europe', in these elections and in other words, functioned largely as a proxy for deeper challenges of domestic politics, including widespread support for a renewal of the political class and, for some, a desire for *le dégagisme* entirely (out with the old).

A significant election

Much as Reynolds predicted above, the question of Europe, and specifically the EU, was electorally significant in the 2017 French presidential elections, as was the case in 2012. Similar to five years previously, the political supply of positions on Europe in 2017 came from presidential candidates along the entire political spectrum and not just at the margins: as

Parsons wrote above, voters *were* invited, in 2017, to '…connect […] their views on Europe to choices of representatives' (2). The electorate *did* choose a president – Emmanuel Macron – who throughout his campaign spoke and signalled without apology his passionate support for Europe: its values, its languages, its peoples – especially its youth; its future: for Macron's supporters voting in the first round of the 2017 presidential elections, more than those of any other candidate, 'European questions' were a key issue informing their preference (IPSOS, 2017a).

Yet in the first round of the 2017 presidential elections, over 14 million people voted for the overtly Eurosceptic candidates of François Asselineau, Jean-Luc Mélenchon and Marine le Pen (Ministère de l'Intérieur, 2017); and in the second round, le Pen won over 10 million votes (a record for a le Pen). Her top priority had been to 'recover France's sovereignty in a Europe of independent nations at the service of its peoples' (cited in Drake, 2018, 98), and she had mooted a referendum in France on a renegotiated form of EU membership. Her first round opponent on the political left, Jean-Luc Mélenchon, had been equally radical in his vision of EU reform which alone could ensure continued French membership.

Other candidates on both left and right had to a greater or lesser extent envisioned the reorganisation of France–EU relations, and Emmanuel Macron was no exception to this rule. Schön-Quinlivan claims that '[o]ut of the 11 candidates, 10 […] were either for some form of Frexit or extremely critical of the direction of European integration' (2017, 294). Setting himself and France a 10-year horizon, Macron's vision was one where Europe would strengthen its collective 'sovereignties' in policy areas ranging from defence to food security. He too expressed the Euroscepticism – the questioning of the status quo at national and EU levels – that Reynolds showed above to have become endemic in French presidential discourse by the time of the 2012 presidential elections. In 2017, candidate Macron (see Drake, 2018 *op. cit.*) was critical, if not dismissive, of the EU's current *modus operandi* and proposed ways to democratise and rejuvenate the bloc. However, this was a critique delivered from within a positive and strategic discourse of presidential love and hope towards the future of Europe; of fervent attachment to European values; of a belief in a 'political Europe'; and of heavy symbolic representation of these preferences. This was no more in evidence than the night of his victory when he declared in his first address as president that he would work to 'retisser le lien entre l'Europe et les peuples qui la forment, entre l'Europe et les citoyens' before later crossing the courtyard of the Louvre to the backdrop of the European anthem to reiterate his intention to 'refonder notre Europe'.[1] Such carefully crafted symbolism was a culmination of the months of presidential campaigning and confirmed that, in tone alone, Macron offered a more fervently optimistic future for France in the EU than either his 2017 opponents or those who had preceded him in the Elysée in the previous decade (Drake, 2017). Thus armed, and into the European leadership vacuum temporarily created by the UK government's preoccupation with the internal UK politics of 'Brexit', and the German Chancellor Angela Merkel's domestic political troubles, strode French President Macron, publicly and purposefully so.

Parties in pieces

Macron's election as president and that of his party, *La République en Marche* (*LREM*), in the 2017 parliamentary (legislative) elections came against the backdrop of ever-higher abstention levels, and spoilt and blank ballot papers, at both the presidential and the parliamentary elections (Ministère de l'intérieur, 2017: *ibid.*). The Eurosceptic populist appeal of Marine le Pen and Jean-Luc Mélenchon was insufficient to carry these presidential candidates into either the Elysée Palace or the second round of the presidential elections, respectively, and neither candidate's political movement was strongly supported in the June 2017 parliamentary elections; but we saw above that they scored record numbers of votes and were part of a picture in which the 2017 elections appeared to have laid waste to the party system and the parties themselves.

On the left and for the PS, 2017 must surely rank in its own right as a key period or moment in the party's history, alongside the three historical episodes explored by Hanley in this volume (25–43). The French *parti socialiste* came spectacularly and ignominiously undone in the 2017 presidential and parliamentary elections, losing popularity, votes, leaders, deputies, members and even its premises in central Paris (Clift and McDaniel, 2017; Clavel, 2017). Its undoing was the product of numerous factors and forces, including, but not exclusively so, the matter of its contradictions and paper-thin veneer of consensus on Europe, as discussed above by Hanley. Internally, for example, the party had begun to fray when in government under François Hollande's presidency, as party members in both government and parliament (*les frondeurs*) openly defied the president; and as midterm elections piled loss upon loss at local and regional levels (Clift and McDaniel, *op. cit.*). The primaries that created Benoît Hamon as presidential candidate for the PS and the centrifugal forces this unleashed amongst party leadership hopefuls made 2017 a risky electoral venture for the PS; the disruptive emergence and competitive appeal of 'En Marche!', and then LREM compounded the damage.

With regards more specifically to the matter of Europe, irreconcilable differences within the French Socialist Party over macroeconomic policy specifically, and globalisation in general, stood as proxies for differing visions over the EU, its future and France in that picture. The presidential candidate Benoît Hamon propounded and stood for a post-national, post-statist vision of Europe that in other circumstances could well have rallied the party, but not in the state in which it found itself since as far back as 'the first Mitterrand presidency and the U-turn of 1983' (Hanley above, 26). That about turn unleashed opposing forces within the party that by 2017 had undermined Mitterrand's 'political acumen and strength to achieve an enduring synthesis between the "first" and "second" lefts, historically a necessity for a dominant left party within the Fifth Republic' (Clift and McDaniel, 414).

What of the right and, in particular, the Gaullists? The party political remains of the Gaullist movement, *les Républicans*, emerged just as shattered from the 2017 elections as those of PS, despite its presidential candidate François Fillon coming very close to entering the second round of the presidential election. The fissiparous effect of the primaries made itself felt on this side of the political spectrum too (see Lees, 2017). Moreover, the Gaullist message itself, on European matters, was arguably embodied in those elections and subsequently by none other than Emmanuel Macron himself, as seen above and developed further below. Marine le Pen and Jean-Luc Mélenchon also channelled certain of the General's antipathies towards 'Brussels' – the institutions, rules and procedures that make up the functioning of the EU – but were rather more lacking in the grandiose visions of *la construction européenne* and French rank and grandeur that characterised de Gaulle's preferences for a European union of states.

Policies and ideas

What of such visionary policies and ideas? Howarth and Schild wrote above of the 'obduracy' of French ideas over monetary policy and macroeconomic governance (61–81). Did Macron promise to breach the defences here, Robert Schuman style? There are certainly grounds to suggest that he was venturing close to Germany's red lines, perhaps revealing the latter to be as obdurate as France. On the other hand, there were suggestions of his willingness to relinquish more national autonomy in fiscal affairs. But the signs in 2018 were that the EU27 were no more likely to rush towards a federal Europe after the UK's withdrawal than it was when 'held up' by the UK or before the wonders of Macron. The federal future of transnational European democracy envisioned by Dehousse, and discussed in this volume by O'Connor (99–114), was not a feature of Macron's political language any more than it was of de Gaulle's in his day. It could be argued that this is indicative of how nothing has really changed; 'political Europe' was indeed back on the table, but would it have any more meaning? For example, how should we read the failure of Macron's suggestion for 73 transnationally elected MEPs following Brexit and the departure of the UK's MEPs from the European Parliament's chambers?

What of the future of Europe per se following the 2017 French elections, particularly in the era of Brexit? Much in the way that Brown's chapter looks at the discussion around the place of France's former colonies in the emergent European project (81–98), could it be argued that France is leading the charge to redraw Europe's boundaries to include where previously had been excluded? Macron's Europe seems fluid in relation to the question of membership: he did not even rule out the possibility of 'Frexit' given the wrong circumstances and went as far as to suggest in a BBC interview that the French would probably have voted to leave the EU if offered a referendum.[2] In his expansive view of European integration, there would even be a place for a post-Brexit UK. More generally, for Macron, Brexit is a double-edged sword. On the one hand, an EU without the enduring obstacle the UK has become will facilitate his mission of imposing his reformist vision for the project. However, on the other hand, the UK withdrawal could potentially offset the delicate balance that has prevented Germany from confirming its outright dominance of the EU and lead to its unassailable hegemony over the project. Nevertheless, it would appear that Macron is a president in a hurry. He sees the UK's choice as a *fait accompli* but fears that a protracted Brexit process will serve as a major distraction and stumbling block for his vision for the future of Europe.

In our Introduction we set out a number of important questions to be addressed. These included whether the France–EU relationship had become as transactional as that of the UK–EU and thereby vulnerable to relatively shallow swings in public opinion and political fashion; if the relationship had become a series of compromises that were 'undoing' France from within; if the national political party system and political institutions were simply too resilient to accommodate a genuine moment of change in the course of French membership of the EU; if there was 'national inertia'.

Looking back just one year after the (notably understated and arguably uncelebrated) 60th anniversary of the Treaty of Rome in France, the picture is unclear. The Macron moment certainly presented characteristics of disruptive change that could in time prove to be transformational. President Macron's governing team has explicitly linked domestic reform in France with strategic change at the EU level (Lemaire, 2018). Emmanuel Macron probably possesses the sort of charisma that is associated with transformational leaders (Cole, 2018), and that is not unfamiliar to French political culture. As we saw above, the mainstream parties by and large collapsed in the 2017 elections, and those voters who bothered to vote seemed to be expressing a desire for change above all else. However, the enduring self-identification of French voters with left and right (Raymond, 2017) suggests that the system per se may endure but under new administration. The institutional and political obstacles in the way of Macron's 10-year vision of a renewed France were formidable. The EU27 were divided over their collective future. Populism, *le dégagisme* and the politics of outrage stalked the continent, and France was no exception. All bets are off on whether the 65th anniversary of the Treaty of Rome, in 2022, will be a cause for national pride or a wake.

Notes

1. Emmanuel Macron's initial victory declaration on 7 May 2017 from his party's headquarters: https://en-marche.fr/articles/discours/allocution-emmanuel-macron-7-mai-2017-president. Video of the Louvre speech can be viewed here: www.youtube.com/watch?v=2cJh_v5 mmuc. The full text of this speech can be found here: https://en-marche.fr/articles/discours/ emmanuel-macron-president-louvre-carrousel-discours.
2. Andrew Marr show, *BBC 1*, 21/01/2018

References

Clavel, G. (2017), 'Le Parti socialiste annonce la mise en vente de son siège rue de Solférino', *Huffington Post*, 19 September 2017.

Clift, B. and S. McDaniel (2017), 'Is this crisis of French socialism different? Hollande, the rise of Macron, and the reconfiguration of the left in the 2017 presidential and parliamentary elections', *Modern and Contemporary France* 25, 4: 403–415.

Cole, A. (2018), 'France – President Macron's political leadership: the personal dimension', *Presidential Power (blog)*, https://presidential-power.com/?p=7438

Drake, H. (2017) 'Macron and the future of the EU. The UK in a Changing Europe', 9th May 2017, http://ukandeu.ac.uk/macron-and-the-future-of-the-eu/

Drake, H. (2018), 'France, Britain and Brexit', in B. Martill and U. Staiger (eds.), *Brexit and Beyond. Rethinking the Futures of Europe* (UCL Press), 97–104.

Embassy of France in London (2018), 'French minister calls on UK to help reform globalization. "France-Europe-UK: what the future holds", Speech by M. Bruno Le Maire, Minister of the Economy and Finance, at Chatham House', https://uk.ambafrance.org/French-Minister-calls-on-UK-to-help-reform-globalization

IPSOS (2017a), '1er tour présidentielle 2017. Comprendre le vote des Français' Présidentielle, 2017', www.ipsos.com/sites/default/files/files-fr-fr/doc_associe/sondage-ipsos_soprasteria_1er-tour-presidentielle-2017-comprendre-le-vote-des-francais.pdf

IPSOS (2017b), '2ème tour présidentielle 2017. Comprendre le vote des Français' Présidentielle, 2017', www.ipsos.com/sites/default/files/files-fr-fr/doc_associe/sondage_ipsos_soprasteria_-_6_mai_19h.pdf

Lees, D. (2017), 'A controversial campaign: François Fillon and the decline of the centre-right in the 2017 presidential elections', *Modern and Contemporary France* 25, 4: 391–402.

Lemaire, B. (2018), 'France, the UK and the EU: what the future holds', *Chatham House*, www.chatham-house.org/file/france-uk-and-eu-what-future-holds-0

Ministère de l'Intérieur (2017), Résultats de l'élection présidentielle 2017, www.interieur.gouv.fr/Elections/Les-resultats/Presidentielles/elecresult__presidentielle-2017/(path)/presidentielle-2017/FE.html

Raymond, G. (2017), 'Beyond left and right?', *Modern and Contemporary France* 25, 4: 417–428.

Schön-Quinlivan, E. (2017), '"The elephant in the room" no more: Europe as a structuring line of political cleavage in the 2017 presidential election', *French Politics* 15: 290–302.

Index

Adenauer, Konrad 88
Algeria: enforcing long reach of Treaty of Rome 87–9; Eurafrica for independent 89–90; L'Algérie française and integrating French Union 84–7
Algerian War 27, 83, 85
Alliot-Marie, Michèle 55
Asselineau, François 116
Atlantic Alliance 28
Aubry, Martine 36

Balladur, Édouard 73
Balladur Memorandum of 1988 72
banking and sovereign debt crises 74–7
Bank of France 73
Barre, Raymond 64, 70
Basel–Nyborg Accords 73
Bayrou, François 12
Ben Bella, Ahmed 89, 91
Benelux Union 101
Bérégovoy, Pierre 15, 73
Bertrand, Louis 84
Bidault, Georges 1
Boegner, Jean-Marc 89
Brandt, Willy 71
Bretton Woods system 3, 62–3, 65–7; collapse of 67, 70–1; embedded liberalism in 63; negotiations 63; support mechanisms for weaker currencies in 65; and United States 67
Brexit 116
Brown, Megan 4

Cambadélis, Jean-Christophe 35
Cartier, Raymond 86
CERES (Centre d'é tudes, de recherches et d'éducation socialistes) 31–2
Chaban-Delmas, Jacques 48
Chatel, Luc 55
Chevènement, Jean-Pierre 31–3
Chirac, Jacques 9, 33, 44; 'a ppel de Cochin' 49; on European Union 51; second presidential term 9

CICE (Crédit d'Impôt pour la Compétitivité et l'Emploi) 35
Coal and Steel Community 28
Cointat, Michel 49
Cold War 27–8, 29, 69
Common Agricultural Policy (CAP) 47, 67, 69
Conference of Venice 85
Congress of the European People 102
Constantine Plan 88
Conway, Martin 101–2, 104–5, 111
Coudenhove-Kalergi, Richard 84
Council of Europe 101
Council of Europe Consultative Assembly 102

Debré, Michel 48, 88, 107
de Carbonnel, Eric 88
Defferre, Gaston 85
de Gaulle, Charles 3, 5, 44, 62, 67, 70, 88; Common Agricultural Policy (CAP) 47; death 47; democracy and 105–8; and 'empty chair crisis' 46–7; European community and 108; on European cooperation 46; Fifth Republic and 88, 106
Dehousse, Fernand 99, 100, 102
Dehousse, Renaud 5, 19
Dehousse Plan 101–5
de Larosière, Jacques 73
Delors, Jacques 32
Depreux, Édouard 30
Désir, Harlem 36
de Villiers, Philippe 51
Draghi, Mario 75
Duflot, Cécile 35–7

ECOFIN Council 71
Economic and Monetary Union (EMU) 52, 64; bold plans, modest outcomes 72–3; macroeconomic imbalances in discussions from 1969 70–2
Economist Intelligence Unit 3
EELV (Europe- Écologie Les Verts) 35
Elliot, Larry 37

INDEX

'embedded currency area theory' 62–4
'embedded liberalism' 62–4; collapse of 67; decline of 66–7; 'embedded currency area' and 62–4; features of 67; Ruggie on 63
'empty chair crisis' 46–7
Eurafrica for independent Algeria 89–90
Eurafrique 4
Euratom 82
euro area sovereign debt crisis 61–78
Euro-Federalism 45–8
Europe: and French presidential elections 7–20; and Gaullist movement 43–58; parties in pieces 116–17; policies and ideas 3–5, 117–19; presidents and parties 2–3; 2017 French presidential elections and 115–16
European Banking Union 75
European Central Bank 38, 74
European Clearing House 68–9
European Coal and Steel Community (ECSC) 1, 4, 84, 101, 106–7
European Coal and Steel Community Common Assembly 102
European Commission 69, 70
European Common Market 85
European Community (EC) 31
European Competition Policy 67
European Constitutional Treaty (ECT) 33
European Council 31
European Currency Units (ECUs) 70
European Defence Community (EDC) 1, 2, 28, 85, 102, 107, 109
European democracy: Charles de Gaulle and 105–8; Dehousse Plan 101–5; stalemate, 1960 108–10
'European Democracy Deferred: de Gaulle and the Dehousse Plan, 1960' 5
European Deposit Insurance Scheme and Commission 76
European Economic Community (EEC) 1, 82; membership, of France 27–30; Pompidou vision of 48
European Financial Stabilisation Mechanism (EFSM) 75
European Financial Stability Facility (EFSF) 75
European integration 4–5; and Euro-Federalism 45–8; and Euro-Populism 45–8; and Euro-Pragmatism 45–8; and French Socialist Party 25–39; and Sarkozy 51–3
European (EC/EU)-level macroeconomic policy coordination: banking and sovereign debt crises 74–7; decline of 'embedded liberalism' 66–7; 'embedded currency area theory' 62–4; 'embedded liberalism' 62–4; EMU and macroeconomic coordination 73–4; European monetary system 72–3; French deficits and unilateral adjustment 64–6; French preferences 64–6; ideas behind

French preferences 62–4; Keynesianism 62–4; macroeconomic imbalances EMU discussions 70–2; neglected in Treaty of Rome 67–70; overview 62
European Monetary Agreement (EMA) 68
European Monetary Authority 69
European Monetary Cooperation Fund 72
European Monetary Fund 72–3
European Monetary System (EMS) 31, 72–3; Exchange Rate Mechanism (ERM) of 62
European Monetary Union 71
European Parliament (EP) 99
European Payments Union (EPU) 68
European Political Community 109
European Reserve Fund (ERF) 62, 71, 73
European Stability Mechanism (ESM) 75
European Union (EU) 26, 99, 115; treatment of Greece after 2008 financial crash 37–8; United Kingdom's entry to 44
Euro-Populism 45–8
Euro-Pragmatism 45–8
Euroscepticism 9, 44
Eurozone crisis 2–4, 33–8; and France 33–8; and Germany 37–8; Greece financial crisis 37–8

Featherstone, Kevin 33
Fifth Republic 1–2, 32, 44, 88–9, 106–8, 117
Five Presidents' Report on the Future of EMU 76
Fourcade, Jean-Pierre 72
'Françafrique' strategy 4
France: banking and sovereign debt crises 74–7; Constitutional Treaty 52; EEC membership 27–30; and Greece financial crisis 38; macroeconomic policy coordination 74–7; parties in pieces 116–17; policies and ideas 3–5, 117–19; presidents and parties 2–3; relationship with Germany 4, 9, 11; 60 years on 115–19; Stability and Growth Pact 34; 2012 presidential elections 1, 10–18; 2017 presidential elections 1, 115–16
'France First' 44, 46–7, 52
France macroeconomic policy: challenging unilateral adjustment 64–6; economic interests behind French preferences 64–6; tackling French deficits 64–6
France moderne et humaniste 55
Franco-German axis 9, 11, 48
Franco-German Economic and Financial Council 73
French *grandes écoles* 63
French Socialist Party (Parti socialiste, PS): and European integration 25–6; and PCF 30
French Union: EEC, exclusion from 85; Fourth Republic and 84; L'Algérie française and case for integrating 84–7; Ministry of Overseas France and 86

INDEX

Gaullism 30, 45–8; European dimension of 46; tenets of 46; *see also* de Gaulle, Charles
Gaullisme chiraquien de deuxième génération 48
Gaullisme chiraquien de première génération 48
Gaullisme de Gauche 47
Gaullisme de Résistance 47
Gaullisme pompidolien 48
Gaullistes en mouvement 55–6
Gaullist movement: and Europe 43–58; Les Républicains (LR) 44; UMP 44; *see also* de Gaulle, Charles
'Gaullist movement' 2
German Bundesbank 72
Germany: France relationship with 4, 9, 11; and Greece financial crisis 37–8; revival of its economy 34; Stability and Growth Pact 34
Giscard d'Estaing, Valéry 31, 48, 49, 55
global financial crisis of 2008 10–11, 19, 37
Gorse, Georges 88
Great Depression 63
Greece: EU's treatment of 37–8; and financial crash of 2008 37; financial crisis and France 38
Grunstein, J. 53
Guaino, Henri 55
Guernier, Eugène 84
Guyomarch, A. 47

Hague European summit 71
Hallstein, Walter 88
Hamon, Benoît 35, 117
Hanley, David 2
Hanover European Council 73
Heath, Edward 48
Hollande, François 2–3, 53, 64, 75–6; and crisis of the eurozone 33–8; disillusion with policies of 35–7; and presidential campaign of 2012 14–15; presidential election win in 2012 33; Treaty on Stability, Co-ordination and Governance 35, 37
Hooghe, Liesber 10

International Monetary Fund 63–4

Jackson, Julian 105
Jospin, Lionel 33
Juhem, Philippe 35
Juppé, Alain 49, 50

Karoutchi, Roger 55
Keynes, John Maynard 63, 68, 76
Keynesianism 62–4
Knapp, A. 47
Kopecký, P. 46

La construction européenne 16
La Droite forte 54

La Droite populaire 56–7
La Droite sociale 54–5
'La France Forte' manifesto 54
La France Solidaire programme 12
La Lettre de la Nation 50
L'Algérie française 84–7
La République en Marche (LREM) 116
Le Figaro 55
Le Marché commun contre l'Europe (Rocard) 32
Le Pen, Marine 11–12, 51, 116–17
Leruth, Ben 2
L'Humain d'abord manifesto 12
Lienemann, Marie-Noëlle 36
Lisbon Treaty 10, 19, 33

Maastricht Treaty 8, 34, 44, 50–1
Machin, H. 47
McNamara, Kathleen R. 67, 74
Macroeconomic Imbalance Procedure (MIP) 62, 76
Macron, Emmanuel 3, 35, 115–19
Mariani, Thierry 56
Marjolin, Robert 69
Marks, Gary 10
Marshall Plan 28
Maurel, Emmanuel 36
Mazower, Mark 111
Melenchon, Jean-Luc 11–12, 33–4, 37, 116–17
Merkel, Angela 36–7, 116
Mes Propositions pour une France Forte et Juste 11
Messmer, Pierre 48
Mittelafrika 84
Mitterrand, François 2, 8, 18; presidency and the turning of 1983–1984 30–3
Mollet, Guy 27–9, 68
'money-in-the-display-window theory' 75
Monnet, Georges 85
Monnet, Jean 103
Mon Projet 52
Montarsolo, Yves 91
Montebourg, Arnaud 35
moteur de l'Europe 9
'Mouvement pour la France,' 51
Mudde, C. 46
Müller, Jan-Werner 111
Mundell, Robert 73

Nordic Council 101
North Atlantic Treaty Organization 101

O'Connor, Eric 4, 5
Ollier, Patrick 55
Ordoliberalismus 36
Organisation for European Economic Co-operation 69

INDEX

Parsons, C. 1, 2
Parti communiste français (PCF) 27; and French Socialist Party 30; opposition to EEC membership 29
Pasqua, Charles 50–1
Pélissier, Jacques 87
Peltier, Guillaume 54
Peyrefitte, Alain 49
Philip, André 28
Pinay–Rueff Plan 70
Pineau, Christian 85
Pleven Plan 46, 56
Polanyi, Karl 63
Pompidou, Georges 44, 48, 52, 71
populism 45
presidential elections: French and Europe 7–20; 1995–2007 8–10; of 2012 8–10

Raffarin, Jean-Pierre 55
Rassemblement pour la R é publique (RPR), and UDF 49–50
Rassemblement p our le Non campaign 50
Ritchie, E. 47
Rittberger, Berthold 100
Rocard, Michel 30
Rome Treaty *see* Treaty of Rome
Ruggie, John 62–3

Sapin, Michel 36, 38
Sarkozy, Nicolas 2, 35, 44, 64, 75; and European integration 51–3; and Eurozone crisis 53; first round of the 2012 election campaign 11–14; on importance of Franco-German axis 11; 'La France Forte' 54; *Mon Projet* 52; policy on Europe 11; presidential elections in 2012 10–11; second round of the 2012 election campaign 14–18
Schäuble, Wolfgang 38
Schild, Joachim 117
Schmidt, Helmut 31, 48
Schmitter, P. 45
Schroeder, Gerard 9
Schuman, Robert 46
Schuman Plan 28
Second World War 63
Séguin, Philippe 50
SFIO (Section française de l'Internationale ouvrière): Atlantic Alliance 28; formation of 27; involvement in French government 30; Marshall Plan 28; role 27; Schuman Plan 28
Shields, J. G. 47, 48–9
Single Market Programme 73
Single Resolution Fund 75
Sinn, Hans-Werner 75

'Six Pack' legislation 76
Smith, Julie 100
Snake in the Tunnel 71–2
Spinelli, Altiero 102
Stability and Growth Pact 34
Startin, Nick 2, 46
Stiglitz, Joseph 37
Stoquer, Nicolas 51
Szczerbiak, A. 45

Tacea, Angela 19
Taggart, P. 45
Tamzali, Abdennour 84–5
Target II Payments system 74
Taubira, Christiane 35
Third Force 27–8
Tindemans Report 48
trade liberalisation 67
Treaty of Paris 1, 84
Treaty of Rome 2, 85; Algeria and 87–9; Article 138 5; enforcing the long reach of 87–9; French administrators negotiating 86; neglected European macroeconomic policy coordination in 67–70; negotiations of 4; poster celebrating 82; signing of 1, 27; 60th anniversary of 99, 118
Treaty of the European Economic Community (EEC) 69
Treaty on Stability, Co-ordination and Governance 35, 37
Triffin, Robert 62, 68–9
Tsipras, Alexis 38

Union of European Federalists Extraordinary General Assembly 102
Union pour la démocratie française (UDF) 46; and RPR 49–50
Union pour un m ouvement populaire (UMP) 44; factions 53–7; France moderne et humaniste 55; Gaullistes en mouvement 55–6; La Droite forte 54; La Droite populaire 56–7; La Droite sociale 54–5
United Nations 85

Valls, Manuel 3, 35
Varoufakis, Yannis 37

Warlouzet, Laurent 110
'Washington Consensus' 67
Wauquiez, Laurent 54–5
Werner Plan 62
Western European Union 101
World War II 84
Wright, V. 47